THE ART OF FAILURE
THE ANTI SELF-HELP GUIDE

Some people would rather die than think. In fact, they do.

Bertrand Russell

THE ART OF FAILURE

FAILURE

THE ANTI SELF-HELP GUIDE

Neel Burton

Acheron Press

Flectere si nequeo superos
Acheronta movebo

© Neel Burton 2010

Published by Acheron Press

All rights reserved. No part of this book may be reproduced or transmitted, in any form or by any means, without permission.

A CIP catalogue record for this book is available from the British Library.

ISBN 978 0 9560353 3 2

Typeset by Phoenix Photosetting, Chatham, Kent, UK
Printed and bound in the UK

About Neel Burton

Neel Burton, 31, is a psychiatrist and philosopher who lives and teaches in Oxford, England. He is the recipient of the Society of Authors' Richard Asher Prize, the British Medical Association's Young Authors' Award, and the Medical Journalists' Association Open Book Award. His other books include *The Meaning of Madness* and *Plato's Shadow*, both also with Acheron Press. He can be contacted at neel.burton@ acheronpress.co.uk.

About Acheron Press

Acheron Press was established in 2008 by Neel Burton for the purpose of independently producing and publishing his books.

The name 'Acheron' was inspired by a verse from Vergil's *Aeneid*:

Flectere si nequeo superos, Acheronta movebo

The line is often translated as, 'if I cannot bend Heaven, I shall move Hell', and was chosen by Freud as the epigraph to his *Interpretation of Dreams*.

According to the psychoanalyst Bruno Bettelheim, the line encapsulates Freud's theory that people who have no control over the outside world turn inward to the underworld of their own minds.

For more information about Acheron Press, visit the website at www.acheronpress.co.uk.

Contents

1. Mania

Beware the barrenness of a busy life.

Socrates

A man who is very busy seldom changes his opinions.

Nietzsche

On a Sunday afternoon in the summer of 2009, a 24–year–old stockbroker went to a trendy rooftop restaurant in the City of London and paid in cash for a glass of champagne. With the glass still in his hand, he climbed over the railing and jumped to his death.

While at Oxford, he had led a vibrant life. He got involved with the Union, the student papers, the Entrepreneurs' Society, and several other student societies. He worked as a presenter for the local radio, in which capacity he interviewed one of the former Spice Girls. Upon coming second in the UK Graduate of the Year Awards, he told a newspaper, 'I have learnt that the sky is the limit since going to university – and that with successful time management skills, one can achieve so much more.'

After leaving Oxford, he became a stockbroker with a large bank and started a company organising club nights in London. He split his time between his home in London and a recently acquired penthouse on the *Costa del Sol*, and described himself as 'living the dream'. According to one of his many friends, he had appeared 'completely normal' only hours before the tragedy. His suicide came as a shock to all those who knew him: how could someone with so much to live for have done such a terrible thing?

It emerged that, two days previously, he had been ordered to leave his desk at the bank, where he was being investigated for the inappropriate use of his office computer. The alleged offence was not particularly egregious, and he had been neither sacked nor suspended. However, a friend told the press that he would have been mortified at the idea of being in any trouble at work, and would have found such a setback hard to deal with. 'He'd always been a high-flyer and nothing had ever got in his way. He was also very concerned with keeping up appearances and how he seemed to other people.' 'He was a good guy who didn't drink too much, didn't take drugs, but worked damned hard and probably pushed himself too hard ...

He never slept and lived on Red Bull.' He had recently written on Twitter of his grief over the death of Michael Jackson, which, he confessed, had made him cry for the first time in a decade.

The Rubin vase (Figure 1) is a famous optical illusion developed in around 1915 by the psychologist Edgar Rubin. The illusion presents the viewer with a choice of two mental interpretations, either (1) two black faces on a white background or (2) a white vase on a black background. A typical person 'sees' one of the two mental interpretations, and only 'discovers' the other after some time or prompting. From then on he only ever 'sees' one mental interpretation at a time, but never both at the same time. The one that he 'prefers' to see is determined by his so-called perceptual set, which is in turn determined by factors such as context, past experiences, and personal interests and preferences. A person's perceptual set acts so as to strengthen the mental interpretations that fit with it and to weaken those that do not. For example, a Democrat and a Republican who listen to the same political speech will 'hear' different things, as will a Tibetan monk, if he can at all be bothered to listen. Anyone who later asks them about the speech might be forgiven for thinking that they had been listening not to one speech, but to three entirely different speeches.

Figure 1: The Rubin vase

Just as there are radically different ways of seeing or hearing the same thing, so there are radically different ways of thinking about the world, radically different worldviews. One of the central tenets of the Western worldview is that one should always be engaged in some kind of outward task. Thus, the Westerner structures his time – including, sometimes, even his leisure time – as a series of discrete programmed activities which he must submit to in order to tick off from an actual or virtual list. One needs only to observe the expression on his face as he ploughs through yet another family outing, cultural event, or gruelling exercise routine to realise that his aim in life is not so much to live in the present moment as it is to work down a never-ending list. If one asks him how he is doing, he is most likely to respond with an artificial smile, and something along the lines of, 'Fine, thank you – very busy of course!' In many cases, he is not fine at all, but confused, exhausted, and fundamentally unhappy. In contrast, most people living in a country such as Kenya in Africa do not share in the Western worldview that it is noble or worthwhile to spend all of one's time rushing around from one task to the next. When Westerners go to Kenya and do as they are wont to do, they are met with pearls of heavy laughter and cries of *'mzungu'*, which is Swahili for 'Westerner'. The literal translation of *'mzungu'* is 'one who moves around', 'to go round and round', or 'to turn around in circles'.

The 20th century psychoanalyst Melanie Klein called it the manic defence: the tendency, when presented with uncomfortable thoughts or feelings, to distract the conscious mind either with a flurry of activity or with the opposite thoughts or feelings. A general example of the manic defence is the person who spends all of his time rushing around from one task to the next like the *mzungu*; other, more specific, examples include the socialite who attends one event after another, the small and dependent boy who charges around declaiming that he is Superman, and the sexually inadequate adolescent who laughs 'like a maniac' at the slightest intimation of sex. It is important to distinguish this sort of 'manic laughter' from the more mature laughter that arises from suddenly revealing or emphasising the ridiculous or absurd aspects of an anxiety-provoking person, event, or situation. Such mature laughter enables a person to see a problem in a more accurate and less threatening context, and so to diffuse the anxiety that it gives rise to. All that is required to make a person laugh is to tell him the truth in the guise of a joke or a tease; drop the pretence, however, and the effect is entirely different. In short, laughter can be used both to reveal the truth or – as in the case of the manic defence – to conceal it or to block it out. Indeed, the essence of the manic defence is to prevent feelings of helplessness and despair from entering the conscious mind by occupying it with opposite feelings of euphoria, purposeful activity, and omnipotent control. This is no doubt why people feel driven not only to mark but also to *celebrate* such depressing things as entering the workforce (graduation), getting ever older (birthdays), and even – more recently – death and dying (Halloween). The manic defence may also take on more subtle forms, such as creating a commotion over something trivial; filling every 'spare moment' with reading, study, or on the phone to a friend; spending several months preparing for Christmas or some civic or sporting event; seeking out status or celebrity so as to be a 'somebody' rather than a 'nobody'; entering into baseless friendships and relationships; even, sometimes, getting married and having children. In Virginia Woolf's novel of 1925, *Mrs Dalloway*, one of several ways in which Clarissa Dalloway prevents herself from thinking about her life is by planning unneeded events and then preoccupying herself with their prerequisites – 'always giving parties to cover the silence'. Everyone uses the manic defence, but some people use it to such an extent that they find it difficult to cope with even short periods of unstructured time, such as holidays, weekends, and long-distance travel, which at least explains why airport shops are so profitable. As Oscar Wilde put it, 'To do nothing at all is the most difficult thing in the world, the most difficult and the most intellectual.'

Virginia Woolf suffered from manic-depressive illness or bipolar disorder, which is a disorder of mood that involves recurrent episodes of abnormally elevated mood ('mania') and clinical depression, interspersed with more or less lengthy periods of normal mood. Although bipolar disorder has a strong hereditary element, episodes of mania may be seen as an extreme form of the manic defence. People with mania are typically euphoric, optimistic, self-confident, and grandiose, although they may also be irritable or tearful, with rapid and unexpected shifts from one extreme to the other. They are often dressed in colourful clothing or in unusual, haphazard combinations of clothing which they complement with inappropriate accessories such as hats and sunglasses and excessive make-up, jewellery, or body art. They are hyperactive, and may appear to others as being entertaining, charming, flirtatious, vigilant, assertive, or aggressive, and sometimes all of these in turn. Thoughts race through their mind at high speed, as a consequence of which their speech is pressured and voluble and difficult to interrupt. The 19th century writer, artist, and art critic John Ruskin described the experience thus: 'I roll on like a ball, with this exception, that contrary to the usual laws of motion I have no friction to contend with in my mind, and of course have some difficulty in stopping myself when there is nothing else to stop me ... I am almost sick and giddy with the quantity of things in my head – trains of thought beginning and branching to infinity, crossing each other, and all tempting and wanting to be worked out.' Sometimes their speech is so rambling or disorganised that they are unable to stick to a topic or to make a point; they may ignore the strictures of grammar, step outside the confines of an English dictionary, and even talk in rhymes and puns. Apart from all this, people with mania are typically full of grandiose and unrealistic plans and projects that they begin to act upon but then soon abandon. They often engage in impulsive and pleasure-seeking behaviour that may involve driving recklessly, taking illegal drugs, spending vast amounts of money with careless abandon, or engaging in sexual activity with near-strangers. As a result, they may end up harming themselves or others, getting into trouble with the police and authorities, or being exploited by the less than scrupulous. In some cases, they may experience psychotic symptoms such as delusions and hallucinations that make their behaviour seem all the more bizarre and irrational. Psychotic symptoms are usually in keeping with the elevated mood, and often involve delusions of grandeur, that is, delusions of exaggerated self-importance – of special status, special purpose, or special abilities. For example, a person with mania may harbour the delusion that he is a brilliant scientist on the verge of finding a cure for AIDS, or that he is an exceptionally talented entrepreneur engaged by the Queen to rid the country of poverty. People with mania invariably have poor insight into their mental state and find it difficult to accept that they are ill. This means that they are likely to delay getting the help that they need, and, in the meantime, to cause tremendous damage to their health, finances, careers, and relationships.

In her extended essay of 1929, *A Room of One's Own*, Virginia Woolf writes, 'I thought how unpleasant it is to be locked out; and I thought how it is worse, perhaps, to be locked in.' At a subconscious level, the person who uses the manic defence seeks to be locked in, to convince himself that he exists, that he is someone, that he is important, and that his life is worth living. He seeks to be locked in not so much for the sake of being locked in, but for the sake of not being locked out, that is, for the sake of avoiding the so-called depressive position, which is frightening, insecure, and lonely. Unfortunately the pretence cannot last forever; the clock strikes midnight and Cinderella's coach turns back into a pumpkin – sometimes with disastrous consequences.

Both the manic defence and the clinical condition of mania can be thought of as a means of avoiding the depressive position. However, the person who uses the manic defence is deemed to have control over his behaviour, whereas the person with mania, that is, with bipolar disorder, is not. Whereas the former is held to be responsible for his actions, the latter is held to be suffering from a mental disorder, and so not to be responsible. If either person went on to commit a serious criminal offence, his conviction would depend on evidence proving beyond reasonable doubt that (1) he carried out the act (*actus reus*) and (2) he *deliberately* intended or risked a harmful outcome (*mens rea*). According to the McNaghten rules prevalent in England and Wales, a plea to insanity can be made if a person was suffering from a mental disorder at the time of the offence, and if this mental disorder led to the absence of *mens rea*. If the jurors decide on the balance of probabilities to accept this defence, then the accused is found 'not guilty by reason of insanity'. This gives rise to an important question: where should the jurors draw the line between sanity and insanity? The McNaghten rules presuppose that people generally exercise free will, but that people with a mental disorder such as bipolar disorder or schizophrenia are, at least in some cases, and at least temporarily, unable to do so. But does anyone ever exercise free will?

2. Freedom

In thoughts more elevate, and reasoned high
Of Providence, Foreknowledge, Will, and Fate –
Fixed fate, free will, foreknowledge absolute,
And found no end, in wandering mazes lost.

John Milton

Like a bird on the wire,
Like a drunk in a midnight choir
I have tried in my way to be free.

Leonard Cohen

In philosophy, libertarians defend the kind of free will that the vast majority of people take for granted, that is, the kind of free will that makes us responsible for our actions – and thus for our lives – in a deep and meaningful sense. However, libertarians are a small minority among philosophers, who, for the most part, believe that this kind of free will is not possible or even intelligible, and that it has no place in our modern scientific picture of the world. How could something that is so deeply ingrained in our psyche and that pervades every aspect of our lives be nothing more than a product of our minds, nothing more than an intricate fantasy? As the 20th century writer Isaac Bashevis once quipped, 'You must believe in free will; there is no choice'. Be this as it may, can a belief in libertarian free will be justified on rational, philosophical grounds? If not, there may be no such thing as an art of success, let alone one of failure.

From the outset, it is important to distinguish the libertarian in matters of free will from the libertarian in matters of politics, who essentially believes that governments should circumscribe themselves to protecting the liberties of the individual, so far as these liberties do not interfere with those of other individuals. The free will libertarian does not necessarily share in the political libertarian's societal ideal. However, there is a clear sense in which the political libertarian relies upon the existence of libertarian free will, which he implicitly takes for a given. Thus, if a belief in libertarian free will cannot be justified on philosophical grounds, nor can a belief in libertarian politics, in criminal justice, and in many other things besides.

On what basis do most philosophers believe that libertarian free will is impossible? Given the physical state of the universe at any given point in time, and given the laws of physics which are universal and constant, (1) it is impossible for the past or future history of the universe to be any other than it is, and (2) it is theoretically possible to map out every single past and future event in the universe. In other words, all past and future events are written out in the very fabric of the universe. Some 200 years ago, the Marquis de Laplace transmogrified this concept of 'causal determinism' into a super-intelligent daemon who could accurately predict the future, first, by knowing every single physical fact about the universe, and, second, by applying Newton's Laws to those facts. Of course, Newtonian physics has since been superseded by quantum mechanics, which allows for chance or indeterminism in the behaviour of elementary particles. Even so, quantum mechanics has not put paid to traditional concerns about causal determinism because (1) even if quantum mechanics is not one day to be superseded by a more comprehensive deterministic theory, indeterminism in the behaviour of elementary particles need not translate into indeterminism in human behaviour and, (2) even if it did, the human behaviour that resulted would be random and unpredictable rather than free and responsible. In short, while free will appears to be incompatible with determinism, it also appears to be incompatible with indeterminism!

A widespread response to the problem of causal determinism is so-called 'compatibilism', according to which 'freedom' is (1) the ability to do something and (2) to be unimpeded in doing it. Thus, I am free to cook a soup if I have the ability to cook a soup, but I am not free to cook a soup if, for example, I do not have the time, ingredients, or equipment to do so, if I am called out in an emergency, or if an intruder is holding me at gunpoint. According to the 17th century philosopher Thomas Hobbes, who was one of the chief exponents of compatibilism, a person is free when 'he finds no stop in doing what he has the will, desire, or inclination to do'. And if this is freedom, then a person is free even if what he has the will, desire, or inclination to do happens to have been determined. A common objection to the compatibilist position is that freedom involves not only the ability to do something, but also the ability to do otherwise. The compatibilist response to this objection is to define 'the ability to do otherwise' in the same way that he defined 'freedom'. Thus, 'the ability to do otherwise' is (1) the ability to do otherwise and (2) to be unimpeded in doing it. If I had wanted to do otherwise than cook a soup, nothing would have impeded me from doing so. However, I did not want to do otherwise than cook a soup (because what I wanted to do had been determined), and in that sense I was free. As 'the ability to do otherwise' has a conditional or hypothetical meaning, it is not strictly speaking incompatible with determinism.

While the compatibilist account seems to capture surface freedoms – freedoms such as taking the bus, buying a packet of lentils, or turning on the gas – which involve nothing more than the ability to do or not to do something, it does not seem to capture the freedom of choice that most people equate with free will. When most people talk about 'free will', they do not just mean 'unconstrained choice', but also control over that choice. Compatibilists believe that this kind of deep or libertarian free will is simply incoherent: like it or not, the same past cannot lead to more than one possible future, and that is the end of the story. Imagine that Emma, who is in the final year of her degree course, is deliberating between a career in teaching and a career in investment banking. After giving it much thought, she 'chooses' to have a career in investment banking. Given the same past – the same beliefs and desires, the same thought processes, the same prior deliberation – how could Emma possibly have 'chosen' differently? The only way that Emma could have chosen differently is if her past, that is, the past, had been different. However, the past could not have been different for the simple reason that there is only ever one past. Even if Emma could have chosen differently, this choice would have been arbitrary and inexplicable given the same beliefs and desires and so on. In conclusion, says the compatibilist, it is not just that most people have a confused notion of freedom, but also that they have a confused notion of determinism, which they confuse with constraint or compulsion. Clearing up these confused notions does not help to bring them round to compatibilism because what they actually believe is that

17

determinism is in itself incompatible with free will. In short, they are incompatibilists.

As I have already touched upon, it is not just that libertarian free will appears to be incompatible with determinism, but also that it appears to be incompatible with *in*determinism. If undetermined events such as quantum leaps occur by chance, and if free actions are undetermined events, then free actions also occur by chance. This is an obvious contradiction in terms, since free and responsible actions cannot, by definition, occur by chance. If my actions result from nothing more than undetermined events in my brain, then they are impulsive and unpredictable, and undermine rather than enable my freedom. Imagine that I am deliberating between a fast-food meal such as a double cheese-burger and a healthier but more time-consuming home-cooked meal such as an asparagus risotto, and that after giving it some thought, I choose the asparagus risotto. If my choices are undetermined, I might suddenly and inexplicably choose the double cheese-burger despite going through exactly the same process of thought and deliberation. One might argue as did the 17th century philosopher Gottfried Leibniz that prior reasons or motives do not determine choice or action, but merely 'incline without necessitating'. However, it is precisely because prior reasons and motives inclined me towards the asparagus risotto that I chose it over the double cheeseburger; had I chosen the double cheeseburger, my choice would have been arbitrary and inexplicable rather than deliberate and responsible. Another way of looking at this problem is to imagine that I have a counterpart, Neel*, who lives in an alternative possible world which is in all respects identical to this one. One day, I succumb to the temptation to steal a bicycle, whereas my counterpart Neel* successfully resists this temptation, even though both of us have had exactly the same past up till that point. In the words of the contemporary philosopher Alfred Mele, 'If there is nothing about the agents' powers, capacities, states of mind, moral character and the like that explains this difference in outcome ... the difference is just a matter of luck'.

If libertarians are to hold that free will is compatible with indeterminism, they need to provide an account of how I might be able to act and act otherwise without it seeming inexplicable, irrational, capricious, or arbitrary. To do this, many libertarians postulate the existence of an additional factor such as the mind or soul that is beyond the physical world and hence beyond the laws of physics or nature. Although the mind or soul is beyond the physical world, it is able to intervene in the physical world to influence physical events, most likely by acting upon the indeterminism in the brain. In other words, whereas undetermined events in the brain may not in themselves account for free choices, they might provide the 'point of engagement' for an additional factor such as the mind or soul to influence physical events. Some libertarians believe that such a Cartesian dualism of mind and body is the only possible solution to the problem of free will, but many others are sceptical. Leaving aside traditional concerns about mind–body dualism, it is not even clear that mind–body dualism is an appropriate response to the threat of indeterminism: if Emma's choice to have a career in investment banking is no longer determined by the prior physical activity of her brain, then it is determined by the prior activity of her disembodied mind or soul. Thus, mind-body dualism appears to achieve little more than to shift the problem to one remove, that is, from the brain to a (hypothetical) mind or soul. All that is left to the dualist libertarian is to appeal to mystery and to claim that disembodied minds or souls are beyond the reach of our understanding. This was in effect the line adopted by the 18th century philosopher Immanuel Kant, who believed that the existence of libertarian free will was presupposed by our practical and, in particular, by our moral lives. Kant held that experience and reason can tell us about how things appear in the world ('phenomena'), but not about how they actually are in themselves ('noumena'). While phenomena are subjected to the constraints of scientific or theoretical reasoning, noumena such as our noumenal selves that govern our practical and moral reasoning are not, and cannot therefore be understood in terms of scientific or theoretical reasoning. Perhaps unsurprisingly, many libertarians are just as unconvinced by Kant's metaphysics as they are by Cartesian mind–body dualism.

Another 'additional factor' strategy advanced by some libertarians is the so-called agent-causal strategy, according to which Emma is able to act or act otherwise because her acts are caused not by prior events (determinism) nor by chance (indeterminism), but by Emma herself (self-determinism). This type of 'immanent' causation induced by the agent himself differs from the 'transeunt' causation induced by prior events in that it involves a 'prime mover unmoved', in this case, Emma. Unfortunately, many libertarians think that agent-causation or immanent causation is no less mysterious than Cartesian mind–body dualism or Kantian noumenal selves, and that, like Cartesian mind–body dualism and Kantian noumenal selves, it merely shifts the problem to one remove, in this case, to a prime mover unmoved, uncaused cause, or cause of itself (*causa sui*), and thus to something akin to God. Unfortunately, it seems unlikely that mere human beings can be moved without being moved, that is, without being moved at least in part by a range of physical, psychological, and social factors. The final word on the matter probably goes to Friedrich Nietzsche, who noted in his philosophical treatise of 1886, *Beyond Good and Evil*, that,

> *The causa sui is the best self-contradiction that has been conceived so far; it is a sort of rape and perversion of logic. But the extravagant pride of man has managed to entangle itself ... with just this nonsense. The desire for 'freedom of the will' in the superlative metaphysical sense, which still holds sway, unfortunately, in the minds of the half-educated – the desire to bear the entire and ultimate responsibility for one's actions oneself, and to absolve God, the world, ancestors, chance, and society – involves nothing less than to be precisely this causa sui and, with more than Baron Münchausen's audacity, to pull oneself up into existence by the hair, out of the swamps of nothingness.*

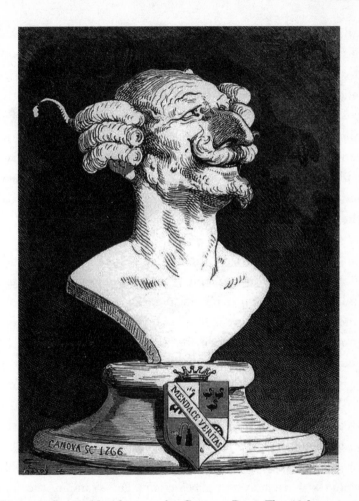

Figure 2: Baron Münchausen, by Gustave Doré. The 18th century Prussian cavalry officer Baron Münchausen was one of the greatest liars in recorded history. One of his many 'hair-raising' claims was to have pulled himself up from a swamp by his hair, or, in an alternative version, by the straps of his boots.

All in all, libertarians have had a hard time defending the kind of free will that makes us responsible for our actions in any deep and meaningful way. Their appeals to various mysterious 'additional factors' such as the mind or soul to explain the possibility of our being uncaused causes of ourselves seem unconvincing. At this point, the question naturally arises as to whether libertarians are able to provide an account of free will that does not make appeal to mysterious forms of agency, but that sits comfortably with our current scientific picture of the world.

One possibility is this. Neuroscience has suggested that electrical signalling in the brain is subject to quantum indeterminacies. Such indeterminacies could translate into undetermined patterns of neurological activity that could provide sufficient latitude for the exercise of free will. Of course, such undetermined patterns of neurological activity would be random, and could not of themselves account for free will, which requires not only alternative possibilities but also free choices. According to chaos theory, small changes in the initial conditions of a physical system can trigger increasingly large events, and thereby lead to enormous and unpredictable changes in that system's behaviour. For example, the flap of a butterfly wing in Kyoto could, at least in theory, result in a violent thunderstorm in Paris or a beautiful sunrise in Mauritius. Similarly, a simple effort of thought or concentration could act on undetermined patterns of neurological activity in the brain so as to culminate in an undetermined action. Most of the time, a person's actions and the neurological activity that they result from would be determined by past events and the cumulative effects of those past events on that person's patterns of thinking. For example, most of the time a person's actions would be determined by a complex amalgamation of addictions, phobias, obsessions, enculturation, socialisation, learned behaviour, and so on. However, on certain occasions, such as when the person was genuinely torn between two competing and potentially life-changing choices, the degree of indeterminacy in his brain would rise to such a high level as to permit an undetermined action. Such a 'window of freedom' would be more or less uncommon, but could exert a profound effect on all subsequent determined and undetermined actions. For example, if Emma had made an undetermined choice to go for a career in teaching rather than in banking, she would, among many other things, have had a very different set of friends. She would have married a man whom she would not otherwise have met. Together they would have had 'other' children, almost certainly in another house, perhaps in a different city, possibly even in a different country, and so forth.

An important and intuitively correct corollary of this 'effort of thought' theory of free will is that some people are freer than others. First, people who are less prone to set patterns of thinking such as those involved in addictions, phobias, obsessions, enculturation, socialisation, learned behaviour, and so on are freer than those who are more prone to them. A small minority of people actively seek to escape from set patterns of thinking, thereby increasing the amount of background indeterminacy in their brain and the number of opportunities that they have for making undetermined choices. In so doing, they are ascending a virtuous spiral in which the more they escape from set patterns of thinking, the more opportunities they have for exercising free will, and the more opportunities they have for exercising free will, the more they escape from set patterns of thinking. Second, people who can 'see into the future', that is, people who have a high degree of insight into the potential ramifications of the choices that they face, are freer than people who cannot or will not see into the future, either because they are lazy or stupid, or, more commonly, because they are afraid to accept responsibility for the choices that they face, and so believe that and behave as though they do not face any (or at least not many). Of course, there is a high degree of overlap between people who are prone to set patterns of thinking and those who cannot or will not see into the future, since both conditions are mutually reinforcing, and both conditions ultimately have their origins in fear. Conversely, there is a high degree of overlap between free thinkers and visionaries. In the game of life as in the game of chess, the best players are those who can see several moves ahead, and who can respond to ever changing circumstances with the boldest and most original moves.

3. Fear

Most people do not really want freedom, because freedom involves responsibility, and most people are frightened of responsibility.

Sigmund Freud

During the first period of a man's life the greatest danger is not to take the risk.

Søren Kierkegaard

According to the 19th century philosopher Søren Kierkegaard, there are three types of lives which a person can lead: the aesthetic life, the ethical life, and the religious life. The person who leads the aesthetic life aims solely at the satisfaction of his desires. If, for example, heroin is what he desires, then he will do whatever it takes to get hold of heroin. In circumstances in which heroin is cheap and legal, this need not include any immoral behaviour. However, in circumstances in which heroin is expensive or illegal, this is likely to include lying, stealing, and much worse. As the aesthete adapts his behaviour to the circumstances in which he finds himself, he does not have a consistent, coherent self. In marked contrast to the aesthete, the person who leads the ethical life behaves according to universal moral principles such as 'do not lie' and 'do not steal', regardless of the circumstances in which he finds himself. As the person has a consistent, coherent self, he leads a higher type of life than that of the aesthete. Despite this, the highest type of life is not the ethical life but the religious life, which shares similarities with both the aesthetic and the ethical lives. Like the aesthetic life, the religious life prioritises individual circumstances and leaves open the possibility of immoral behaviour. However, like the ethical life, the religious life acknowledges the existence and authority of universal, determinate moral principles, as embodied in and promulgated by social norms and conventions. By acknowledging moral principles and yet prioritising individual circumstances, the religious life opens the door for moral indeterminacy. For this reason, the religious life is a life of constant ambiguity and constant uncertainty, and hence of constant anxiety. Anxiety, says Kierkegaard, is the dizziness of freedom.

For Kierkegaard, a paradigm of the religious life is that of the biblical patriarch Abraham, as epitomised by the episode of the Sacrifice of Isaac. According to Genesis 22, God said to Abraham,

> *Take now thy son, thine only son Isaac, whom thou lovest, and get thee into the land of Moriah; and offer him there for a burnt offering upon one of the mountains which I will tell thee of.*

Unlike the aesthete, Abraham clearly recognises the existence and authority of moral principles. However, unlike the moralist, he prioritises individual circumstances over moral principles, and thus obeys God's command to kill Isaac. As Abraham is about to slay Isaac, an angel appears and calls out to him,

> *Abraham, Abraham ... Lay not thine hand upon the lad, neither do thou any thing unto him: for now I know that thou fearest God, seeing thou hast not withheld thy son, thine only son from me.*

At that moment, a ram appears in a thicket, and Abraham spares Isaac and sacrifices the ram is his stead. Abraham then names the place of the sacrifice *Jehovahjireh*, which translates from the Hebrew as, 'The Lord will provide'. The teaching of the Sacrifice of Isaac is that the conquest of doubt and anxiety, and hence the exercise of freedom, requires nothing less than a leap of faith. It is by making such a leap of faith, not only once but over and over again, that a person, in the words of Kierkegaard, 'relates himself to himself' and becomes a true self. Although choice is made in the instant, the consequences of making a choice are irredeemable and everlasting, and this risk and responsibility give rise to intense anxiety.

People with a high level of anxiety have historically been called 'neurotic'. The core feature of neurosis is a high level of 'background anxiety', but neurosis can also manifest in the form of other symptoms such as phobias, panic attacks, irritability, perfectionism, and obsessive-compulsive tendencies, among others. Like the manic defence, neurosis can prevent us from living in the moment, adapting usefully to our environment, and developing a richer, more complex, and more fulfilling outlook on life. The psychiatrist Carl Jung believed that neurotic people fundamentally had issues with the meaning and purpose of their life. In his autobiography of 1961, *Memories, Dreams, Reflections*, he noted that 'the majority of my patients consisted not of believers but of those who had lost their faith'. It is not difficult to hear in Jung echoes of Kierkegaard. The high level of anxiety that is at the core of neurosis accrues from a reluctance or inability to make a leap of faith. The higher the level of anxiety, the more difficult it is to make a leap of faith, and the more difficult it is to make a leap of faith, the higher the level of anxiety. Caught in this vicious spiral, the person with neurosis is unable to exercise freedom, and so is unable to become a true, living self.

The most influential theory of the origins of neurosis is not that of Jung, but that of his one-time mentor and adoptive father, Sigmund Freud. In his book of 1899, *The Interpretation of Dreams*, Freud developed his topographical model of the mind, describing the conscious, the unconscious, and an intermediary layer called the preconscious, which, although not conscious, could readily be accessed by the conscious. Freud later became dissatisfied with the topographical model and replaced it with the so-called structural model according to which the mind is divided into the id, ego, and superego (Figure 3). The wholly unconscious id contains a person's drives and repressed emotions. The id is driven by the 'pleasure principle' and seeks out immediate gratification. However, it is opposed in this by the mostly unconscious superego, a sort of moral judge that arises from the internalisation of parental figures and, by extension, of society itself. Caught in the middle is the ego, which is – in contrast to the id and superego – mostly conscious. The function of the ego is to reconcile the id and the superego, and thereby to enable the person to engage successfully with reality. According to Freud, neurotic anxiety arises when the ego is overwhelmed by the demands of the id, the superego, and reality.

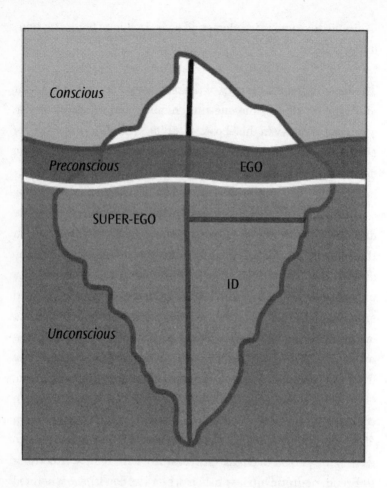

Figure 3: Freud's topographical model superimposed upon his later structural model. The mind is presented as an iceberg with its greater part submerged under an ocean of unconsciousness.

As in Jung, it is not difficult to hear in Freud echoes of Kierkegaard. Freud's tripartite division of the mind corresponds, I think, almost exactly to Kierkegaard's three types of lives. The id and superego, which are both mostly unconscious, correspond, respectively, to the aesthetic and ethical lives, while the ego, which is mostly conscious, corresponds to the religious life. A person who is dominated by the id or the superego cannot be said to be free. Only a person who reconciles the id and superego can become fully conscious of his individuality and of the risk and responsibility that it entails. However, to become conscious of his predicament, the person first needs to overcome the ego defences that it inevitably gives rise to. These ego defences include not only the manic defence and neurosis, but also aesthetic indulgences, moral codes, bourgeois values, habits, customs, culture, and so on. The best education is not that which enables him to make a living (as the government seems to think), nor even that which enables him to make a social contribution (as the universities seem to think), but that which enables him on this path to freedom and individuation, and which, in the longer term, leads to the fullest living and the greatest social contribution. 'Had I to carve an inscription on my tombstone,' said Kierkegaard, 'I would ask for none other than *The Individual*.'

4. Courage

The secret of happiness is freedom; the secret of freedom is courage.

Thucydides

Where is your ancient courage?

Shakespeare

Unfortunately, even the best education may be lost on many people. While knowledge is necessary, it is not sufficient for freedom, since there is often an important gap between knowing something and acting on that knowledge. This gap is commonly called 'courage', and no amount of teaching or learning appears to be able to bridge it. If a lack of courage is that which prevents people with knowledge from exercising freedom, then it becomes important to ask the question, 'What is courage?'

This is precisely the question that Socrates puts to the eminent Athenian general Laches in the *Laches*, which is one of Plato's earlier dialogues. Being the eminent general that he is, Laches thinks that the question is an easy one, and asserts that courage is when a man is willing to remain at his post and defend himself against the enemy. Socrates objects that a man who flees from his post can also sometimes be called courageous. He gives the examples of the Scythian cavalry who fight both in pursuing and in retreating, and of the legendary hero Aeneas who, according to the poet Homer, was always fleeing on horses. Homer praised Aeneas for his knowledge of fear, and called him the 'counsellor of fear'. Laches counters that Aeneas and the Scythian cavalry are cases concerning horsemen and chariots, not hoplites (foot soldiers), for which reason Socrates also gives the example of the Spartan hoplites at the Battle of Plataea (the final land battle of the Second Persian War), who fled the enemy but turned back to fight once the enemy lines had broken. What Socrates really wants to know from Laches is what courage is in every instance, for the hoplite, for the horseman, and for every sort of warrior, and also for those who 'show courage in illness and poverty', 'are brave in the face of pain and fear', and so on. What is it that these instances of courage all have in common? For example, quickness can be found in running, in speaking, and in playing the lyre, and in each of these instances, 'quickness' can be defined as 'the quality that accomplishes much in a little time'. Is there a similar, single definition of 'courage' that might apply to every instance of courage?

Laches this time defines courage as a sort of endurance of the soul. Socrates says that Laches cannot be correct, since endurance can be accompanied by folly rather than by wisdom, in which case it is likely to be harmful. Courage, in contrast, is always a fine thing. Laches accordingly restricts his definition of courage to 'wise endurance'. Who, asks Socrates, is the more courageous, the man who is willing to hold out in battle in the knowledge that he is in a stronger position, or the man in the opposite camp who is willing to hold out nonetheless? Laches admits that the second man is clearly the more courageous, even though his endurance is the more foolish. Yet foolish endurance is both disgraceful and harmful, whereas courage is always a fine, noble thing. Therefore, courage cannot amount to wise endurance.

Despite having been thrown into a state of confusion, Socrates insists that he and Laches should persevere in their enquiry 'so that courage itself won't make fun of us for not searching for it courageously'. Laches still thinks that he knows what courage is, but he does not understand why he cannot express it in words. His companion, the Athenian general Nicias, says that he once heard Socrates say that every person is good with respect to that in which he is wise, and bad in respect to that in which he is ignorant. Thus, courage must be some sort of knowledge or wisdom. If courage is some sort of knowledge, what, asks Socrates, is it the knowledge of? Nicias replies that courage is the knowledge of the fearful and the hopeful in war and in every other sphere or situation. Laches accuses Nicias of talking nonsense, and maintains that wisdom is a very different thing from courage. He gives the example of an illness, in which the doctor is the one who knows best what is to be feared, but the patient is the one who is courageous. Nicias retorts that a doctor's knowledge amounts to no more than an ability to describe health and disease, whereas it is the patient who has knowledge of whether his illness is more to be feared than his recovery. In other words, it is the patient and not the doctor who knows what is to be feared and what is to be hoped. Socrates says that, if Nicias means that courage is knowledge of the grounds of fear and hope, then courage is very rare among men, and animals can never be called 'courageous', but at most 'fearless'. Nicias agrees with Socrates, and surmises that the same is also true of children: 'Or do you really suppose I call all children courageous, who fear nothing because they have no sense?'

Socrates proposes to investigate the grounds of fear and hope. Fear, he affirms, is produced by anticipated evil things, but not by evil things that have happened or that are happening. In contrast, hope is produced by anticipated good things or by anticipated non-evil things. For any science of knowledge, there is not one science of the past, one science of the present, and one science of the future; knowledge of the past, present, and future are the same type of knowledge. Thus, courage is not only the knowledge of fearful and hopeful things, but the knowledge of all things, including those that are in the present and in the past. A person with such knowledge cannot be said to be lacking in courage, but nor can he be said to be lacking in any of the other virtues (namely, justice, piety, and temperance). Thus, in trying to define courage, which is a part of virtue, Socrates has succeeded in defining virtue itself. Virtue is knowledge. Nicias and Laches are suitably impressed, but Socrates insists that he does not as yet fully understand the nature of either courage or virtue.

If Socrates is correct in holding that courage and all of virtue is knowledge, then surely courage and the other virtues can be taught just like other forms of knowledge such as geometry or medicine can be taught. So who is wrong, Socrates in holding that courage is knowledge, or I in holding that courage cannot be taught?

In the *Meno*, which Plato almost certainly wrote several years after the *Laches*, Socrates points out that people of wisdom and virtue seem to be very poor at imparting these qualities. For example, whereas the Athenian soldier and statesman Thermistocles was able to teach his son Cleophantus skills such as standing upright on horseback and shooting javelins, no one ever said of Cleophantus that he was wise and virtuous, and the same could be said of Lysimachus and his son Aristides, Pericles and his sons Paralus and Xanthippus, and Thucydides and his sons Melesias and Stephanus. As there do not appear to be any teachers of virtue, Socrates infers that virtue cannot be taught; and if virtue cannot be taught, then it is not, after all, a form of knowledge.

If virtue cannot be taught, how, asks Meno, did good men come into existence? Socrates replies that he and Meno have so far overlooked that right action is possible under guidance other than that of knowledge. A man who has knowledge of the way to Larisa might make a good guide, but a man who has only correct opinion of the way to Larisa, but has never been and does not know, might make an equally good guide. If the man who thinks the truth is just as good a guide as the man who knows the truth, then correct opinion is just as good a guide to right action as knowledge. In that case, how, asks Meno, is knowledge different from correct opinion, and why should anyone prefer the one to the other? Socrates replies that correct opinions are like the statues of Daedalus (a mythological architect and craftsman of unsurpassed skill), which needed to be tied down if they were not to run away. Correct opinions can be tied down with 'an account of the reason why', whereupon they cease to be correct opinions and become knowledge. Since virtue is not knowledge, all that remains is for it to be correct opinion. This explains why virtuous men such as Thermistocles, Lysimachus, Pericles, and Thucydides were unable to impart their virtue to other men. Virtuous men are no different from soothsayers, prophets, and poets, who say many true things when they are inspired, but have no real knowledge of what they are saying. If ever there was a virtuous man who was able to impart his virtue to another man, he would be said to be amongst the living as Homer says Tiresias was amongst the dead: 'he alone has understanding; but the rest are flitting shades.'

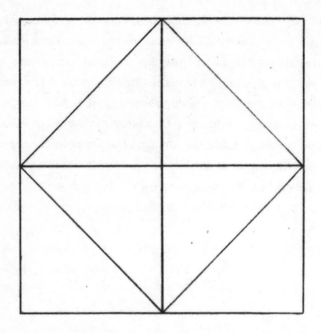

Figure 4: Plato's *Meno* also contains the famous slave boy's 'lesson' in geometry, in which an uneducated slave boy discovers Pythagoras' theorem by calling it up or 'recollecting' it. The knowledge of Pythagoras' theorem was already in him, waiting to be stirred up as in a dream. If the length of the sides of one of the four smaller squares is two feet, Socrates asks of the boy, what is the length of the sides of a square that is twice its area (that is, twice four feet or eight feet in area)? With minimal prompting, the boy understands that (1) the square contained by the four diagonal lines is twice the area of one of the four smaller squares, (2) the length that he is looking for is the length of any one of the four diagonal lines, and (3) twice the area of a square is the square of its diagonal.

Thus, courage, like all the virtues, consists not in knowledge but in correct opinion. The virtues relate to human behaviour and, in particular, to good or moral human behaviour, that is, to ethics. In ethics, the choice of one action over another involves a complex and indeterminate calculus that cannot be condensed into, and hence expressed as, knowledge. Whereas knowledge is precise and explicit, correct opinion is vague and unarticulated, and more akin to intuition or instinct. For this reason, correct opinion – of which courage is a form – cannot be taught, but only encouraged or inspired. In chapter 3, I floated the idea that the best education is not that which enables a person to make a living, nor even that which enables him to make a social contribution, but that which enables him on the path of freedom and individuation, and which, in the longer term, leads to the fullest living and the greatest social contribution. If this is true, then the best education consists not in being taught but in being inspired, which is, I think, a far more difficult thing to do. Unfortunately, it seems that many people are not open to being inspired, not even by the most charismatic people or the greatest works of art or thought. As the 20th century writer Ernest Hemingway once put it, 'He was just a coward and that was the worst luck any man could have.'

5. Death

Was it a dream? Or am I still dreaming now?
And all in all, is life more than a dream
That lights upon dead matter for a moment
And, with it, fades to final dissolution?
Why, why this momentary self-awareness?
That we may see the dread of non-existence?

Imre Madach

It is possible to provide security against other ills,
but as far as death is concerned, we men live in a
city without walls.

Epicurus

In chapter 3, I suggested that only a person who reconciles the id and the superego, or who reconciles the aesthetic and the ethical lives, can become fully conscious of his individuality and of the risk and responsibility that it entails. However, to do this the person first needs to overcome the various ego defences that such a consciousness inevitably gives rise to. If he cannot overcome these ego defences by means of courage, can he do so by any other means? As ego defences arise from a need to suppress or attenuate frightening or anxiety-provoking thoughts, it is likely that a person may be able to overcome his ego defences not only by means of courage, but also by means of a better understanding of the basis of fear and anxiety.

At this stage, one might argue (in my opinion, correctly) that 'the understanding of the basis of fear and anxiety' is, in fact, a part of 'courage'. However, it is at most only a small part of 'courage', and so more precise and more explicit a concept. (1) Since that which is more precise and explicit is closer to knowledge than that which is more vague and unarticulated, 'the understanding of the basis of fear and anxiety' is closer to knowledge than 'courage', which is closer to correct opinion. (2) Since that which is closer to knowledge is more amenable to being taught than that which is closer to correct opinion, 'the understanding of the basis of fear and anxiety' is more amenable to being taught than 'courage'.

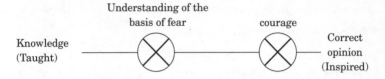

Figure 5a: Compared to 'courage', 'the understanding of the basis of fear and anxiety' is much closer to knowledge, and so more amenable to being taught.

Let us then explore the basis of fear and anxiety. According to its medical definition, anxiety is 'a state consisting of psychological and physical symptoms brought about by a sense of apprehension at a perceived threat'. These psychological and physical symptoms vary greatly according to the nature and magnitude of the perceived threat, as well as from one person to the other. Psychological symptoms may involve feelings of fear, an exaggerated startle reflex or 'alarm reaction', poor concentration, irritability, and difficulty initiating or maintaining sleep. In mild anxiety, physical symptoms arise from the body's so-called 'fight-or-flight' response, a state of high arousal that is associated with a surge in adrenaline in the bloodstream. These physical symptoms include tremor, sweating, muscle tension, a fast heartbeat ('tachycardia'), and fast breathing ('tachypnoea'). In severe anxiety, this fast breathing becomes so fast that it leads to a significant drop in the level of carbon dioxide in the bloodstream ('hypocapnia'), which in turn leads to an additional set of physical symptoms,

47

including chest discomfort, numbness or tingling in the hands and feet, dizziness, and faintness.

Anxiety can be a normal response to life experiences, a protective mechanism that has evolved to prevent us from entering into potentially dangerous situations and to help us in escaping from them should they befall us regardless. For example, anxiety may prevent us from coming into close contact with disease-carrying or poisonous animals such as spiders, rats, or snakes; from engaging with a much stronger enemy to whom we are likely to lose out; and even from declaring our undying love to someone who is unlikely to spare our feelings. Should we find ourselves in a potentially dangerous situation, the physical changes brought about by anxiety may help us to mount an appropriate response by priming our body for action and increasing our performance and stamina. This may enable us to face our foe or scamper up the nearest tree, and thus to improve our chances of escaping danger and, ultimately, death itself.

Although some degree of anxiety can increase our performance, severe anxiety can have the opposite effect and hinder our performance. For example, whereas an experienced actor may perform optimally in front of a live audience, a novice may develop stage-fright and freeze. From a medical standpoint, anxiety is considered to be pathological when it becomes so severe, frequent, or longstanding that it prevents us from doing the sorts of things that most people take for granted, such as caring after our personal needs or enjoying the companionship of our friends and family. In most cases such pathological anxiety is primary, although in some cases it may be secondary to a psychiatric or medical disorder such as depression, schizophrenia, alcohol withdrawal, or an overactive thyroid gland. The prevalence of primary pathological anxiety is difficult to ascertain with any precision as a significant proportion of cases never present to medical attention. However, the condition is very common, and is estimated to affect about one in every five people. It often presents in the form of one or more discrete and well-defined anxiety disorders such as a phobic anxiety disorder, panic disorder, or post-traumatic stress disorder (PTSD).

Table 5.1: Prevalence of anxiety disorders (best estimate)

Phobic anxiety disorders	
Agoraphobia	4.9%
Social phobias	2.0%
Specific (simple) phobias	8.3%
Panic disorder	1.6%
Post-traumatic stress disorder	3.6 %
Generalised anxiety disorder	3.4%

Phobic anxiety disorders are the most common type of anxiety disorder, and can simply and effectively be defined as the persistent and irrational fear of a given object, activity, or situation. Modern psychiatric classifications such as the *International Classification of Diseases 10th Revision* (ICD-10) and the *Diagnostic and Statistical Manual of Mental Disorders 4th Revision* (DSM-IV) recognise three types of phobic anxiety disorder, namely, agoraphobia, social phobia, and specific phobia.

The term 'agoraphobia' derives from the Greek *phobos* (fear) and *agora* (market or marketplace), and so literally means 'fear of the market place'. Contrary to popular belief, agoraphobia does not describe a fear of open places, but a fear of places that are difficult or embarrassing to escape from, such as places that are confined, crowded, or far from home. In time, people with agoraphobia may become increasingly homebound and reliant on one or several trusted companions to accompany them on their outings. A number of scientific studies have found an association between agoraphobia and poor spatial orientation, suggesting that spatial disorientation, particularly in places were visual cues are sparse, may contribute to the development of the disorder. Spatial orientation is important from an evolutionary standpoint since it enables us not only to locate ourselves, but also to locate our friends and foes, sources of food and water, and places of shelter and safety.

The second type of phobic anxiety disorder, social phobia, is the fear of being judged by others and of being embarrassed or humiliated, either in most social situations or in specific social situations such as dining or public speaking. Social phobia has many features in common with shyness, and distinguishing between the one and the other can be a cause for debate and controversy. Whereas social phobia is invariably maladaptive, a certain degree of shyness can be adaptive in that it can protect our reputation and standing in society and dissuade us from interacting too closely with potentially hostile or abusive strangers. In preventing other people from hurting our feelings or our body, shyness can also protect our self-esteem, which in the long run is likely to improve our chances of material and mating success.

The third and last type of phobic anxiety disorder, specific phobia, is by far the most common. As its name implies, specific phobia is the fear of a specific object, activity, or situation. Common specific phobias involve enclosed spaces (claustrophobia), heights (acrophobia), darkness (achluo–phobia), storms (brontophobia), animals (zoophobia), and blood (haematophobia). Unlike other anxiety disorders which begin in adulthood, specific phobias typically begin in early childhood, and there is a strong innate predisposition or 'biological preparedness' for specific phobias such as phobias of spiders (arachnophobia) or snakes (ophidiophobia), or indeed any one of the common specific phobias that I have just listed (claustrophobia, acrophobia, and so on). This biological preparedness is no doubt intended to protect us from the potential dangers that our ancestors commonly faced, and so to increase our chances of surviving and reproducing. Today manmade hazards such as motor vehicles and electric cables are far more likely to strike us than natural dangers such as spiders and snakes, but most phobias are still of natural dangers. This is probably because manmade dangers are comparatively recent arrivals, and have not had enough time to imprint themselves onto our genome.

In a phobic anxiety disorder, the thought alone of the feared object, activity, or situation may provoke a formidable rush of anxiety. During such a panic attack, symptoms of anxiety are so severe that the person begins to fear that he is suffocating, having a heart attack, losing control, or even 'going crazy'. As a result, he may develop a fear of the panic attacks themselves, and this fear may in turn trigger further panic attacks. A vicious spiral takes hold wherein the more he fears panic attacks, the more he suffers from them, and the more he suffers from them, the more he fears them. The panic attacks become ever more frequent and ever more severe, and may even begin to occur 'out of the blue'. This recurrent pattern of panic attacks is referred to as 'panic disorder', and may develop as a result not only of a phobic anxiety disorder but also of any other form of anxiety (see Table 5.1). In many cases, panic disorder can lead to so-called secondary agoraphobia, in which the person becomes increasingly homebound so as to minimise the risk and consequences of having a panic attack. Thus, although primary pathological anxiety often presents in the form of a discrete and well-defined anxiety disorder such as a phobic anxiety disorder or panic disorder, these disorders may and often do co-exist in the same person.

Post-traumatic stress disorder or PTSD results from a highly traumatic event such as a car crash or a physical or sexual assault, and is most common in military personnel and victims of rape. Common symptoms of PTSD include anxiety, numbing, detachment, flashbacks, nightmares, partial or complete loss of memory for the traumatic event, and avoidance of reminders of the traumatic event, although not all of these symptoms need to be present for the diagnosis to be made. The symptoms may last for up to several years, and associated secondary mental disorders such as depression or alcohol misuse and dependence are especially common. PTSD was first recognised in the aftermath of the First World War, and its historical epithets include shell shock, combat neurosis, and survivor syndrome.

The symptoms of PTSD vary significantly from one culture to another, and this has led to the suggestion that PTSD is a culture-specific or 'culture-bound' syndrome. Culture-bound syndromes are mental disorders that only find expression in certain cultures or ethnic groups and that are not easily accommodated by modern psychiatric classifications such as ICD-10 and DSM-IV. DSM-IV simply defines them as 'recurrent, locality specific patterns of aberrant behaviour and troubling experience...' However, many culture-bound syndromes are best understood as idiosyncratic expressions of anxiety and stress-related disorders. Examples include susto or *perdida de la sombra*, which is specific to Latin American populations, and ghost sickness, which is specific to Native American Indian populations. In susto, a sudden and intense fear provokes the 'loss of the soul' (*perdida de la sombra*), leaving the soulless person with symptoms of anxiety, irritability, tearfulness, anorexia, insomnia, listlessness, and despondency. Ghost sickness is brought about by contact or association with the dead, for example, by seeing a dead person or his belongings or even by conjuring up his name, and arises from the fear that the dead person is trying to carry off the living into the realm of the dead. The symptoms of ghost sickness are similar to those of susto or PTSD, but may also include auditory hallucinations, which are uncommon in either susto or PTSD.

In a phobic anxiety disorder, panic disorder, or PTSD, anxiety has a clearly defined cause or object. This is, however, not the case in generalised anxiety disorder or GAD, a condition that is listed both in ICD-10 and in DSM-IV, and that is rather similar to old-fashioned neurosis (see Chapter 3, *Fear*). In GAD, anxiety is not related to any particular object, activity, or situation, but is free-floating and non-specific. There is apprehension about a number of hypothetical events that is far out of proportion to the actual likelihood or potential impact of those events. People with GAD fear the future to such an extent that they behave in a manner that is overly cautious and risk-averse. They are, quite literally, 'paralysed with fear'. But what is it exactly that they are so afraid of?

From our discussion of normal anxiety, phobic anxiety disorders, panic disorder, and PTSD, it appears that the ultimate grounds for all primary anxiety, in whatever form it takes, is, in fact, death. At best, anxiety is an adaptive mechanism that improves our odds of avoiding or escaping from danger and, by extension, death. At worst, it is so severe, frequent, or longstanding that it becomes inhibiting and disabling. Such maladaptive anxiety can adopt one or more of several forms, but whatever form it adopts – whether a phobic anxiety disorder, panic disorder, PTSD, or GAD/neurosis – the final fear is of death. Indeed, if death did not exist, there would be little or no grounds for anxiety. If Emma feels anxious about sitting her exams, choosing a career, taking out a mortgage, or marrying her less than perfect boyfriend, then this is because she only has a finite number of opportunities to 'make good'. If she could live forever, she would have an infinite number of opportunities to get things right, and so she could fail as many times as she liked. However, she is only going to live for perhaps another fifty years (some 18,000 days), and that is all the life that she is going to have. To make things worse, she does not really know what it is to get things right, or even whether it is possible to get things right. Thus, she has no real choice but to make a leap of faith, not only once, but over and over again. In other words, she has no real choice but to be free – wherefore her anxiety. This is not to deny that genetic factors play a predisposing role in the aetiology (or causation) of primary pathological anxiety, as the scientific evidence that they do is strong and incontrovertible. However, such a genetic influence is not at all incompatible with my conclusion that the ultimate ground for all primary anxiety is death.

Figure 5b: Leaping out of the frame. Notice the look of fear in the child's eyes.
Escaping Criticism, by Pere Borrell del Caso (1874)

Earlier on, I suggested that a person could overcome his ego defences not only by means of courage, which is difficult to impart, but also by means of a better understanding of the basis of fear and anxiety. By gaining a better understanding of the basis of fear and anxiety, the person makes it easier to overcome his ego defences, and thereby requires less courage to exercise choice and freedom. The present discussion of anxiety and anxiety disorders led me to conclude that the ultimate basis of fear and anxiety is none other than death. To have this understanding is an important first step, but it is not in itself sufficient to enable a person to overcome his ego defences and the fear and anxiety that they arise from. To go all the distance, the person needs also to contemplate, engage with, and come to terms with death. In the words of the 20th century philosopher Martin Heidegger, 'If I take death into my life, acknowledge it, and face it squarely, I will free myself from the anxiety of death and the pettiness of life – and only then will I be free to become myself.'

And so I turn to the subject of death. In his influential paper of 1970, tersely entitled *Death*, the philosopher Thomas Nagel asks the question: if death is the permanent end of our existence, is it an evil? Either it is an evil because it deprives us of life, or it is a mere blank because there is no subject left to experience the loss. Thus, if death is an evil, this is not in virtue of any positive attributes that it has, but in virtue of what it deprives us from, namely, life. For Nagel, the bare experience of life is intrinsically valuable, regardless of the balance of its good and bad elements.

The longer one is alive, the more one 'accumulates' life. In contrast, death cannot be accumulated – it is not, as Nagel puts it, 'an evil of which Shakespeare has so far received a larger portion than Proust'. Most people would not consider the temporary suspension of life as an evil, nor would they regard the long period of time before they were born as an evil. Therefore, if death is an evil, this is not because it involves a period of non-existence, but because it deprives us of life.

Nagel raises three objections to this view, but only so as to counter them later on. First, it is doubtful whether anything can be an evil unless it actually causes displeasure. Second, in the case of death, there does not appear to be a subject to suffer an evil. As long as a person exists, he has not yet died, and once he has died, he no longer exists. Thus, there seems to be no time at which the evil of death might occur. Third, if most people would not regard the long period before they were born as an evil, then why should they regard the period after they are dead any differently?

Nagel counters these three objections by arguing that the good or evil that befalls a person depends on his history and possibilities rather than on his momentary state, and thus that he can suffer an evil even if he is not here to experience it. For example, if an intelligent person receives a head injury that reduces his mental state to that of a contented infant, this should be considered a serious ill even if the person himself (in his current state) is unable to comprehend it. In other words, if the three objections are invalid, it is essentially because they ignore the direction of time. Even though a person cannot survive his death, he can still suffer an evil; and even though he does not exist during the time before his birth or during the time after his death, the time after his death is time of which he has been deprived, time in which he could have continued to enjoy the good of living.

The question remains as to whether the non-realisation of further life is an absolute evil, or whether this depends on what can naturally be hoped for: the death of Keats at 24 is commonly regarded as tragic, but that of Tolstoy at 82 is not. 'The trouble,' says Nagel, 'is that life familiarises us with the goods of which death deprives us ... Death, no matter how inevitable, is an abrupt cancellation of indefinitely extensive goods.'

Given the sheer pain of this conclusion, it is hardly surprising that philosophers throughout the ages have sought, more or less unsuccessfully, to undermine it. Death not only deprives us of life, but also compels us to spend the life that it deprives us from in the mostly unconscious fear of this deprivation. And it is precisely this unconscious fear that holds us back from exercising choice and freedom. In short, death is an evil not only because it deprives us of life, but also because it mars whatever little life we do have. While we may be able to somewhat postpone our death, there is absolutely nothing that we can do to prevent it altogether. In the words of the ancient philosopher Epicurus, 'It is possible to provide security against other ills, but as far as death is concerned, we men live in a city without walls.' All that we can do is to come to terms with death in the hope of preventing it from preventing us from making the most of our life. Of course, all this does not necessarily mean that an eternal life is desirable, especially if one disagrees with Nagel's premise that the bare experience of life is intrinsically valuable, or if one believes that it is the brevity or finiteness of human life lends it shape or meaning. The 20th century philosopher Bernard Williams in particular argued that human life is not suited to immortality. This is, however, a different debate, and I shall leave it for another time.

At this stage, I should point out that death and anxiety have not always been such a big problem for us human beings. Our ancestors evolved to live in a group and conceived of themselves less as autonomous agents and more as part of a group. In other terms, our ancestors tended to subsume their egos into the collective ego of the group. For this reason, the long-term survival or fulfilment of the group tended to take precedence over their own, comparatively limited, survival or fulfilment. This spirit of self-sacrifice is still prominent in traditional societies and other close knit groups, and lives on, even if only in a dormant or vestigial state, in all of us. As our ancestors conceived of themselves less as autonomous individuals and more as part of a group, they tended to conceive of their personal death less as the end of their life and more as a part of the life of the group. This enabled them to focus more on the present moment and on being, and less on the future and on becoming. To put it differently, by focusing more on the long-term future of the group, they could focus less on the relatively short-term future of a human life-time and more on the present moment. The 20th century philosopher Ludwig Wittgenstein noted in his philosophical treatise of 1921, *Tractatus Logico-Philosophicus*, that, 'If we take eternity to mean not infinite temporal duration but timelessness, then eternal life belongs to those who live in the present.' 'Living in the present' should not, I think, be conceptualised as some form of manic frenzy or aesthetic hedonism, but rather as the capacity and ability to take in the impressions of the moment, and perhaps also to feel the deep and subtle emotions that come from relating these impressions both to our finite, mortal selves and, at the same time, to the eternal and infinite.

In a sense, the perspective of eternity freed our ancestors from the perspective of a human life-time, but only at the price of the modern concept of self-fulfilment, which – I shall continue to assume – is the ultimate goal of freedom. There are, it seems to me, three principal scales of time, the present moment, the future of a human life-time, and the eternal. The problem with modern man is not so much that he situates himself in the future of a human life-time, since he fears death far too much to do that, but rather that he does not situate himself in any of these three scales of time. Instead, he is forever stuck somewhere in-between, this evening, tomorrow morning, next week, next Christmas, in five years' time. As a result, he has neither the joy of the present moment, nor the perspective of a human life-time, nor the immortality of the eternal. To quote from the *Bhagavad Gita*, that most ancient and venerable of Hindu scriptures, 'There is neither this world nor the world beyond nor happiness for the one who doubts.' For various reasons that I shall not presently go into, I think that it is too late for us to go back to living as our ancestors once did, and to subsume our egos into the collective ego of some group. For better or for worse, we have no other real choice but to be autonomous individuals. We have no other real choice but to be free.

6. Values

Most people are other people. Their thoughts are someone else's opinions, their lives a mimicry, their passions a quotation.

Nowadays people die of a sort of creeping common sense, and discover too late that the only things one never regrets are one's mistakes.

Oscar Wilde

In chapter 3, I suggested that only a person who reconciles the id and the superego, or who reconciles the aesthetic and the ethical lives, can become fully conscious of his individuality and of the risk and responsibility that it entails. However, to do this the person first needs to overcome the various ego defences that such a consciousness inevitably gives rise to. These may include neurosis and the manic defence, but also aesthetic indulgences, moral codes, bourgeois values, habits, customs, culture, and so on. If these ego defences are particularly common and particularly marked in the middle classes, then this is at least in part because middle class people have a more ingrained notion of 'success' and come under greater pressure to 'succeed', that is, to become something like an accountant, doctor, or lawyer, to live in a big house, to get married to a similar thinking and similar looking partner of the opposite sex, and to have children to perpetuate this ideal of middle class felicity. A middle class person deviating even slightly from this paradigm is thought of as a failure, not only by others but also – and often most of all – by himself. For this reason, every choice that he makes is especially fraught with risk and responsibility, and he is paralysed with fear and anxiety. If Emma feels anxious about sitting her exams, choosing a career, and so on, then this is because she only has a finite number of opportunities to 'make good'. And if she comes from a particularly middle class background, then 'to make good' means not only something that is particularly desirable, but also something that is particularly specific and particularly difficult to attain to.

Nothing illustrates the emptiness of society's conception of 'success' better than Leo Tolstoy's novella of 1886, *The Life of Ivan Ilyich*, which is, among other things, an acerbic attack on the artificiality and limitations of the middle classes. The novella begins with the death of a judge called Ivan Ilyich and the gathering of a number of people, among whom judges, family members, and acquaintances, to mark his passing. As these people have not yet come to terms with the possibility of their own death, they are unable to understand or empathise with that of Ivan. Instead, they begin to consider the various advantages such as money or promotion that Ivan's passing is likely to mean for them. The novella then goes back in time by thirty years, with Ivan still in the prime of his life. The younger Ivan leads a carefree existence that is 'most simple and ordinary and therefore most terrible'. He devotes most of his time and efforts to climbing the social ladder and to 'doing everything properly', but his gradual social ascent comes at the price of his family life and, more importantly, of his intellectual and emotional development. Then one day, while hanging curtains in his house, he suffers a fall and injures his side. The pain gets worse and worse until his wife insists that he consult a physician. The physician makes it clear to him that his condition is terminal and that there is absolutely nothing that he can do to remedy it. Ivan is going to die. As he lies on his deathbed passing in and out of consciousness, he has nothing for comfort but the friendship and sympathy of a peasant boy called Gerasim. Then, soon before his death, he has a revelatory exchange with his inner voice.

> *Then [Ivan] grew quiet and not only ceased*
> *weeping but even held his breath and became all*

attention. It was as though he were listening not to an audible voice but to the voice of his soul, to the current of thoughts arising within him.

'What is it you want?' was the first clear conception capable of expression in words, that he heard.

'What do you want? What do you want?' he repeated to himself.

'What do I want? To live and not to suffer,' he answered.

And again he listened with such concentrated attention that even his pain did not distract him.

'To live? How?' asked his inner voice.

'Why, to live as I used to – well and pleasantly.'

'As you lived before, well and pleasantly?' the voice repeated.

And in imagination he began to recall the best moments of his pleasant life. But strange to say none of those best moments of his pleasant life now seemed at all what they had then seemed – none of them except the first recollections of his childhood. There, in childhood, there had been something really pleasant with which it would be possible to live if it could return. But the child who had experienced that happiness existed no longer, it was like a reminiscence of somebody else.

As soon as the period began which had produced the present Ivan Ilyich, all that had then seemed joys now melted before his sight and turned into something trivial and often nasty.

And the further he departed from childhood and the nearer he came to the present the more worthless and doubtful were the joys. This began with the School of Law. A little that was really good was still found there – there was light-heartedness, friendship, and hope. But in the upper classes there had already been fewer of such good moments. Then during the first years of his official career, when he was in the service of the governor, some pleasant moments again occurred: they were the memories of love for a woman. Then all became confused and there was still less of what was good; later on again there was still less that was good, and the further he went the less there was. His marriage, a mere accident, then the disenchantment that followed it, his wife's bad breath and the sensuality and hypocrisy: then that deadly official life and those preoccupations about money, a year of it, and two, and ten, and twenty, and always the same thing. And the longer it lasted the more deadly it became. 'It is as if I had been going downhill while I imagined I was going up. And that is really what it was. I was going up in public opinion, but to the same extent life was ebbing

> *away from me. And now it is all done and there*
> *is only death.*
> *'Then what does it mean? Why? It can't be that*
> *life is so senseless and horrible. But if it really has*
> *been so horrible and senseless, why must I die and*
> *die in agony? There is something wrong!*
> *'Maybe I did not live as I ought to have done,' it*
> *suddenly occurred to him.*

. . .

> *And whenever the thought occurred to him, as it*
> *often did, that it all resulted from his not having*
> *lived as he ought to have done, he at once recalled*
> *the correctness of his whole life and dismissed*
> *so strange an idea.*

The film *Trainspotting* opens on the character of Renton, who flatly rejects the sort of unexamined middle class life that Ivan devoted all his time and efforts to achieving. For Renton, the middle class life is even more worthless than a life spent on heroin, that is, even more worthless than the paradigm of the aesthetic life, which is the most escapist and ignoble of Kierkegaard's three types of life. If the aesthetic life is aimed solely at the satisfaction of desires, that is, at pleasure, then – bar the occasional, fleeting experience – the middle class life is not even able to provide that. At the beginning of the film, Renton says,

> *Choose a job. Choose a career. Choose a family. Choose a f***ing big television. Choose washing machines, cars, compact disc players and electrical tin openers. Choose good health, low cholesterol, and dental insurance. Choose fixed interest mortgage payments. Choose a starter home. Choose your friends. Choose leisurewear and matching luggage. Choose a three-piece suit on hire purchase in a range of f***ing fabrics. Choose DIY and wondering who the f*** you are on a Sunday morning. Choose sitting on that couch watching mind-numbing, spirit-crushing game shows, stuffing f***ing junk food into your mouth. Choose rotting away at the end of it all, p***ing your last in a miserable home, nothing more than an embarrassment to the selfish, f***ed up brats you spawned to replace yourselves. Choose your future. Choose life... But why would I want to do a thing like that? I chose not to choose life. I chose something else. And the reasons? There are no reasons. Who needs reasons when you've got heroin?*

If all there is to life is middle class life, then Renton would rather choose 'something else', even though he is unable to fully articulate his reasons for doing so. For the middle class person, happiness is always in sight, yet always out of reach, and then 'it is all done and there is only death'. For this reason, it does not really matter that the sort of life that Ivan relentlessly pursued was somewhat more of an upper middle class life than that which Renton 'chose not to choose'. The various kinds of middle class life are fundamentally all the same.

Despite the impression that one might get from reading *The Life of Ivan Ilyich*, the middle class or other attitudes, beliefs, and values (henceforth 'values') that constrain a person's freedom are not timeless and universal, but the product of a given community, in a given society, at a given time in history. This subjectivity of values is often apparent in psychiatric practice, when the values of the patient clash with those of the psychiatrist and of the system and community that the psychiatrist represents. A failure on the part of the psychiatrist to recognise the subjectivity of his values can open the door for the abuse of psychiatry.

Beginning in the early 1970s, reports began appearing that political and religious dissidents in the Soviet Union were being incarcerated in maximum-security psychiatric hospitals. In 1989, the Soviet government authorised a delegation of psychiatrists from the United States to make site visits to some of these hospitals and to conduct extensive interviews of 27 suspected victims of abuse, of whom 24 had at some time received a diagnosis of schizophrenia. The investigation unearthed unequivocal evidence that psychiatry had been abused to imprison people whose only symptoms of 'mental disorder' had been the articulation and expression of dissenting political and religious opinions. In 14 out of the 27 cases, no evidence of any mental disorder whatsoever could be found, let alone mental disorder of a nature and degree that required hospitalisation in a maximum-security psychiatric hospital. The living conditions in the hospitals were primitive and highly restrictive, with 'patients' forbidden from keeping books and writing materials, and subjected both to physical restraints and to high dose injections of antipsychotic and other drugs. In a paper of 2002, *Political Abuse of Psychiatry in the Soviet Union and China: Complexities and Controversies*, Richard Bonnie writes, 'In some cases, abuse was undoubtedly attributable to intentional misdiagnosis and to knowing complicity by individual psychiatrists in an officially directed effort to repress dissident behaviour. In other cases [however] the elastic conception of mental disorder used in Soviet psychiatry was probably bent to political purposes, with individual psychiatrists closing their eyes to whatever doubts they may have had about the consequences of their actions.' In this regard, it should be noted that the prevailing psychiatric classification in the Soviet Union accommodated a broad concept of schizophrenia with mild ('latent' or 'sluggish') and moderate forms that could be diagnosed on the basis of little more than 'personality changes'. Such a loose definition of schizophrenia made it especially easy for individual psychiatrists to justify making a diagnosis of the disorder on the basis of nothing more than a minority opinion and the courage or 'madness' to express it.

Unfortunately, clashes of values such as this one are not confined to distant lands and history books. Some three years ago, a young African woman presented to me complaining of hair loss. She had recently been started on an antipsychotic drug for a psychotic episode involving auditory hallucinations, and (quite rightly) suspected the drug of being responsible for the thinning of her beautiful braided hair. I established that the auditory hallucinations consisted in the voices of several of her dead ancestors, and that the voices were castigating her for having left her native country and community. While the voices were distressing, the antipsychotic drug had not touched them, so please could I discontinue the drug and give her my blessing to consult with a witch doctor. After discussing the various options available, such as decreasing the dose of the drug or switching to another drug, I turned to her brother who had come with but mostly remained silent, and, almost as an afterthought, asked him whether he too could hear the voices. 'Yes', he replied sheepishly, 'we all do.' 'But they upset her most.'

These examples taken from psychiatric practice illustrate that even psychiatrists, that is, medically qualified prof–essionals who are accustomed to intimate interaction with a broad cross-section of people, are often blind to the parochial values that shape their perceptions, judgements, and behaviours. More generally, many of the values that are held by the vast majority of people living in Britain today are far from being timeless and universal. For example, the values of equality, fairness, and political correctness that have come to pervade almost every aspect of public life in Britain are completely alien to traditional societies, and completely alien even to the Britain of not so long ago, which, among others, governed the largest empire that history records (Figure 6a). Other examples of values that are far from being timeless and universal include those surrounding risk ('health and safety'), ideal body image, pre-marital and homosexual sexual relations, single-parenting, and the rearing of children.

Figure 6a: Cartoon by Edward Linley Sambourne published in *Punch* after Cecil Rhodes announced plans for a telegraph line and railroad from Cape Town to Cairo. The values that define our sense of self are not timeless and universal, nor are they truly ours.

People tend either not to be conscious of their values, or not to be conscious that they are just that, values, and therefore subjective. As a result, they tend to be blind to the determining role that their values play in shaping their perceptions, judgements, and behaviours. Recall from Chapter 1 that the viewer of the Rubin vase 'prefers' one mental interpretation of the optical illusion to the other, but is nonetheless able to 'see' the other after some time or prompting. Unfortunately, this is not generally the case with values. If most people living in Kenya laugh at *wazungu* (the plural form of *mzungu* or 'Westerner') who rush around from one task to the next, then this is because they are unable or unwilling to appreciate the values that define the Western worldview. Similarly, if many Westerners pour scorn over the Kenyan way of life, then this is because they too are unable or unwilling to appreciate the values that define the Kenyan worldview. In contrast, people do not generally laugh at or pour scorn over one another for preferring one mental interpretation of the Rubin vase to the other. Why the difference? A person's values are closely related to his sense of self, whereas his 'preference' for one or other mental interpretation of the Rubin vase is almost not at all. If a person's values are pitted against rival values, his sense of self comes under attack and he is compelled to defend himself against what are, in effect, uncomfortable reminders of his subjectivity, and hence of his fallibility, absurdity, and tragic insignificance. He commonly defends himself either by failing to recognise the existence of the rival values or by refusing to accept their validity. He may, for example, debase or trivialise the rival values by belittling them, pouring scorn over them, or laughing them off. As I argued in Chapter 1, humour can be used either to deny the significance or validity of something uncomfortable, or to reveal or emphasise its ridiculous or absurd aspects, in either case diffusing the anxiety that it gives rise to. When Kenyans laugh at *wazungu*, they are almost certainly doing both things at the same time, even though they are mostly unconscious of doing so. Freud held that jokes are one of only four direct routes into the unconscious, the other three being parapraxes or slips of the tongue, free association, and dreams, which he famously called 'the royal road to the unconscious'. In the words of Plato, who lived more than 2,000 years before Freud, 'every man seems to know all things in a dreamy sort of way, and then again to wake up and know nothing.'

Although a person's values are closely related to his sense of self, their origins lie far more in the family, community, and society that he happened to be born into than they do in himself as a conscious and self-determining human being. Thus, a person's worldview is not only subjective, but also, for the most part, fundamentally alien. To see this, one need only to question a person's motivations in greater depth than is usual or socially acceptable, almost as though one had 'regressed' to being an insatiably curious and fiercely insistent child (or a philosopher).

So, Emma, are you looking forward to
  graduation day?
Yes, very much so! It's so nice not to have to be a
  student anymore!
Why, what didn't you like about being a student?
Oh, er, nothing really, it's just nice to move on.
Move on?
Yeah, I'm going down to London. I've got a job in
  an investment bank. (Smiles and nods gently.)
Why?
What do you mean, why?
Well, for example, why investment banking rather
  than, say, teaching? Didn't I once hear you say
  that you wanted to be a teacher?
Well, investment banking has many downsides, of
  course.
I'm sure the money's very good.
That is certainly a part of the equation.
So you want to make a lot of money?
(Becomes silently irritated) *Of course.*
Why?
Why? So that I can afford nice things, a nice
  house, a nice car, and so on. It's a compromise,
  I guess.
A nice house and a nice car, is that all?
No, no... If I made enough money, I would retire
  early.

How much money do you think you would need?

*I don't know, two or three million quid? Cash, I
mean, not assets.*

Then what?

*(Lightens up) Then I could do what I really want
to do!*

Which is what?

That would depend.

I see.

I could do some charity work.

Why would you do that?

*To help people, of course, make a difference and
so on.*

Help people?

Yes, make a difference, give something back.

What else would you do?

*I think I'd have a family. Yes, I'd definitely have
a family. It would make my parents happy, if
nothing else.*

I see.

*I'd have to get married first, of course. I'm old-
fashioned like that.*

You're religious, aren't you?

*Well, yes, kind of. You know, it's always been
important to us.*

So you'd get married to have a family.

And out of love, of course.

What kind of person would you fall in love with?
Well, that's what people do. Why, what about
you? Did you watch the football last night?
England beat Croatia, three to one. There was
one hell of a party at the Union. Did you go?

The 20th century philosopher Jean-Paul Sartre called it 'bad faith', the habit that people have of deceiving themselves into thinking that they do not have the freedom to make choices for fear of the potential consequences of making a choice. By sticking with the safe, easy, default 'choice' and failing to recognise the multitude of other choices that are available to him, a person places himself at the mercy of the circumstances in which he happens to find himself. Thus, the person is more akin to an object than to a conscious human being, or, in Sartrean terminology, more akin to a 'being–in–itself' than to a 'being–for–itself'. People may pretend to themselves that they do not have the freedom to make choices by pursuing pragmatic concerns and adopting social roles and value systems that are alien to their nature as conscious human beings. However, to do so is in itself to make a choice, and thereby to acknowledge their freedom as conscious human beings.

One example of bad faith that Sartre gives is that of a waiter who does his best to conform to everything that a waiter should be. For Sartre, the waiter's exaggerated behaviour is evidence that he is play-acting at being a waiter, an automaton whose essence is to be a waiter. However, in order to play-act at being a waiter, the waiter must at some level be aware that he is not in fact a waiter, but a conscious human being who is deceiving himself about being a waiter. Another example of bad faith that Sartre gives is that of a young woman on a first date. The young woman's date compliments her on her physical appearance, but she ignores the obvious sexual connotations of his compliment and chooses instead to direct the compliment at herself as a conscious human being. He then takes her hand, but she neither takes it nor rejects it. Instead, she lets her hand rest indifferently in his so as to buy time and delay having to make a choice about accepting or rejecting his advances. Whereas she chooses to treat his compliment as being unrelated to her body, she chooses to treat her hand (which is a part of her body) as an object, thereby acknowledging her freedom to make choices.

For Sartre, people may pretend to themselves that they do not have the freedom to make choices, but they cannot pretend to themselves that they are not themselves, that is, conscious human beings who actually have little or nothing to do with their pragmatic concerns, social roles, and value systems. In pursuing such and such pragmatic concerns or adopting such and such social roles and such and such value systems, a person may pretend to himself that he does not have the freedom to make choices, but to do so is in itself to make a choice, namely, the choice of pretending to himself that he does not have the freedom to make choices. Man, Sartre concludes, is condemned to be free.

People adopt the values of their family, community, and society not only so as avoid the responsibility for making choices, but also so as to submit to the strong peer and social pressure to conform. 'Conformism' refers to the suspension of a person's self-determined values in favour of those shared by a group. It results, on the part of the group, from subtle unconscious influences and overt pressure, and, on the part of the person, from a desire to avoid criticism, bullying, and rejection, and to achieve a sense of security within the group. Note, however, that the dynamic of group conformism can itself be interpreted in terms of the desire to avoid the responsibility for making choices, that is, in terms of bad faith. Thus, at a subconscious level, the person's desire to conform to the group is in no small part motivated by a desire to engage in bad faith, whereas the group's desire for the person to conform to its values is in large part motivated by a desire to dissimulate its bad faith in the supposed universality of its values.

The desire to conform is advantageous in that it helps society to run smoothly and predictably, but it is disadvantageous in that it discourages the innovation, creativity, self-expression, and self-fulfilment that are the fruits of individuation and self-realisation. Moreover, the desire to conform can lead to error, as has been demonstrated by the Asch Experiment, and even to evil, as has been demonstrated by the Milgram Experiment.

First carried out in the 1950s, the famous Asch Experiment into conformity involved eight people seated around a table. Of those eight people, only one was a genuine test subject, and the other seven were confederates tutored to give the same answers as one another. Each person in turn was asked to answer an easy question such as which line is the longest or which line matches the reference line (Figure 6b), with the test-subject always the last person to be asked the question. So as not to arouse the suspicion of the test-subject, the confederates began by giving correct answers and only gradually moved to giving wrong answers. The experimenters found that, whenever the confederates gave the same wrong answer, the likelihood of the test-subject also doing so was as high as 33%. Overall, 75% of all test-subjects gave at least one wrong answer. More optimistically, follow-ups to the Asch experiment found that test-subjects were significantly more likely to resist pressure to conform if one of the confederates was 'out of tune' with the others, thereby confirming the commonly held suspicion that even a small dissenting minority can exert a strong influence within a group.

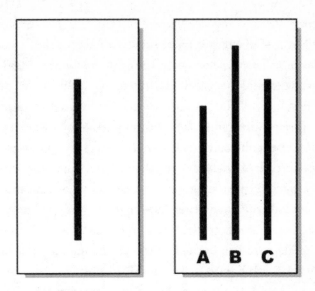

Figure 6b: One of the pairs of cards used in the Asch experiment. The reference line is on the left-hand side with the three comparison lines on the right-hand side.

In the even more famous Milgram experiment of the early 1960s, an experimenter ordered a 'teacher', who was the subject of the experiment, to give what the latter believed were painful electric shocks to a 'learner' who was actually a confederate of the experimenter. The role of the experimenter was played by a stern, impassive biology teacher dressed in a grey technician's coat, and the role of the learner was played by a 47–year–old Irish-American accountant trained for the role. The experimenter told the teacher and learner that they would be participating in a study on learning and memory in different situations. He then asked them to draw lots to 'determine' their roles, but the lots were rigged so that the subject of the experiment invariably ended up in the role of the teacher. The teacher and the learner were separated into neighbouring rooms where they could hear but not see each other. The teacher was instructed to administer a shock to the learner for each wrong answer that he gave and to increase the voltage on the apparatus by 15 volts after each shock administered. Each time the teacher administered a shock, a tape recorder that played pre-recorded sounds including screams from the learner was activated. After a number of increasingly powerful shocks, the learner began to bang on the wall. After banging on the wall and complaining about his heart condition several times, all responses by the learner ceased. If the teacher indicated that he wanted to stop the experiment, he was given a verbal prod by the experimenter. If he still wanted to stop the experiment after four increasingly authoritarian prods by the experimenter, the experiment was stopped. Otherwise, the experiment was stopped after the teacher had given the maximum 450-volt shock three times in succession. In the first set of experiments, 65% (26/40) of subjects ultimately administered the massive 450-volt shock and only one subject steadfastly refused to administer shocks below the 300-volt level.

A phenomenon that is related to conformism is 'groupthink'. Groupthink arises when the members of a group seek to minimise conflict by failing to critically test, analyse, and evaluate the ideas that are put to them as a group. As a result, the decisions reached by the group are hasty and irrational, and more unsound than if they had been taken by either member of the group alone. Even married couples can fall into groupthink, for example, when they decide to take their holidays in places that neither spouse wanted, but thought that the other wanted. Groupthink principally arises from the fear of being criticised, the fear of upsetting the group, and the hubristic sense of invulnerability that comes from being in a group. The 20th century philosopher Ludwig Wittgenstein once remarked that 'it is a good thing that I did not let myself be influenced'. In a similar vein, the 18th century historian Edward Gibbon wrote that '...solitude is the school of genius ... and the uniformity of a work denotes the hand of a single artist'. In contrast to Wittgenstein or Gibbon, modern society constantly reinforces the notions that man is a social animal, that he needs the companionship and affection of other human beings from cradle to grave, and that the chief source of his happiness should come mostly if not exclusively from intimate relationships with other similarly gregarious human beings. In the realm of the nine to five or eight to eight, large corporations glorify and reinforce conformism, decisions are taken by committees dominated by groupthink, people are evaluated according to their 'team playing skills', and any measly time out is seen as an opportunity for 'team building', 'group bonding', 'networking', or, at best, 'family time'. Yet solitude also has an important role to play in any human life, and the capacity and ability for solitude are a pre-requisite for individuation and self-realisation. In his book of 1988, *Solitude – A Return to the* Self, the psychiatrist Anthony Storr convincingly argues that 'the happiest lives are probably those in which neither interpersonal relationships nor impersonal interests are idealised as the only way to salvation. The desire and pursuit of the whole must comprehend both aspects of human nature.'

7. Ghosts

I can't explain myself, I'm afraid, Sir, because I'm not myself you see.

Lewis Carroll

There has never been a time when you and I have not existed, nor will there be a time when we will cease to exist ... the wise are not deluded by these changes.

Bhagavad Gita

Despite its subjectivity and alien origins, a person's sense of self is that which confers upon him unity and direction, that is, coherence and meaning. Without it, the person would be almost as good as dead. For this reason, he uses the same ego defences to protect himself against attacks on his sense of self as he does to protect himself against fear and anxiety, the ultimate grounds for which is death (see Chapter 5, *Death*). To understand why and in what way a person without a sense of self would be 'almost as good as dead', it is necessary to ask the question, what is a person?

A person is a self-conscious mental being who, according to the 17th century philosopher John Locke, is 'a thinking, intelligent being, that has reason and reflection, and can consider itself as itself, the same thinking thing, in different times and places'. In short, a person is a person because he can think about himself in the past, future, and conditional, and in a variety of different places: 'Next year I hope to buy a house in Dorset', 'Last August, in the South of France, I fell in love', 'Last month I could have won the lottery, if only I had bought a ticket'. If a person is a 'self-conscious mental being', what is it that makes him so? Is it his body, his brain, his 'soul'? Imagine that he has a serious accident that leaves him lying brain-dead on a hospital bed. His body is still alive but he is no longer self-conscious nor can he ever be again. Is he then still a person? If not, then his physical body is not what makes him a person.

Some argue that a person at a time A can be the same as a person at a time B because his body or brain is the same body or brain at both times, in the sense that they are spatiotemporally continuous, that is, continuous in space and time. Others argue that this is not the case, and that a person at a time A can be the same as a person at a time

B because they are psychologically continuous, that is, the mental states of the person at a time B derive or descend from the mental states of the person at a time A. To help elucidate this problem, the contemporary philosopher Sydney Shoemaker asks us to imagine that science has advanced to such an extent that it has become possible to carry out brain transplants. Two men, Mr Brown and Mr Robinson, each have their brains removed and operated on at the same time. However, a poorly trained assistant inadvertently puts Brown's brain into Robinson's head, and Robinson's brain into Brown's head. One of these men dies, but the other – say the one with Brown's brain and Robinson's head (let us call him 'Brownson') – eventually regains consciousness. When asked his name, he replies 'Brown'. Subsequently, he is able to recognise Brown's wife and family and to recount Brown's childhood memories, but he cannot recognise Robinson's wife and family nor recount Robinson's childhood memories. Who then is this man Brownson with Brown's brain and Robinson's head? If he is Brown, as most people would argue, then a person cannot be reduced to a body (as the earlier brain dead scenario may already have demonstrated). This leaves us with two possibilities: either Brownson is Brown because he has Brown's brain, or he is Brown because he is psychologically continuous with Brown.

To help decide between these two possibilities, let us carry our thought experiment further still. Let us imagine that

Brownson's brain is now divided into two equal halves or hemispheres and that each hemisphere is transplanted into a brainless body. After the operation, two people awake who are psychologically continuous with Brownson. If they are both psychologically continuous with Brownson, are they then both Brownson? And if so, are they then both also each other? Most people would argue that, even though the two people may be very similar at the time of awaking from the operation, they are not in fact the same person, and in time will develop into two very different people.

So what can we conclude from this mind-boggling discussion? It seems that what makes a person a person, what makes him a 'self-conscious mental being', depends causally upon the existence of his brain, but at the same time amounts to something more than just his brain. What this might be is unclear, and perhaps for a reason. As human beings we have a tendency to think of our personhood as something concrete and tangible, something that exists in the 'real world' and that extends through time. However, it is possible that our personhood is in fact nothing more than a product of our minds, merely a convenient concept or schema that enables us to relate our present self with our past, future, and conditional selves, and so to lend to our life a sense of coherence and meaning. This concept or schema amounts to our sense of self, which is the very basis of our ego, and which is, therefore, tantamount to one gigantic ego defence, or the sum total of all our ego defences.

A number of Eastern philosophies also hold that the ego is something of an illusion. For example, in Buddhist thought, *anattā* or *anātman* refers to the concept of the 'not-self', which is composed of five *skandhas* or elements, namely, body, sensation, perception, will, and consciousness. These five *skandhas* are in a constant state of change, but they create for the not-self the illusion of continuity, that is, the illusion of the self. For this reason, if a person consciously tries to become aware of his self, he only ever becomes aware of such and such feeling, such and such perception, or such and such thought, but never of his actual self. The 18th century empirical philosopher David Hume, who was certainly no mystic, expressed this idea eloquently in his philosophical treatise of 1739, *A Treatise of Human Nature*,

> *When I enter most intimately into what I call myself, I always stumble on some particular perception or other, of heat or cold, light or shade, love or hatred, pain or pleasure. I can never catch myself at any time without a perception, and never can observe anything but the perception. When my perceptions are removed for any time, as by sound*

> *sleep, so long am I insensible of myself, and may*
> *truly be said not to exist.*

The Buddha taught that the source of all ignorance and unhappiness is none other than the failure to recognise the illusion of the self. It is important to note that, although Buddhist thought rejects the notion of a permanent self, it does not reject the notion of an 'empirical self' that can be referred to in terms such as 'I', 'you', 'being', and 'person', nor does it reject the ultimate reality of the 'true self' or *ātman*, which corresponds to every person's potential to realise enlightenment and Buddhahood and to enter into a state of everlasting transcendental happiness. In terms of the three scales of time that I explored in Chapter 5, Buddhist thought rejects the future of a human life-time (permanent self), but not the present moment (empirical self) nor the eternal (true self or *ātman*). This emphasis on the eternal is also present in Hindu thought. In the *Bhagavad Gita*, the god Krishna appears to the archer Arjuna in the midst of the battlefield of Kurukshetra to allay his scruples about engaging in battle and shedding the blood of his cousins the Kauravas. In either case, explains Krishna, all the men on the battlefield are one day condemned to die, as are all men. Their deaths are trivial, because the spirit in them, their human essence, does not depend on their particular forms or incarnations for its continued existence. Krishna tells Arjuna, 'When one sees eternity in things that pass away and infinity in finite things, then one has pure knowledge.'

Plato takes this idea even further in the *Phaedo*, which was known to the Ancients as *On the Soul*. In the *Phaedo*, Socrates tells the philosophers Simmias and Cebes that absolute justice, absolute beauty, or absolute good cannot be apprehended with the eyes or any other bodily organ, but only by pure thought, that is, with the mind or soul. For this reason, the philosopher seeks in as far as possible to separate his soul from his body and to become pure soul. As death is the complete separation of the soul from the body, the philosopher aims at death, and indeed can be said to be almost dead. Only a person who does not fear death can be said to be a true philosopher and to possess courage and the other virtues. Most people with supposed courage endure death simply because they are afraid of yet greater evils, just as most people with supposed temperance abstain from one class of pleasures simply because they are overcome by another class of pleasures.

> *Yet the exchange of one fear or pleasure or pain for another fear or pleasure or pain, which are measured like coins, the greater with the less, is not the exchange of virtue. O my dear Simmias, is there not one true coin for which all things ought to exchange?– and that is wisdom; and only in*

> *exchange for this, and in company with this, is*
> *anything truly bought or sold, whether courage or*
> *temperance or justice.*

The idea of metaphorical reincarnation can be found not only in Eastern philosophies but also, of all places, in Plato's *Republic*, which was written as far back as the 4th century BC. At the end of the *Republic,* Plato relates an eschatological myth (a myth of death), the so-called 'myth or Er'. Er was slain in battle but came back to life twelve days later to tell the living of what he saw during the time that he was dead. During this time, his soul went on a journey to a meadow with four openings, two into the heavens above and two into the earth below. Judges sat in this meadow and ordered the good souls up through one of the openings into the heavens and the bad ones down through one of the openings into the earth. Meanwhile, clean and bright souls floated down to the meadow from the other opening into the heavens, and dusty and worn out souls rose up to the meadow from the other opening into the earth. Each soul had returned from a thousand year journey, but whereas the clean and bright souls spoke merrily of that which they enjoyed in the heavens, the dusty and worn out souls wept at that which they had endured in the underground. Souls that had committed heinous crimes, such as those of tyrants or murderers, were not permitted to rise up into the meadow, and were condemned to an eternity in the underground. After seven days in the meadow, the souls travelled for five more days to the spindle of Necessity, a shaft of intensely bright light that extends into the heavens and that holds together the universe. The souls were then asked to come forth one by one and to choose their next life from a scattered jigsaw of human and animal lives. Not having known the terrors of the underworld, the first soul hastily chose the life of a powerful dictator, only to discover that he was fated, among many other evils, to devour his own children. Although he had been virtuous in his previous life, his virtue had arisen out of habit rather than out of philosophy, and so his judgement was poor. In contrast, the souls that had known the terrors of the underworld often chose a better, more virtuous life, but this they did on no other basis than harsh experience. Thus, many of the souls exchanged a good destiny for an evil or an evil for a good. The soul of the wily Odysseus, which was the last to come forth, sought out the life of a private man with no cares. This he found easily, lying about and neglected by everybody else. After having chosen their next life, the souls travelled through the scorching Plain of Oblivion and encamped by the River of Forgetfulness. Each soul was required to drink from the river's water so as to forget all things, but the souls which had not been saved by wisdom drank more than was strictly necessary. In the night, as they slept, the souls shot up like stars to be reborn into their chosen lives. As they did so, Er opened his eyes to find himself lying on his funeral pyre.

Our attitudes, beliefs, and values may give us a sense of self, but they also define us as such and such, and, in so doing, place limits on our range of thought and action, and hence on our freedom. In chapter 3, I suggested that only a person who reconciles the id and the superego, or who reconciles the aesthetic and the ethical lives, can become fully conscious of his individuality and of the risk and responsibility that it entails. However, to do this the person first needs to overcome the various ego defences that such a consciousness inevitably gives rise to. If he cannot overcome these ego defences by means of courage (see Chapter 4, *Courage*), he might do so by means of coming to terms with the basis of fear and anxiety, which is death (see Chapter 5, *Death*). Here I suggest that he might also do so by means of renouncing his sense of self and thereby opening himself up to different modes of thinking and behaving. As 'renouncing one's sense of self' amounts to metaphorical suicide, it is related to 'coming to terms with the basis of fear and anxiety', which is death, and so to courage, of which it is also a part. However, if our sense of self is the sum total of all our ego defences, and if our ego defences are designed to protect us against fear and anxiety, then 'renouncing one's sense of self' is not so much an alternative to 'coming to terms with the basis of fear and anxiety' as it is its outcome. In other words, coming to terms with the basis of fear and anxiety is a pre-requisite for renouncing one's sense of self. As Socrates intimates in the *Phaedo*, one can hardly commit metaphorical suicide if one is still afraid of death.

An interesting corollary to the theory that our sense of self is nothing but a product of our mind is that the death of the self is not actually possible. However, one must be careful not to confuse the permanent self with the empirical self (nor, for that matter, with the true self), which obviously does exist, even if only in its parts, for example, in the five *skandhas* of the Buddhist *anattā*. The empirical self is both the sum of its parts and more than the sum of its parts, but it is not – and this is an important distinction – other than the sum of its parts. As an analogy, a car is the sum of its parts and also more than the sum of its parts, but it not something other than a car. Thus, whereas the death of the empirical self is possible, the death of the permanent self is not, if only because there is no such thing as a permanent self. Thinking of the self in these terms can help us not only to renounce the ego defences that make up the self and that limit our freedom, but also to relate to other selves and to the eternal. This, I think, is best understood by looking more closely at the Buddhist doctrine of death and rebirth.

In Buddhist thought, the death of the empirical self leads to the disaggregation of the *skandhas* and to their re-aggregation into another self which is neither identical to nor entirely different from the previous self, but which forms part of a causal continuum with it. An analogy that is often used to describe this process of rebirth or *samsāra* is that of a flame passing from one candle to the next. This cycle of rebirth can only be broken if the empirical, changing self is able to transcend its subjective and distorted image of the world, which is both conscious and unconscious, and which has the 'I am' conceit as a crucial reference point. This, then, is heaven or *nibbana*. *Nibbana*, as I see it, rests on the understanding that consciousness is a sequence of conscious moments rather than the continuous consciousness of the 'I am' conceit. Each moment is an experience of an individual mind-state such as a perception, feeling, or thought; the consciousness of an empirical self is made up of the birth and death of these individual mind-states, and 'rebirth' is nothing more than the persistence of this process.

Note that the Buddhist doctrine of rebirth is not normally amalgamated with the Hindu doctrine of reincarnation, which holds that there is a fixed or permanent entity called *ātman* that is reborn. However, if *ātman* is thought of less in terms of a 'permanent self' and more in terms of a 'human essence', then the Hindu doctrine of reincarnation begins to look more like the Buddhist doctrine of rebirth. This latter interpretation of *ātman* I think makes even more sense out of some of Krishna's pronouncements in the *Bhagavad Gita*, such as, 'There has never been a time when you and I have not existed, nor will there be a time when we will cease to exist,' or again, 'When one sees eternity in things that pass away and infinity in finite things, then one has pure knowledge.'

That a person should become fully conscious of his individuality by renouncing his sense of self may seem paradoxical. However, the 'sense of self' that he is renouncing derives not so much from himself as a conscious human being as it does from the family, community, and society that he happened to be born into (see Chapter 6, *Values*). To find his true self and the possibility of developing and expressing it, he needs in as far as possible to see beyond the vagaries of fate, to rise above parochial ties such as family and community, and to become timeless and universal – to become, so to speak, a pure essence of humanity, and then to re-cast himself as his true self. In his book of 1978, *The Unheard Cry for Meaning*, the neurologist, psychiatrist, and holocaust survivor Victor Frankl writes, 'Only to the extent that someone is living out this self transcendence of human existence is he truly human or does he become his true self. He becomes so, not by concerning himself with his self's actualisation, but by forgetting himself and giving himself, overlooking himself and focusing outward.'

Figure 7a: Hans Holzer (1920–2009), the celebrated parapsychologist and 'ghost hunter'. Ghosts, Holzer explained, were perfectly natural. They were simply human beings who were not aware that they were dead.

Shining examples of people who transcended human existence include Socrates and Diogenes the Cynic. When Socrates was still a young man, his friend Chaerephon asked the oracle at Delphi if anyone was wiser than Socrates, and the *pythia* or priestess replied that no one was wiser. To discover the meaning of this divine utterance, Socrates questioned a number of wise men, and in each case concluded, 'I am likely to be wiser than he to this small extent, that I do not think I know what I do not know.' From then on, he dedicated himself to the service of the gods by seeking out anyone who might be wise and, 'if he is not, showing him that he is not'. In the *Apology*, Socrates says that the gods attached him to Athens as upon a great and noble horse which 'needed to be stirred up by a kind of gadfly'. In the *Theaetetus*, he compares himself to a midwife who attends not to the labour of the body but to the labour of the soul, helping others to 'discover within themselves a multitude of beautiful things, which they bring forth into the light'. The method that he devised, the celebrated *elenchus* or Socratic dialogue, consists in questioning one or more people about a certain concept, for example, courage (as in the *Laches*) or friendship (as in the *Lysis*), so as to expose a contradiction in their initial assumptions about the concept, and thereby to provoke a reappraisal of the concept. As the process is iterative, it leads to an increasingly precise or refined definition of the concept or, more often than not, to the conclusion that the concept cannot be defined, and thus that we know far less than we thought that we did.

Socrates devoted himself entirely to discussing philosophy, for which he never accepted payment. It is unclear how he earned a living, but a combination of meagre needs and rich friends may have been enough to get him by. In 399 BC, at the age of 70, he was indicted by three men for offending the Olympian gods and thereby breaking the law against impiety. He was accused of 'studying things in the sky and below the earth', 'making the worse into the stronger argument', and 'teaching these same things to others'. In the *Apology*, he gives a defiant defence, intimating to the jurors that they should be ashamed of their eagerness to possess as much wealth, reputation, and honours as possible, while not caring for or giving thought to wisdom or truth, or the best possible state of their soul. 'Wealth', he says 'does not bring about excellence, but excellence makes wealth and everything else good for men, both individually and collectively.' After bringing on his conviction, he tells the jurors that he was sentenced to death not because he lacked words, but because he lacked shamelessness and the willingness to say what they would most gladly have heard from him. 'It is not difficult to avoid death, gentlemen; it is much more difficult to avoid wickedness, for it runs faster than death.'

Throughout his lifetime, Socrates was a beacon of courage. He served in the Athenian army during the campaigns of Potidaea (432 BC), Delium (424 BC), and Amphipolis (422 BC), which were, with one or two exceptions, the only times he ever left Athens. In the *Laches*, Laches calls upon Socrates for advice because of his courageous behaviour during the retreat from Delium. Athens, Laches opines, would have emerged victorious if only the other Athenians could have behaved like him. In the *Symposium*, the infamous Athenian general and statesman Alcibiades says that Socrates singlehandedly saved his life at Potidaea, and that he took the hardships of the campaign 'much better than anyone in the whole army'. In the *Apology*, Socrates warns that 'a man who really fights for justice must lead a private, not a public, life if he is to survive for even a short time', a warning that is almost as relevant today as it was in the 5th century BC. He cites the time in 406 BC when he was chairing the assembly meeting and alone opposed the trial as a body of the generals who, after the naval Battle of Arginusae, failed to pick up the Athenian survivors because of a violent storm. At the time the orators had been ready to prosecute him and take him away, although later everyone realised that the prosecution would have been illegal. He also cites the time in 404 BC when the Thirty Tyrants asked him and four others to bring the innocent Leon of Salamis to be executed. He alone refused, even though his refusal may have cost him his life. Such was the courage of Socrates, who in the end was condemned for being, in the words of Plato, 'the wisest, justest, and best of all the men whom I have ever known'.

Diogenes of Sinope or Diogenes the Cynic was a contemporary of Socrates' pupil Plato, whom Plato described as 'a Socrates gone mad'. Like Socrates and, to a lesser extent, Plato,

Diogenes favoured direct verbal interaction over the written account. When a man called Hegesias asked to be lent one of his writing tablets, he replied, 'You are a simpleton, Hegesias; you do not choose painted figs, but real ones; and yet you pass over the true training and would apply yourself to written rules.' After being exiled from his native Sinope for having defaced its coinage, Diogenes moved to Athens, took up the life of a beggar, and made it his mission to metaphorically deface the coinage of custom and convention, which, he maintained, was the false coin of morality. He disdained the need for conventional shelter or any other such 'dainties' and elected to live in a tub and survive on a diet of onions. He proved to the later satisfaction of the Stoics that happiness has nothing whatever to do with a person's material circumstances, and held that human beings had much to learn from studying the simplicity and artlessness of dogs, which, unlike human beings, had not 'complicated every simple gift of the gods'. The terms 'cynic' and 'cynical' derive from the Greek *kynikos*, which is the adjective of *kyon* or 'dog'.

Diogenes placed reason and nature firmly above custom and convention, which he held to be incompatible with happiness. It is natural for a human being to act in accord with reason, and reason dictates that a human being should live in accord with nature. Thus, he taught that, if an act is not shameful in private, then it should not be shameful in public either. Upon being challenged for masturbating in the marketplace, he replied, 'If only it were so easy to soothe hunger by rubbing an empty belly'. Upon being asked, on another occasion, where he came from, he replied, 'I am a citizen of the world' (*cosmopolites*), a radical claim at the time and the first recorded use of the term 'cosmopolitan'. Although Diogenes privileged reason, he despised the sort of abstract philosophy that was being practiced elsewhere and in particular at Plato's Academy. When, to great acclaim, Plato defined a human being as an animal, biped, and featherless, Diogenes plucked a fowl and brought it to the Academy with the words, 'Behold! I have brought you Plato's man.' Plato consequently revised his definition, adding to it 'with broad nails'.

Diogenes was not impressed with his fellow men, not even with Alexander the Great, who came to meet him one morning while he was lying in the sunlight. When Alexander asked him whether there was any favour he might do for him, he replied, 'Yes, stand out of my sunlight.' Much to his credit, Alexander still declared, 'If I were not Alexander, then I should wish to be Diogenes.' In another account of the conversation, Alexander found Diogenes looking attentively at a pile of human bones. Diogenes explained, 'I am searching for the bones of your father (King Philip of Macedon), but cannot distinguish them from those of a slave.' Diogenes used to stroll about in broad daylight with a lamp. Whenever curious people asked him what he was doing, he would reply, 'I am just looking for a human being.' Much to his chagrin, all he ever found were rascals and scoundrels. When asked how he wished to be buried, he left instructions to be thrown outside the city wall so that wild animals could feast upon his body. After his death in the city of Corinth, the Corinthians erected to his memory a pillar upon which they rested a dog of Parian marble. Diogenes taught by living example that wisdom and happiness belong to the person who is independent of society. He was, I think, a shining example of the art of failure.

Figure 7b: Diogenes searching for a human being. Attributed to JHW Tischbein (c 1780)

8. Madness

True, we love life, not because we are used to living, but because we are used to loving. There is always some madness in love, but there is also always some reason in madness.

Friedrich Nietzsche

To be normal is the ideal aim of the unsuccessful.

CG Jung

To summarise the position that has so far been reached, if a person is to become fully conscious of his individuality, he needs to come to terms with the basis of fear and anxiety, which is death, and then to renounce his acquired sense of self, which amounts to metaphorical suicide. This is not going to happen overnight, but only, if at all, very gradually over several months and years. A person's beliefs, attitudes, and values (henceforth, 'beliefs') are stored in his brain in the form of nerve cell pathways. Over time and with frequent use, these neural pathways become increasingly worn in, such that it becomes increasingly difficult to alter them, and so to alter the beliefs that they correspond to. If these beliefs are successfully challenged, the person begins to suffer from 'cognitive dissonance', which is the psychological discomfort that results from holding two or more inconsistent or contradictory beliefs ('cognitions') at the same time. To reduce this cognitive dissonance the person may either (1) adapt his old beliefs, which is difficult or (2) maintain the *status quo* by justifying or 'rationalising' his old beliefs, which is not so difficult and therefore more common. The ego defence of rationalisation involves the use of feeble but seemingly plausible arguments either to justify one's beliefs ('sour grapes') or to make them seem 'not so bad after all' ('sweet lemons'). 'Sour grapes' is named after one of the fables attributed to Aesop, *The Fox and the Grapes*.

> *One hot summer's day a Fox was strolling through an orchard till he came to a bunch of Grapes just ripening on a vine which had been trained over a lofty branch. 'Just the thing to quench my thirst', quoth he. Drawing back a few paces, he took a run and a jump, and just missed the bunch. Turning round again with a One, Two, Three, he jumped up, but with no greater success. Again and again*

*he tried after the tempting morsel, but at last had
to give it up, and walked away with his nose in the
air, saying: 'I am sure they are sour.'*

In the case of Aesop's fox, the cognitive dissonance arises from the cognitions 'I am an agile and nimble fox' and 'I can't reach the grapes on the branch', and the rationalisation, which is a form of 'sour grapes', is 'I am sure the grapes are sour'. Had the fox chosen to use 'sweet lemons' instead of 'sour grapes', he might have said something like, 'In any case, there are far juicier grapes in the farmer's orchard.' Another example of rationalisation is the student who fails his exams and who blames the examiners for being biased. In this case, the cognitive dissonance arises from the cognitions 'I am an intelligent, capable person' and 'I failed my exams', and the rationalisation, which is once again a form of 'sour grapes', is 'I am sure the examiners are biased'. Had the student chosen to use 'sweet lemons' instead of 'sour grapes', he might have said something like, 'In any case, failing my exams has given me more time to study / gain experience / examine my career options / enjoy student life. One of the most famous examples of rationalisation comes from Leon Festinger's book of 1956, *When Prophecy Fails*, in which Festinger discusses his experience of infiltrating a UFO doomsday cult whose leader had recently prophesised the end of the world. When the end of the world failed to materialise, most of the cult's members dealt with the cognitive dissonance that arose from the cognitions 'the leader prophesised that the world is going to end' and 'the world did not end' not by abandoning the cult or its leader, but by introducing the rationalisation that the world had been saved by the strength of their faith.

Human beings are not rational, but rationalising animals. If they find it frightening to think and painful to change, this is in large part because thinking and changing represent major threats to the beliefs that make up their sense of self. Given this state of affairs, any tectonic shift in a person's outlook is only ever going to occur incrementally and over a long period of time. Moreover, such a tectonic shift is likely to be provoked by a significant deterioration in the person's circumstances, a deterioration that overwhelms his ego defences and leaves him with no alternative but to adopt the depressive position. In *Remembrance of Things Past*, the early 20th century novelist Marcel Proust tells us, 'Happiness is good for the body, but it is grief which develops the strengths of the mind.'

I discussed the subject of depression in quite some detail in my book of 2008, *The Meaning of Madness*, in which I argued, among others, that the concept of depression as a mental disorder may be useful for the more severe cases of clinical depression seen by hospital psychiatrists, but probably not for the majority of cases of 'depression', which, for the most part, are mild and short-lived and easily interpreted in terms of life circumstances, human nature, or the human condition. Thus, rather than talk about depression, I prefer to talk about the much broader concept of the depressive position, which I intend to mean the polar opposite of the manic defence or position. A person who uses the manic defence or indeed any other ego defence seeks to avoid the depressive position by pretending to himself that things matter, that he is important, and that his life is worth living. Sometimes, however, the gap between the person's actual reality and desired reality may become so large that his ego defences can no longer carpet over it. As in Psalm 41, *abyssus abyssum invocat* – 'hell brings forth hell' or, in an alternative translation, 'the deep calls onto the deep'.

The person has no alternative but to adopt the depressive position, and thereby to signal to himself that there is something seriously wrong in his life, and that this something is going to need thinking through and changing. For a person to adopt the depressive position is for him to give himself the time and the space to stand back at a distance, examine his bigger picture, re-evaluate his needs, and formulate a modest but realistic plan for fulfilling them. Although the adoption of the depressive position may serve such a mundane purpose, it may also enable a person to develop a deeper understanding of himself and a more refined perspective on his life and on life in general. From an existential standpoint, the adoption of the depressive position obliges a person to become aware of his mortality and freedom, and challenges him to exercise the latter within the framework of the former. By meeting this difficult challenge, the person is able to break out of the cast that has been imposed upon him, discover who he truly is, and, in so doing, begin to give deep meaning to his life. Around the world, every mythology has a hero who retreats, even to Hades itself in the case of Odysseus, to find himself and re-emerge as a Hero. In the *Divine Comedy*, Dante also had to journey through hell and purgatory before he could reach the gates of heaven and find his Beatrice (Latin, 'happiness').

> *In the middle of our life's walk*
> *I found myself alone in a dark forest*
> *Where my path was confused.*
>
> *Ah how hard it is to retell*
> *How dense, dark, and dangerous*
> *The thought of it alone fills me with fear!*
>
> *So bitter that death is scarcely worse;*
> *But to speak of the good I found there,*
> *I shall tell of the other things that I saw.*

> Dante, *The Divine Comedy: Hell*,
> Opening verses, trans. N Burton

Figure 8: This crayon drawing by a hospital in-patient with severe depression alludes to her temporary withdrawal from mainstream society. The months that she spent in hospital gave her the time and the solitude to think over her life, and the motivation to make difficult but necessary changes to it. She went on to make a full recovery.

If, as I suggest, the depressive position is the outcome of an unbridgeable gap between actual reality and desired reality, then it follows that the depressive position can be adopted either (1) if actual reality is especially bad, or (2) if desired reality is especially good. Thus, not all people who adopt the depressive position do so because of a marked deterioration in their life circumstances; some do so because they have high standards and expectations for themselves and for life in general, and come to be disillusioned by the comparative baseness of their life circumstances, human nature, or the human condition. In other words, the adoption of the depressive position is just as much a sign of nobility as it is a symptom of failure. Furthermore, whereas the adoption of the depressive position may provoke a tectonic shift in a person's outlook, it may also result from, or be prolonged by, the aftershocks of such a shift. Thus, the adoption of the depressive position may be either the cause or the symptom of an existential re-appraisal, or, more often than not, both the cause *and* the symptom. In existential terms, by refusing to face up to 'non-being', a person is acting in bad faith and living out a life that is inauthentic and unfulfilling. Facing up to non-being can bring about a sense of calm, freedom, even nobility, but it can also bring about responsibility, loneliness, and insecurity, and hence the adoption or prolongation of the depressive position.

So far I have spoken only of the depressive position. However, an existential re-appraisal may also cause and be caused by a range of other 'abnormal' mental states and disturbances. In Plato's *Phaedrus*, Socrates says,

> *Madness, provided it comes as the gift of heaven, is the channel by which we receive the greatest blessings ... the men of old who gave things their names saw no disgrace or reproach in madness; otherwise they would not have connected it with the name of the noblest of arts, the art of discerning the future, and called it the manic art ... So, according to the evidence provided by our ancestors, madness is a nobler thing than sober sense ... madness comes from God, whereas sober sense is merely human.*

To see this, one need look no further than the unending list of highly insightful and accomplished people to have suffered from a mental disorder such as depression or bipolar disorder. Snippets from this list might include Balzac, Beethoven, and Blake; Faulkner, Fitzgerald, and Foucault; Handel, Hemingway, and Hugo; Schopenhauer, Schumann, and Shelley; Tchaikovsky, Tennyson, and Tolstoy; Waugh, Whitman, and Woolf. Many of these people have gone so far as to credit their creative genius with their 'moods of the mind'. For example, Edgar Allen Poe had the narrator of his semi-autobiographical short story of 1842, *Eleonora*, relate,

> *I am come of a race noted for vigor of fancy and ardour of passion. Men have called me mad; but the question is not yet settled, whether madness is or not the loftiest intelligence – whether much that is glorious – whether all that is profound – does not spring from disease of thought – from moods of the mind exalted at the expense of the general intellect. They who dream by day are cognizant of many things which escape those who dream only by night. In their grey visions they obtain glimpses of eternity ... They penetrate, however rudderless or compassless, into the vast ocean of the 'light ineffable'.*

Is his poem of 1845, *The Raven*, Poe tells of the mysterious visit of a talking raven to a distraught lover on the brink of madness. The poem is noted for its musicality, stylised language, and supernatural atmosphere, and it is likely that the raven personifies either Poe's mental disorder or his related alcoholism. In the final stanza of the poem Poe alludes to 'Pallas', which is another name for Athena, the goddess of wisdom who was born by bursting out of the forehead of her father Zeus.

And the Raven, never flitting, still is sitting, still
*   is sitting*
On the pallid bust of Pallas just above my
*   chamber door;*
And his eyes have all the seeming of a demon's
*   that is dreaming,*
And the lamplight o'er him streaming throws his
*   shadow on the floor;*
And my soul from out that shadow that lies
*   floating on the floor*
Shall be lifted – nevermore!

Jung's life story is, I think, especially illustrative of the relationship that can exist between mental disturbance and individuation and self-realisation. Carl Gustav Jung was born in 1875 in the canton of Thurgau to Paul Jung, a poor rural pastor in the Swiss reformed Church, and to Emilie Preiswerk, a melancholic woman who claimed to be visited by spirits at night. His paternal grandfather Carl Gustav Jung, after whom he was named, was a physician who was rumoured to be the illegitimate son of Goethe, and who rose to become Rector of

Basel University and Grand Master of the Swiss Lodge of Freemasons. His maternal grandfather Samuel Presiwerk was an eccentric theologian who had visions, conversed with the dead, and devoted his life to learning Hebrew in the belief that it was the language spoken in heaven. He used to make his daughter Emilie (Jung's mother) sit behind him while he composed his sermons, so as to prevent the devil from peering over his shoulder. When Jung was three years old, his mother had a nervous breakdown for which she needed to spend several months in hospital. In his autobiography of 1961, *Memory, Dreams, Reflections*, he wrote 'From then on I always felt mistrustful when the word 'love' was spoken. The feeling I associated with 'woman' was for a long time that of innate unreliability.' Jung's father was kind but weak-willed, and all too accepting of the religious dogma in which he had long lost all faith.

Jung was a solitary and introverted child who imagined that he had two personalities, that of a typical schoolboy of his time (Personality No 1), and that of a dignified, authoritative, and influential man from the past (Personality No 2). He once carved a tiny mannequin into the end of a wooden ruler, which he kept together with a painted stone in a pencil case in his attic. He periodically returned to the mannequin, bringing to it scrolls inscribed in a secret language of his invention. Perhaps unsurprisingly, he was not popular at school. At the age of 12, he received a blow to the head and for a moment was unconscious. He lay on the ground for much longer than necessary and thought, 'Now you won't have to go to school anymore'. For the next six months, he avoided school by fainting each time he was made to go, an experience which gave him an early insight into hysteria.

Inspired by a dream, Jung entered the University of Basel in 1895 to study natural science and medicine. His father's premature death one year later prompted his mother to comment, rather eerily, 'He died in time for you'. During his early years at the University of Basel, Jung had a dream in which he was making painful headway through dense fog, with a tiny light in the cup of his hands and a gigantic black figure chasing after him. When he awoke he realised that the black figure was his own shadow, brought into being by the light that he was carrying: '...this light was my consciousness, the only light that I have. My own understanding is the sole treasure I possess, and the greatest.' After presenting a paper on *The Limits of the Exact Sciences*, he spent two years attending and recording the séances of a young medium, his cousin, Hélène Preiswerk. He submitted his observations in the form of a doctoral thesis entitled *On the Psychology and Pathology of So-Called Occult Phenomena*.

Towards the end of his studies, a reading of Krafft-Ebing's textbook of psychiatry led Jung to choose psychiatry as a career. The Preface alone had such a profound effect on him that he had to stand up to catch his breath: Here alone the two currents of my interest could flow together and in a united stream dig their own bed. Here was the empirical field common to biological and spiritual facts, which I had everywhere sought and nowhere found.' Jung was taken on at the renowned Burghölzli Psychiatric Hospital in Zürich as an assistant to Eugen Bleuler, who went down in history as the man who coined the term 'schizophrenia'. Bleuler set Jung to work on Galton's word-association test, and in 1906 he published 'Studies in Word Association', which he thought provided hard evidence for the existence of unconscious complexes. He sent a copy to Freud, and on their first meeting in Vienna the two men conversed without interruption for thirteen hours.

Jung needed a father as much as Freud needed a son, and Freud formally anointed Jung his 'son and heir'. However, as time passed, it became increasingly clear that Jung was unable to accept Freud's assumptions that human motivation is exclusively sexual, or that the unconscious mind is entirely personal. For Jung, sexuality was but one aspect or mode of expression of a broader 'life force', and beneath the personal unconscious there was a deeper and more important layer that contained the entire psychic heritage of mankind. The existence of this 'collective unconscious' had been hinted at by Jung's childhood dreams and experiences, and confirmed by the delusions and hallucinations of psychotic patients which contained symbols and images that occurred in myths and fairy-tales from all around the world. In his book of 1912, *Transformations and Symbols of the Libido*, Jung replaced Freud's concept of libido with a much broader concept of undifferentiated psychic energy, arguing that undifferentiated psychic energy could 'crystallise' into the universal symbols contained in dreams and myths, for example, into the hero's slaying of the dragon, which represents the struggle of the adolescent ego for deliverance from parental dominance. For Jung, the purpose of life was 'individuation', which involves pursuing one's own vision of the truth and, in so doing, realising one's fullest potential as a human being. If this meant disagreeing with Freud, then so be it. In 1913, on the eve of the First World War, Jung and Freud broke off their relationship.

Once again Jung was alone, and he spent the next few years in a troubled but highly creative state of mind that verged on psychosis and led him to a 'confrontation with the unconscious'. By then Jung had had five children with his wife Emma Rauschenbach, the daughter of a rich industrialist. Despite being happily married, he felt that he needed a muse as well as a home-maker, observing that 'the pre-requisite of a good marriage ... is the license to be unfaithful'. The marital strife that resulted from his affairs, and particularly from his affair with a former patient called Toni Wolff, contributed to his troubled state of mind, and Emma accepted Toni as much from a concern for Jung's sanity as from a desire to save her marriage. During his confrontation with the unconscious, Jung gained first-hand experience of psychotic material in which he found a 'matrix of mythopoeic imagination which has vanished from our rational age'. Like Gilgamesh, Odysseus, Heracles, Orpheus, and Aeneas before him, he travelled deep down into an abyssal underworld where he conversed with Salome, a beautiful young woman who was the archetype of the feminine, and with Philemon, an old man with a white beard and the wings of a kingfisher who was the archetype of the wise old man. Although Salome and Philemon were products of his unconscious, they had a life of their own and said things that he had not previously thought. In Philemon, Jung had at long last found the father-figure that both Freud and his own father had singularly failed to be. More than a father-figure, Philemon was a guru, and the projection of what Jung himself was later to become – the 'wise old man of Zürich'. At the end of the First World War, Jung re-emerged into sanity, and considered that he had found in his madness 'the prima materia for a lifetime's work'.

It is true that mental disturbance may provoke a change in outlook and thereby promote individuation and self-realisation. For all this, the varieties of mental disturbance that are severe and prolonged enough to qualify as mental disorder should not be romanticised, sought out, or left untreated. Many cases of mental disorder have a strong biological basis and are not simply the outcome of environmental or psychological factors. All mental disorders are drab and intensely painful, and most people who suffer from one would not wish it on anyone, least of all on themselves. In many cases, mental disorder can lead to serious harm or even to death by accident, self-neglect, or self-harm. Even highly successful people with a mental disorder such as Sylvia Plath or Virginia Woolf committed suicide in the end, and more than 90% of people who die by suicide are thought to have been suffering from a mental disorder at the time of killing themselves. To paraphrase Plato, madness may be the channel by which we receive the greatest blessings, but only provided it comes as the gift of heaven.

9. Happiness

Don't fear god,
Don't worry about death,
What is good is easy to get, and
What is terrible is easy to endure.

Epicurus, *Tetrapharmakos* or 'four-part cure'

I have found power in the mystery of thought.

Euripides

Having freedom is one thing, but deciding what to do with it is quite another. Freedom requires judgement, and judgement requires perspective, which is a combination of knowledge and understanding, and which is therefore, like courage, a kind of wisdom. The question of deciding what to do with freedom approximates to the question of the purpose or 'meaning' of life, which is one that many people would rather not ask for fear of the answer – or lack thereof.

Historically and still today, many people believe that humankind is the creation of a supernatural entity called God, that God had an intelligent purpose in creating humankind, and that this intelligent purpose is the 'meaning of life'. I do not propose to go through the various arguments for and against the existence of God. However, even if God exists, and even if He had an intelligent purpose in creating humankind, no one really knows what this purpose might be, or that it is especially meaningful. The Second Law of Thermodynamics states that the entropy of a closed system such as the universe increases up to the point at which equilibrium is reached, and God's purpose in creating humankind and, indeed, all of nature, might have been nothing more lofty that to catalyse this process. If our God-given purpose is to act as super-efficient heat dissipaters, then having no purpose at all is better than having this sort of purpose because it frees us to be the authors of our own purpose or purposes and thereby to lead truly dignified and meaningful lives. For this same reason, having no purpose at all is better than having any kind of purpose, even a more traditional and uplifting purpose such as 'serving God' or 'improving our karma'. In short, even if God exists, and even if He had an intelligent purpose in creating humankind (and why should He have had?), we do not know what this purpose might be and, whatever it might be, we would rather be able to do without it. Unless we can be free to become the authors of our own purpose or purposes, our lives may have, at worse, no purpose at all, and, at best, only some unfathomable and potentially trivial purpose that is not of our choosing.

Some might object that not to have a pre-determined purpose is, really, not have any purpose at all. However, this is to believe (1) that for something to have a purpose, it must necessarily have been created with a purpose in mind, and (2) that something that was created with a purpose in mind must necessarily have the same purpose for which it was created. Last summer, I visited the vineyards of Châteauneuf-du-Pape in the South of France. One evening, I picked up a beautiful rounded stone called a *galet* which I later took back to England and put to excellent use as a book-end. In the vineyards of Châteauneuf-du-Pape, the declared purpose of these stones is to absorb the heat from the sun during the daytime and then to release it during the night time. Of course, these stones were not created with this or any other purpose in mind. Even if they were created with a purpose in mind, then this purpose was almost certainly not to make great wine, serve as book-ends, or be beautiful. That same evening over supper, I got my friends to blind-taste a bottle of claret that I had brought along from England. As I did not have a decanter to hand, I kept the wine in its bottle and masked the identity of the bottle by slipping it into one of a pair of socks. Unlike the *galet*, the sock had been created with a purpose in mind, even though this purpose was very different from (although, note, not strictly incompatible with) the one that it eventually found.

Some might yet object that talk about the purpose of life is neither here nor there because life is merely a prelude to some form of eternal afterlife and this is, if you like, its purpose. One can marshal up at least four arguments against this position. (1) If only from our discussion of personhood (see Chapter 7, *Ghosts*), it is not at all clear that there is or even can be some form of eternal afterlife that involves the survival of the personal ego. (2) Even if there is such an eternal afterlife, living for ever is not in itself a purpose, and so the question naturally arises, what is the purpose of the eternal afterlife? If the eternal afterlife has a pre-determined purpose, again, we do not know what this purpose might be and, whatever it might be, we would rather be able to do without it. Instead of having a pre-determined purpose, we would rather be free to determine our own purpose or purposes, which we could just as well do in this life as in an eternal afterlife. (3) It is not just that reliance on an eternal afterlife effectively postpones the question of life's purpose, but also that it prevents us from determining a purpose or purposes for that which may well be the only life that we have. (4) If it is the brevity or finiteness of human life that gives it shape and purpose, then an eternal afterlife cannot, by definition, have any purpose. I personally do not believe that it is the brevity or finiteness of human life that gives it shape and purpose, and rather suspect that the idea is just another ego defence against death. This is, however, a different debate, and I shall leave it for another time.

In conclusion, whether or not God exists, whether or not He has a purpose for us, and whether or not there is an eternal afterlife, we should strive to create our own purpose or purposes. In Sartrean terms, whereas for the *galet* it is true only that existence precedes essence, for the sock it is true both that essence precedes existence (when the sock is used on a foot) *and* that existence precedes essence (when the sock is used other than on a foot, for example, as a bottle sleeve). Human beings are either like the rock or like the sock, but whichever one they are like, they are better off creating their own purpose or purposes. To re-iterate, unless we can be free to be the authors of our purpose or purposes, our lives may have, at worse, no purpose at all, and, at best, only some unfathomable and potentially trivial purpose that is not of our choosing. Plato once defined a human being as an animal, biped, featherless, and with broad nails (see Chapter 7, *Ghosts*), but another much better definition that he gave was simply this, 'A being in search of meaning.'

The pessimistic 19th century philosopher Arthur Schopenhauer opened his essay of 1851, *On the Vanity of Existence*, thus,

> *The vanity of existence is revealed in the whole form existence assumes: in the infiniteness of time and space contrasted with the finiteness of the individual in both; in the fleeting present as the sole form in which actuality exists; in the contingency and relativity of all things; in continual becoming without being; in continual desire without satisfaction; in the continual frustration of striving of which life consists.*

There is a lot of truth in Schopenhauer's assessment of human nature and the human condition. At a cosmic level, the earth is something like a small piece of Stilton or Roquefort cheese, with human beings and the rest of creation making up the greenish mould that feeds upon it and gives it its distinctive character. If the naturalist account is correct – and so far there is no reason to suppose that it is not – human beings are the outcome of a long process of natural selection that occurs not at the level of organism but at the level of the gene. Thus, human beings are mere apparatuses for the survival and propagation of their genes, nothing more than the incidental by-products of the purposes of 'their' genes. Needless to say, this is a state of affairs far worse than even Schopenhauer could have imagined.

Figure 9: According to Arthur Schopenhauer, the vanity of existence is revealed, among other things, in the infiniteness of time and space contrasted with the finiteness of the individual in both.

Mercifully, it is not necessary for something to have been created with a purpose for it to have a purpose, nor is there any reason to suppose that a pre-determined purpose is better than a created one. For example, in 1949 the psychiatrist and researcher John Cade serendipitously discovered the calming properties of lithium. The naturally occurring salt soon became the first effective drug for the treatment of bipolar disorder, ushering in an era of hope and optimism for bipolar sufferers and their relatives and carers. Clearly, the fact that lithium had not been created with any purpose, let alone the purpose of stabilising the mood of human beings, did not make it any less effective or invaluable in the treatment of bipolar disorder. Moreover, mood stabilisation is not the only purpose that lithium has found, as it is also used in the manufacture of aircraft parts, batteries, focal lenses, mobile phones, rocket propellants, and many other things besides. Just as with lithium, human life may not have been created with any pre-determined purpose, but this does not mean that it cannot have a purpose, nor that this purpose cannot be just as good as, or even better than, any pre-determined one.

In trying to think about what our purpose or meaning might be, a good place to start is with Aristotle's *Nicomachean Ethics*, which is named for or after Aristotle's son Nicomachus. In the *Nicomachean Ethics*, Aristotle tries to discover 'the supreme good for man', that is, the best way for man to lead his life and to give it purpose and meaning. For Aristotle, a thing is best understood by looking at its end, goal, or purpose (*telos*). For example, the goal of a knife is to cut, and it is by grasping this that one best understands what a knife is; the goal of medicine is good health, and it is by grasping this that one best understands what medicine is (or ideally should be). If one does this for some time, it soon becomes apparent that some goals are subordinate to other goals, which are themselves subordinate to yet other goals. For example, a medical student's goal may be to qualify as a doctor, but this goal is subordinate to his goal to heal the sick, which is itself subordinate to his goal to earn a living by doing something useful. This could go on and on, but unless the medical student has a goal that is an end-in-itself, nothing that he does is actually worth doing. What, asks Aristotle, is this goal that is not a means to an end but an end-in-itself? This Supreme Good, says Aristotle, is happiness (*eudaimonia*).

> *And of this nature Happiness is mostly thought to be, for this we choose always for its own sake, and never with a view to anything further: whereas honour, pleasure, intellect, in fact every excellence we choose for their own sakes, it is true, but we choose them also with a view to happiness,*

> *conceiving that through their instrumentality we shall be happy: but no man chooses happiness with a view to them, nor in fact with a view to any other thing whatsoever.*

All well and good, but what is 'happiness'? Recall that, for Aristotle, it is by understanding the distinctive function of a thing that one can understand its essence. For example, one cannot understand what it is to be a gardener unless one can understand that the distinctive function of a gardener is 'to tend to a garden with a certain degree of skill'. Whereas human beings need nourishment like plants and have sentience like animals, their distinctive function, says Aristotle, is their unique capacity to reason. Thus, the Supreme Good, or Happiness, for human beings is to lead a life that enables them to exercise and to develop their reason, and that is in accordance with rational principles. In contrast to amusement or pleasure, which can be enjoyed even by animals, happiness is not a state, but an activity, and it is profound and enduring. Aristotle acknowledges that our good or bad fortune can play a part in determining our happiness; for example, he acknowledges that happiness can be affected by such factors as our material circumstances, our place in society, and even our physical appearance. Yet he maintains that, by living our life to the full according to our essential nature as rational beings, we are bound to become happy regardless of our good or bad fortune. For this reason, happiness is more a question of behaviour and of habit – of 'excellence' and of 'virtue' – than of luck. A person who cultivates reason and who lives according to rational principles is able to bear his misfortunes with equanimity, and thus can never be said to be truly unhappy.

In short, happiness for Aristotle consists in developing and exercising reason. A person's ability to exercise reason may be severely restricted by addictions, phobias, obsessions, neurosis, enculturation, socialisation, learned behaviour, and so on. At the same time, it is only by exercising reason that the person can free himself from these various prisons. Thus, the more a person exercises reason, the more he is able to exercise reason, and the more he is able to exercise reason, the more he exercises reason. Just as freedom begets freedom, so reason begets reason, and reason begets freedom, and freedom begets reason, and both together beget knowledge of the truth (that is, wisdom), which for Aristotle is supreme happiness.

Epicurus of Samos, who flourished not long after Aristotle died, founded a school of philosophy that convened at his home and garden in Athens and that dedicated itself to attaining happiness through the exercise of reason and the application of rational principles. According to Epicurus, reason teaches that pleasure is good and that pain is bad, and that pleasure and pain are the ultimate measures of good and bad. This has often been misconstrued as a call for rampant hedonism, rather than the absence of pain and tranquillity of mind that Epicurus actually intended. Indeed, Epicurus explicitly warned against overindulgence, because overindulgence so often leads to pain.

Epicurus wrote prolifically, but the early Christians thought of him as especially ungodly among the ancient philosophers, and almost none of his works survived their disapprobation. Epicurus held that the gods exist, but that they have absolutely no concern for, or even awareness of, humankind. Indeed, for them to get involved in the menial matters of human beings would be to perturb the supreme happiness and tranquillity that characterises and even defines them. Human beings should seek to emulate the gods in their supreme happiness and tranquillity, but they need not to fear them.

Neither need they to fear death, this for two principal reasons. (1) The mind of a person is a part of his body, and, just like other parts of his body (and everything else in the universe), it consists of atoms. The death of the person entails the death of both his body and his mind and the dispersion of their atoms. As there is no longer any person to be troubled, death cannot trouble the person after he is dead. And if death cannot trouble the person after he is dead, then nor should it trouble him while he is alive (this is the famous 'no subject of harm argument'). (2) The eternity that comes before a person's birth is not regarded as an evil. Therefore, nor should the eternity that comes after his death (this is the famous 'symmetry argument'). The reader may recall from Chapter 5 that Thomas Nagel countered both the no subject of harm argument and the symmetry argument by positing that the good or evil that befalls a person depends on his history and possibilities rather than on his momentary state, and thus that he can suffer an evil even if he is not here to experience it. Who of Epicurus or Nagel one decides to side with I think ultimately depends on how one chooses to think about a person (see Chapter 7, *Ghosts*).

Epicurus himself died at the age of 72 from renal colic (kidney stones), which is associated with one of the sharpest and most intense of all bodily pains. On the last day of his life, he penned this remarkable letter to his friend and follower Idomeneus, which is nothing if not a testament to the overriding powers of philosophy.

> *I have written this letter to you on a happy day to me, which is also the last day of my life. For I have been attacked by a painful inability to urinate, and also dysentery, so violent that nothing can be added to the violence of my sufferings. But the cheerfulness of my mind, which comes from the recollection of all my philosophical contemplation, counterbalances all these afflictions. And I beg*

> *you to take care of the children of Metrodorus, in*
> *a manner worthy of the devotion shown by the*
> *young man to me, and to philosophy.*

Epicurus agrees with Aristotle that happiness is an end-in-itself and the highest good of human living. However, he identifies happiness with the pursuit of pleasure and the avoidance of pain rather than with the pure exercise of reason. Pleasure is the highest good, and anything else that is good is so only by virtue of the immediate or deferred pleasure that it can procure. The behaviour of infants confirms that human beings instinctively pursue pleasure and that all of their actions, including those that may be construed as being either virtuous or altruistic, are ultimately aimed at obtaining pleasure for themselves. Just as human beings can immediately feel that something is hot or cold, colourful or dull, so they can immediately feel that something is pleasurable or painful. However, not everything that is pleasurable should be pursued, and not everything that is painful should be avoided. Instead, a kind of hedonistic calculus should be applied to determine which things are most likely to result in the greatest pleasure over time, and it is above all this hedonistic calculus that people are unable to handle.

To help them a bit, Epicurus proceeds to distinguish between two different types of pleasure, 'moving pleasures' and 'static pleasures'. Moving pleasures involve the satisfying of a desire, for example, eating a meal when hungry. Static pleasures on the other hand involve the state of having had a desire satisfied, for example, feeling sated after having eaten the meal. Static pleasures, says Epicurus, are better than moving pleasures because they free us from the pain of need or want. Epicurus also distinguishes between physical and mental pleasures and pains, and argues that anxiety about the future, especially fear of the gods and fear of death, are the greatest obstructions to happiness. To attain a state of perfect mental tranquillity or *ataraxia*, a person needs to avoid anxiety, which he can do by learning to trust in the future.

Pleasure often arises from the satisfaction of desire and pain from its frustration. Thus, any desire should either be satisfied to yield pleasure or eliminated to avoid pain, and, overall, it is elimination that should be preferred. There are, Epicurus says, three types of desires, (1) natural and necessary desires such as those for food and shelter which are difficult to eliminate but naturally limited and both easy and highly pleasurable to satisfy, (2) natural but non-necessary desires such as those for luxury food and accommodation, and (3) vain desires such as those for fame, power, or wealth which are inculcated by society and which are not naturally limited and neither easy nor highly pleasurable to satisfy. Natural and necessary desires should be satisfied, natural but non-necessary desires can be satisfied but should not be depended upon, and vain desires should be entirely eliminated. By following this prescription for the selective elimination of desires, a person can minimise the pain and anxiety of harbouring unfulfilled desires, and thereby bring himself as close as possible to *ataraxia*. Given the prime importance that he attaches to the avoidance of pain, the elimination of desire, and peace of mind, Epicurus is far more of a 'tranquillist' than a hedonist. 'If thou wilt make a man happy', he says, 'add not unto his riches but take away from his desires.'

10. Meaning

Our main motivation for living is our will to find meaning in life.

Victor Frankl

When one maintains his proper attitude in life, he does not long after externals. What would you have, O man?

Epictetus

Epicurus did not give a painted fig for fame, power, or wealth, nor, indeed, for anyone who did. He once remarked, 'I have never wished to cater for the crowd; for what I know they do not approve, and what they approve I do not know.' However, he spoke very highly of friendship, which he thought of as the surest way of securing a pleasurable and tranquil life. 'Of all the things which wisdom provides to make us entirely happy', he said, 'much the greatest is the possession of friendship.' Epicurus' disdain for worldly things or 'vain desires' such as fame, power, or wealth has been echoed through the ages by every ancient and modern philosopher. For instance, the ancient philosopher Thales of Miletus had so little regard for worldly things that he once fell into a well while gazing at the stars. In the *Theaetetus*, Plato recounts that,

> *Thales was studying the stars and gazing into the*
> *sky, when he fell into a well, and a jolly and witty*
> *Thracian servant girl made fun of him, saying*
> *that he was crazy to know about what was up in*
> *the heavens while he could not see what was in*
> *front of him beneath his feet.*

Thales was a geometer who travelled to Egypt to receive instruction from Egyptian priests. While in Egypt he measured the height of the pyramids by measuring their shadows at the time of day when his own shadow was as long as he was tall. He discovered that triangles with one equal side and two equal angles are congruent, and applied this knowledge to calculate the distances of ships at sea. He also discovered the method for inscribing a right-angled triangle into a circle, and celebrated by sacrificing an ox to the gods. Apart from being a geometer, Thales was an astronomer and a meteorologist who determined the dates of the summer and winter solstices and predicted the solar eclipse of 585 BC which halted the battle of Halys between the Lydians and the Medes. As a philosopher, Thales sought to explain the origin and nature of the world without resorting to myths and gods, for which reason he is often regarded as the first genuine philosopher, as well as the first genuine scientist. He held that all things are one, that water is the basic constituent of the universe, and that the earth floats upon water like a log upon a stream. Despite the great number and magnitude of his achievements, the people of his native Miletus used to mock him for his material poverty. So one year he predicted a bumper crop of olives, took out a lease on all the olive presses in Miletus, and made himself a fortune, simply to prove to the Milesians that a thinker could easily be rich, if only he did not have better things to do with his time.

Other shining examples of the art of failure among the philosophers include Pythagoras and Heraclitus. Pythagoras was born in Samos, not far from Miletus. As a young man, he took the advice of Thales and travelled to Memphis to take instruction from Egyptian priests. At the age of 40, he fled the tyranny of Polycrates to Croton in Southern Italy, where he established a philosophical and religious community which became a prototype for the monastic life and for later philosophical institutions such as Plato's Academy, Aristotle's

Lyceum, and Epicurus' Garden. Those who entered the community's inner circle were governed by a strict set of ascetic and ethical rules, forsaking personal possessions, assuming a mainly vegetarian diet, and – since words are so often careless and misrepresentative – observing the strictest silence. Music had an important place in the community; Pythagoreans recited poetry, sang hymns to Apollo, and played on the lyre to cure illnesses of the body and soul. One day, Pythagoras passed by some blacksmiths at work and was taken in by the pure and harmonious sounds produced by their hammering on anvils. He then discovered that the anvils consisted of simple ratios of one another, one being half the size of the first, another being two thirds of the size, and so on. This discovery of a relationship between numerical ratios and musical intervals led him to believe that the study of mathematics is the key to understanding the structure and order of the universe. According to his 'harmony of the spheres', the heavenly bodies move according to mathematical equations which correspond to musical notes and form part of a grand cosmic symphony. Pythagoras never separated religion from science and philosophy which, even in his day, left him open to accusations of mysticism. He believed in the transmigration of the soul, that is, in the reincarnation of the soul over time into the bodies of human beings, animals, or plants ('metempsychosis'), until such a time as it became moral. He claimed to have lived four lives and to remember them all in detail, and once recognised the cry of a dead friend in the yelping of a puppy. All in all, Pythagoras held that there are three sorts of men, just as there are three classes of strangers who go to the Olympic Games. There are the lovers of gain who come to buy and sell, the lovers of honour who come to compete, and the lovers of wisdom who come simply to look on. After his death, Pythagoras' followers deified him and attributed him with a golden thigh and the gift of bilocation. However, during his lifetime he had always remained a modest man, declining to be called a 'wise man' (*sophos*) and preferring instead to be called a 'lover of wisdom' (*philosophos*). Had it not been for such modesty, the word 'philosopher' might never have been coined.

In stark contrast to Pythagoras or Epicurus, Heraclitus of Ephesus was a misanthrope with no interest in the vast majority of people, who he found to be singularly lacking in understanding, and who he compared to cattle. Heraclitus was an aristocrat with a claim to be king (*basileus*). However, he abdicated in favour of his brother, explaining that he much preferred talking to children than to politicians. The Persian king Darius once invited him to his resplendent court, but he refused to go, replying, 'All men upon earth hold aloof from truth and justice, while, by reason of wicked folly, they devote themselves to avarice and thirst for popularity'. He once wished the citizens of his native Ephesus great wealth as a punishment for their worthless lives. Although fragments of his writings have survived, they take the form of obscure and ambiguous aphorisms, for which reason he is sometimes known as 'Heraclitus the Obscure' or 'Heraclitus the Riddler'. His big idea was that everything is in a constant state of flux or becoming, as epitomised by his saying that 'You cannot step into the same river twice, for fresh waters are ever flowing in upon you'. In his *Metaphysics* Aristotle reasoned that, if everything is in a constant state of flux, then nothing can be known, and it is likely that Heraclitus thought this too. Since fire is a symbol of perpetual change, Heraclitus pronounced it to be the primary substance. The underlying order of change is the product of God's reason or *Logos*, and fire is the expression of *Logos*, and thus of God. Accordingly, an enlightened man's soul is hot and dry, whereas a drunk 'is led by an unfledged boy, stumbling and not knowing where he goes, having his soul moist'. It is a testament to Heraclitus' enduring influence that the *Logos* entered the Bible at John 1:1, with '*Logos*' mistranslated from Greek into English as 'the Word': 'In the beginning was the Word, and the Word was with God, and the Word was God.' Heraclitus also taught about the 'unity of the opposites', for instance, that hot and cold are the same, as are light and dark and day and night. These opposites appear to be in a constant state of strife, but the resulting cosmic tension is, in fact, an expression of essential harmony. He wrote, 'It is wise to agree that all things are one. In differing it agrees with itself, a backward-turning connection, like that of a bow and a lyre. The path up and down is one and the same.' Heraclitus eventually removed himself to the loneliness of the mountains, where he lived out his days feeding on grasses and other plants.

The question as to whether these philosophers were right or wrong to disdain worldly things such as fame, power, or wealth barely seems worth entertaining. In the past 50 or 60 years, real term incomes in countries such as the UK and USA have increased dramatically, but happiness has not kept apace. In fact, people today are considerably less happy than back then: they have less time, they are more alone, and so many of their number are on antidepressants that trace quantities of fluoxetine (Prozac) have been detected in the water supply. Although economists focus on the absolute size of salaries, several sociological studies have found that the effect of money on happiness results less from the things that money can buy (absolute income effect) than from comparing one's income to that of others, and particularly to that of one's peers (relative income effect). This is an important part of the explanation as to why people today are no happier than people 50 or 60 years ago; despite being considerably richer, healthier, and better trained, they have only barely managed to 'keep up with the Joneses'.

But there is more. If I am to believe everything that I see in the media, happiness is to be six foot tall or more and to have bleached teeth and a firm abdomen, all the latest clothes, accessories, and electronics, a picture-perfect partner of the opposite sex who is both a great lover and a terrific friend, an assortment of healthy and happy children, a pet that is neither a stray nor a mongrel, a large house in the right sort of postcode, a second property in an idyllic holiday location, a top-of-the-range car to shuttle back and forth from the one to the other, a clique of 'friends' with whom to have fabulous dinner parties, three or four foreign holidays a year, and a high-impact job that does not distract from any of the above. There are at least three major problems that I can see with this ideal of happiness. (1) It represents a state of affairs that is impossible to attain to and that is in itself an important source of unhappiness. (2) It is situated in an idealised and hypothetical future rather than in an imperfect but actual present in which true happiness is much more likely to be found, albeit with great difficulty. (3) It has largely been defined by commercial interests that have absolutely nothing to do with true happiness, which has far more to do with the practice of reason and the peace of mind that this eventually brings. In short, it is not only that the bar for happiness is set too high, but also that it is set in the wrong place, and that it is, in fact, the wrong bar. Jump and you'll only break your back.

So much for wealth and its trappings; what about celebrity, fame, or, better still, honour? In the *Symposium*, Plato says that animals enter into a state of love because they seek to reproduce and thereby to become immortal. Human beings, he explains, also seek to become immortal, and are prepared to take great risks, even to die, to attain fame and honour. Some human beings are pregnant in body and beget children to preserve their memory, whereas others are pregnant in soul and beget wisdom and virtue. As their children are more beautiful and more immortal, human beings who are pregnant in soul have more to share with each other and a stronger bond of friendship between them. Everyone, says Plato, would rather have their children than human ones.

> *Who when he thinks of Homer and Hesiod and other great poets, would not rather have their children than ordinary human ones? Who would not emulate them in the creation of children such as theirs, which have preserved their memory and given them everlasting glory?*

Plato thereby distinguishes between the lesser immortality of leaving behind children and grandchildren, which is relatively easy to achieve but which only preserves one's memory for at most three or four generations, and the greater immortality of leaving behind a significant artistic, intellectual, or social legacy, which preserves one's memory for much longer but which is much more difficult to achieve. Some 2,500 years after his time, Thales continues to be studied by every student of philosophy, but no one remembers the names of the Milesians who mocked him for his poverty. Even so, a day will surely come when students no longer study Thales (or even Plato), if only because there are no longer any students left. For this reason, to search for happiness in immortality, even greater immortality, is never anything more than a vain attempt to delay the inevitable, a manic defence aimed at fooling oneself into thinking that one is a 'somebody' rather than a 'nobody' like everybody else. More fundamentally, it is once again to fall into the trap of searching for happiness in an idealised and hypothetical future rather than in an imperfect but actual present in which true happiness is much more likely to be found, albeit with great difficulty. Of course, this is not to say that a person should not seek out individuation and self-realisation – far from it – but only that he should not do so in some vain attempt to secure immortality, or even to secure celebrity, fame, or honour within his lifetime. This also frees the person from having to rely on public recognition, which can be just as painful as it can be pleasurable, and which is neither dependable nor indispensible.

By seeking out individuation and self-realisation, a person is likely not only to help himself, but also to help others, and many people think of helping others or being useful as 'the meaning of life'. However, it should be remembered that, at its best, altruism is a means to an end (for example, alleviating hunger or poverty), and not an end-in-itself. If altruism were an end-in-itself, then (1) the person to benefit most from altruism would be the altruist himself, and (2) the person actually being helped by the altruist would not himself be able to lead a purposeful, happy life. In psychoanalytic theory, the kind of altruism that is an end-in-itself is thought of as an ego defence in which a person copes with his fear and anxiety by, so to speak, stepping out of his life and into those of other people. By concentrating on the needs of other people, the person is able to push his own needs into the background, and so to avoid ever having to address or even to acknowledge them. For example, carers of a disabled or chronically ill person often experience profound anxiety and distress if their responsibilities are taken away from them, and the same is also true of many people employed in caring professions such as teaching and nursing. Obviously, this is not to say that people should not help others or be useful, but only that they should see this as a means to an end rather than as an end-in-itself.

It can be tempting to substitute altruism with 'the good of the species'. However, just as with altruism, 'the good of the species' is a means to an end rather than an end-in-itself. And just as with immortality, it is to fall into the trap of searching for happiness in an idealised and hypothetical future rather than in an imperfect but actual present in which true happiness is much more likely to be found, albeit with great difficulty.

In any case, it can sometimes seem that all 'the good of the species' has ever achieved is the destruction of the planet, and that it is only a matter of time before it also achieves the destruction of the species whose good it supposedly seeks. That, however, is a different debate, and I shall leave it for another time.

11. Friendship

A man is happy if he has merely encountered the shadow of a friend.

Menander

Friendship is ... complete sympathy in all matters of importance, plus goodwill and affection, and I am inclined to think that with the exception of wisdom, the gods have given nothing finer to men than this.

Cicero

All in all, it seems that Epicurus was right to disdain worldly things in favour of a pleasurable and tranquil life which, he thought, could best be attained to by the possession of friendship. Plato and Aristotle also gave an important place to friendship in the good life; Plato devoted the major part of three books (the *Lysis*, *Phaedrus*, and *Symposium*) to friendship and to love, and in Book VIII of the *Nicomachean Ethics* Aristotle lavished extravagant praise upon the Greek concept of friendship or *philia*, which included not only voluntary relationships but also those relationships that hold between the members of a family. Friendship, says Aristotle, is a virtue which is 'most necessary with a view to living ... for without friends no one would choose to live, though he had all other goods'.

If friendship is so important to the good life, then it is important to ask the question, what is friendship? According to Aristotle, for a person to be friends with another 'it is necessary that [they] bear goodwill to each other and wish good things for each other, without this escaping their notice'. A person may bear goodwill to another for one of three reasons, that he is good (that is, rational and virtuous), that he is pleasant, or that he is useful. While Aristotle leaves room for the idea that relationships based on advantage alone or pleasure alone can give rise to friendships, he believes that such relationships have a smaller claim to be called friendships than those that are based partly or wholly on virtue. 'Those who wish good things to their friends for the sake of the latter are friends most of all, because they do so because of their friends themselves, not coincidentally.' Friendships that are based partly or wholly on virtue are desirable not only because they are associated with a high degree of mutual benefit, but also because they are associated with companionship, dependability, and trust.

More important still, to be in such a friendship and to seek out the good of one's friend is to exercise reason and virtue, which is the distinctive function of human beings, and which amounts to happiness (see Chapter 9, *Happiness*).

For Aristotle, an act of friendship is undertaken both for the good of one's friend and for the good of oneself, and there is no reason to think that the one precludes the other. In any case, to have a perfect friend is like to have 'another self', since perfect friends make the same choices as each other and each one's happiness adds to that of the other. Unfortunately, the number of people with whom one can sustain a perfect friendship is very small, first, because reason and virtue are not to be found in everyone (never, for example, in young people, who are not yet wise enough to be virtuous), and, second, because a perfect friendship can only be created and sustained if a pair of friends spend a great deal of exclusive quality time together. Thus, even if one lived entirely surrounded by virtuous people, one would only ever have the time for at most a small handful of perfect friends. Aristotle is not nearly as interested in erotic love as he is in friendship. 'As for the pleasure of sex,' he tells us with a whiff of disdain, 'no one could have any thoughts while enjoying that.'

The ideal of perfect friendship may strike the modern reader as being somewhat elitist, but Aristotle is surely right in holding that the best kinds of friendship are both rare and demanding.

If the best kinds of friendship are those that are based on virtue, then this is above all because such friendships call upon the exercise of reason and virtue, which is the distinctive function of human beings, and which amounts to happiness. However, it could be argued that the distinctive function of human beings is not the exercise of reason and virtue, but the capacity to form loving and meaningful relationships. If this is the case, then friendships that are based on virtue are even more important to the good life than Aristotle thinks. Despite the extravagant praise that he lavishes upon friendship, Aristotle is quite clear that the best and happiest life is not the life spent in friendship, but the life spent in the contemplation of those things that are most true and therefore most beautiful and most dependable. There is a contradiction here: if the best life is a life of contemplation, then friendship is either superfluous or inimical to the best life, and therefore undeserving of the high praise that Aristotle lavishes upon it. It may be, as Aristotle tentatively suggests, that friendship is needed because it leads to contemplation, or that contemplation is only possible some of the time and friendship is needed the rest of the time, or again that a life of friendship is just as good as a life of contemplation.

Figure 11: Both Plato and Aristotle gave an important place to friendship in the good life. In this detail from Raphael's masterpiece, *The School of Athens* (c. 1511), Plato is holding a copy of the *Timaeus* and pointing vertically to the lofty vault above their heads, while a younger Aristotle is holding a copy of his *Nicomachean Ethics* and gesturing horizontally towards the descending steps at their feet. The line 'Where both are friends, it is right to prefer truth' from the *Nichomachean Ethics* is often paraphrased as, 'Plato is my friend, but Truth is a greater friend still'.

So much for Aristotle, one might say. Plato also gives an important place to friendship in the good life. He ostensibly devotes an entire book, the *Lysis*, to defining friendship or *philia*, which he is reluctant to distinguish from erotic love or *erôs*. In the *Lysis*, Socrates is in conversation with two youths, Lysis and Menexenus. Socrates tells the youths that, whereas some people desire horses, or dogs, or gold, or honour, he would rather have a good friend than 'the best cock or quail in the world': 'Yea, by the dog of Egypt, I should greatly prefer a real friend to all the gold of Darius, or even to Darius himself: I am such a lover of friends as that'. Lysis and Menexenus appear to possess this treasure in each other, so perhaps Menexenus can tell him: when one person loves another, which of the two becomes the friend of the other, the lover or the beloved? Menexenus replies that either may be the friend of the other, that is, they both are friends. Socrates says that this cannot be the case, since one person may love another who does not love him back, or even who hates him. Menexenus suggests that, unless they both love each other, neither is a friend. Socrates disagrees, and explains that if something that does not love in return is not beloved by a lover, then there can be no lovers of things such as horses, dogs, wine, or wisdom. Thus, what is beloved, whether or not it loves in return, may be dear to the lover of it. Such is the case, for example, with children who are too young to love, or who hate their parents for punishing them. This suggests that the beloved is the friend of the lover and the hated one is the enemy of the hater, but the implication is that some people are loved by their enemies and hated by their friends, which seems absurd. Thus, neither the lover not the beloved can always be said to be a friend to the other.

Socrates suggests that they may have been wrong in their conclusions. He turns for guidance to the poets and philosophers, who say that 'like loves like'. Socrates argues that this aphorism must only apply to good people, since bad people are in some way unlike themselves and are just as likely to hate other bad people as anyone else. This implies that good people are friends with other good people, whereas bad people do not have any friends at all. However, Socrates remains unconvinced: like cannot be of any use to like, and if people cannot be of any use to one another, then they cannot love each other. It remains possible that they love each other because they are both good, but the good is by definition self-sufficient, and so has no desire for friendship.

> *What place then is there for friendship, if, when absent, good men have no need of one another (for even when alone they are sufficient for themselves), and when present have no use of one another? How can such persons ever be induced to value one another?*

Socrates suspects that he may have been wrong in thinking that like loves like. He quotes Hesiod in saying that 'the most like are most full of envy, strife, and hatred of one another, and the most unlike, of friendship'. Menexenus thinks that Hesiod is right in saying that friendship is born not in likeness but in dissimilarity, but Socrates is sceptical as the implications are not only that the enemy is the friend of the friend and the friend the friend of the enemy, but also that the just man is the friend of the unjust, the good man the friend of the bad, and so on. This, he says, is simply monstrous. Thus, neither like and like nor unlike and unlike can be friends.

If neither like and like nor unlike and unlike can be friends, then the friend of the good is neither the good nor the bad, but the neither–good–nor–bad. Since like and like cannot be friends, the neither–good–nor–bad cannot be friends with the neither–good–nor–bad, and since no one can be friends with the bad, the neither–good–nor–bad cannot be friends with the bad either. Thus, the neither–good–nor–bad must be friends with the good, who, Socrates says, are also possessed of beauty, that 'soft, smooth, slippery thing' that 'easily slips in and permeates our souls'. While the good and beautiful cannot be friends with the good and beautiful or with the bad, there is nothing to stop them from being friends with the neither–good–nor–bad. For example, the body is neither good nor bad, but if it is corrupted by sickness, which is bad, then it becomes the friend of the physician. The fact that the body is corrupted by something bad does not make it bad, just as covering Menexenus' auburn locks with white lead does not make them white. Socrates concludes that they have at long last discovered the nature of friendship: 'it is the love which, by reason of the presence of evil, the neither good nor evil has of the good, either in the soul, or in the body, or anywhere.' However, an 'unaccountable suspicion' comes over him, and he begins to doubt this conclusion.

If medicine, which is good, is a friend, then it is a friend for the sake of health. However, health is also good and, if good, then good for the sake of something, something which must also be good, and so on. Surely, there must some first principle of friendship or dearness for the sake of which all other things are dear. For example, if a father values his son above all things, he also values other things for the sake of his son. If, for instance, his son had drunk poisonous hemlock, and he thought that wine would save him, then he would value the wine and even the vessel that contains it. However, it is not really the wine or the vessel that he is valuing, but his son. 'That which is only dear to us for the sake of something else is improperly said to be dear, but the truly dear is that in which all these so called dear friendships terminate.' Socrates infers that the truly dear is the good, but points out that the good appears to be loved not for its own sake but for the sake of the bad. However, if the bad were eradicated, love and friendship would still exist, suggesting that there must be some other cause of friendship.

Socrates suggests that desire is the cause of friendship, and that he who desires, desires that of which he is in want, and hence that which is dear to him. Thus, desire, love, and friendship appear to be of the congenial, whether in soul, character, manners, or form. Socrates adds that if love is of the congenial, then the true lover must necessarily have his love returned. However, he points out that this theory falls flat if the congenial is merely the like, since the like cannot be friends with the like.

> *Then what is to be done? Or rather is there anything to be done? I can only, like the wisemen who argue in courts, sum up the arguments: If neither the beloved, nor the lover, nor the like, nor the unlike, nor the good, nor the congenial, nor any other of whom we spoke – for there were such a number of them that I cannot remember all – if none of these are friends, I know not what remains to be said... O Menexenus and Lysis, how ridiculous that you two boys, and I, an old boy, who would fain be one of you, should imagine ourselves to be friends – this is what the bystanders will go away and say – and as yet we have not been able to discover what is a friend!*

The *Lysis* may seem to fail in its task of defining friendship, and on one level of course it does. There is, however, far more to it than a couple of interesting but misguided thoughts about friendship. By discussing friendship with Lysis and Menexenus as he does, Socrates is not only discussing friendship, but also demonstrating to the youths that, even though they count each other as close friends, they do not really know what friendship is, and that, whatever friendship is, it is something far deeper and far more meaningful than the puerile 'friendship' that they count themselves to have. In contrast to the youths, Socrates knows perfectly well what friendship is, and is only feigning ignorance so as to teach the youths: '...and I, an old boy, who would fain be one of you...' More than that, by discussing friendship with Lysis and Menexenus as he does, Socrates is himself in the process of befriending them. He befriends them not with the pleasant banter, gossipy chitchat, or small kindnesses with which most people befriend one another, but with the sort of philosophical conversation that is the hallmark of the deepest and most meaningful of friendships. In the course of this philosophical conversation, he tells the youths that he should 'greatly prefer a real friend to all the gold of Darius', thereby indicating not only that he places friendship on the same high pedestal as philosophy, to which he has devoted (and will sacrifice) his life, but also that the kind of friendship that he has in mind is so rare and uncommon that even he does not possess it. If friendship ultimately escapes definition, then this is because, like philosophy, friendship is not so much a thing-in-itself as it is a process for becoming. True friends seek together to live truer, fuller lives, not only by relating to each other authentically, but also by teaching each other about the limitations of their beliefs and the defects in their character, which are a far greater source of error than mere rational confusion. For Socrates as for Plato, friendship and philosophy are aspects of one and the same impulse, one and the same love – the love that seeks to know.

Just as philosophy leads to friendship, so friendship leads to philosophy. In the *Phaedrus*, which was most probably written several years after the *Lysis*, Socrates and Phaedrus go out into the idyllic countryside just outside Athens and have a long conversation about the anatomy of the soul, the nature of true love, the art of persuasion (rhetoric), and the merits of the spoken over the written word. At the end of this conversation, Socrates offers a prayer to the local deities. This is the famous Socratic prayer, which is notable both in itself and for the response that it elicits from Phaedrus.

> *Beloved Pan, and all ye other gods who haunt*
> *this place, give me beauty in the inward soul;*
> *and may the outward and inward man be at*
> *one. May I reckon the wise to be the wealthy,*
> *and may I have such a quantity of gold as*

> *a temperate man and he only can bear and*
> *carry. – Anything more? The prayer, I think, is*
> *enough for me.*
> Ask the same for me, for friends should have all
>   things in common.
> *Let us go.*

Plato may fail to define friendship in the *Lysis*, but in the *Phaedrus* he gives us its living embodiment. Socrates and Phaedrus spend their time together enjoying the beautiful Attic countryside while engaging in honest and open philosophical conversation. By exercising and building upon reason, they are not only furthering each other's understanding, but also transforming a life of friendship into a life of joint contemplation of those things that are most true and hence most beautiful and most dependable.

At one point, during a lull in their conversation, Socrates insists that they continue talking, lest the cicadas laugh at them for avoiding conversation at midday, and mistake them for a pair of slaves who have come to their resting place as cattle to a waterhole. On the other hand, he explains, if the cicadas see that they are not lulled by their chirruping, they may, out of respect, offer them their god-given gifts. For once upon a time, before the birth of the Muses, the cicadas used to be human beings. Then the Muses were born and song was created, and they were so overwhelmed with the pleasure of singing that they forgot to eat or drink *and died without even realising it*. As a gift from the Muses, they were reborn as cicadas, singing from the moment they are born to the moment they die without ever feeling hunger or thirst. After dying, the cicadas report back to the Muses in heaven about who is honouring them on earth, and win the love of Terpsichore for the dancers, of Erato for the lovers, and of Calliope, the eldest Muse, for the philosophers.

If only on the basis of his response to the Socratic prayer, it is obvious that Phaedrus is another self to Socrates, since he makes the same choices as Socrates and even justifies making those choices on the grounds that their friendship requires it. Thus, whereas Aristotle tries to tell us what perfect friendship is, Plato lets us feel it in all its allure and transformative power.

12. Truth

*Man's creative struggle, his search for wisdom
and truth, is a love story.*

Iris Murdoch

*At the touch of love everyone becomes a poet,
even though he had no music in him before ...
He whom love touches not walks in darkness.*

Plato

In the *Lysis* as elsewhere, Plato is reluctant to distinguish between friendship or *philia* and erotic love or *erôs*, and he has good reasons for not doing so. Whereas Aristotle is not nearly as interested in erotic love as he is in friendship, for Plato the best kind of friendship is that which lovers can have for each other. It is a *philia* that is born out of *erôs*, and that in turn feeds back into *erôs* to strengthen and to develop it. Like philosophy itself, *erôs* aims at transcending human existence, at connecting it with the eternal and infinite, and thereby at achieving the only species of immortality that is open to us as human beings. Not only does *philia* strengthen and develop *erôs*, but it also transforms it from a lust for possession into a shared desire for a higher level of understanding of the self, the other, and the universe. In short, *philia* transforms *erôs* from a lust for possession into an impulse for philosophy. As Nietzsche put it in his book of 1882, *The Gay Science*,

> *Here and there on earth we may encounter a kind of continuation of love in which this possessive craving of two people for each other gives way to a new desire and lust for possession – a shared higher thirst for an ideal above them. But who knows such love? Who has experienced it? Its right name is friendship.*

In other words, if erotic love can be transformed into the best kind of friendship, then it can open up a blissful life of shared understanding in which desire, friendship, and philosophy are in perfect resonance with one another. Plato's theory of love is fleshed out in the *Phaedrus* and the *Symposium*. Like many Greeks of his era and social position, Plato is most interested in the same-sex desire that can exist between an older and a younger man, but there is no reason to suppose that his theory of love does not also apply to other kinds of erotic relationship. That having been said, Plato distinguishes the kind of love that can give rise to *philia* from a baser kind of love that is enjoyed by those who are more given to the body than to the soul. Rather than underpin the search for truth, this baser kind of love is almost designed to impede it, and calls into my mind the song of Fanny Crowne in Aldous Huxley's dystopian novel of 1932, *Brave New World*. In this song, Fanny Crowne compares love to soma, a hallucinogenic drug that has been engineered to take users on enjoyable, hangover-free 'holidays', and that is described as having 'all the advantages of Christianity and alcohol [but] none of their defects'.

> *Hug me till you drug me, honey;*
> *Kiss me till I'm in a coma:*
> *Hug me, honey, snugly bunny;*
> *Love's as good as soma.*

In the *Phaedrus*, Socrates says that, although madness can be an illness, it can also be the source of man's greatest blessings (see Chapter 8, *Madness*). There are four forms of such 'divine madness', prophecy from Apollo, holy prayers and mystic rites from Dionysus, poetry from the Muses, and – the highest form – love from Aphrodite and Eros. The madness of love arises from seeing the beauty of the earth and being reminded of true, universal beauty. Unfortunately, most earthly souls are so corrupt by the body, 'that living tomb which we carry about', that they lose all memory for the universals. When their eyes fall upon the beauty of the earth, they are merely given over to pleasure, and 'like a brutish beast' rush on to enjoy and beget. In contrast, the earthly soul that is able to remember true, universal beauty and so to feel true love gazes upon the face of his beloved and reverences it as an expression of the divine – of temperance, justice, and knowledge absolute. As his eyes catch those of his beloved, a shudder passes into an unusual heat and perspiration. The parts of the soul out of which the wings grew, and which had hitherto been closed and rigid, begin to melt open, and small wings begin to swell and grow from the root upwards.

> *Like a child whose teeth are just starting to grow in, and its gums are all aching and itching – that is exactly how the soul feels when it begins to grow wings. It swells up and aches and tingles as it grows them.*

The lover feels the utmost joy when he is with his beloved and the most intense longing when they are separated. When they are separated, the parts out of which the lover's wings are growing begin to dry out and close up, and the pain is such that he prizes his beloved above all else, utterly unable to think a bad thought about him, let alone to betray or forsake him. The lover whose soul was once the follower of Zeus among all the other gods seeks out a beloved who shares in his god's philosophical and imperial nature, and then does all he can to confirm this nature in him. Thus, the desire of the divinely inspired lover can only be fair and blissful to the beloved. In time, the beloved, who is no common fool, comes to realise that his divinely inspired lover is worth more to him than all his other friends and kinsmen put together, and that neither human discipline nor divine inspiration could have offered him any greater blessing.

Thus great are the heavenly blessings which the friendship of a lover will confer upon you ... Whereas the attachment of the non-lover, which is alloyed with a worldly prudence and has worldly and niggardly ways of doling out benefits, will breed in your soul those vulgar qualities which the populace applaud, will send you bowling round the earth during a period of nine thousand years, and leave you a fool in the world below.

There is in terms of the ideas covered quite a lot of overlap between the *Phaedrus* and the *Symposium*. However, whereas in the *Phaedrus* Plato emphasises the relationship that love has to the divine and hence to the eternal and infinite, in the *Symposium* he emphasises more the relationship that it has to the practice of philosophy, the search for happiness, and the contemplation of truth. In the *Symposium*, Socrates argues that, if love is not of nothing, then it is of something, and if it is of something, then it is of something that is desired, and therefore of something that is not possessed. He then relates a conversation that he once had with a priestess called Diotima of Mantinea, from whom he learned the art of love. Diotima ('honoured by the gods') told him that the something that love desires but does not possess consists of extremely beautiful and extremely good things, and particularly of wisdom, which is both extremely beautiful and extremely good. Love, said Diotima, must not be confused with the object of love, which, in contrast to love itself, is perfectly beautiful and perfectly good. If love desires but does not possess beautiful and good things, then love cannot, as most people think, be a god. Love is in truth the child of Poverty and Resource, always in need, but always inventive. He is not a god but a great spirit (*daimon*) who intermediates between gods and men. As such, he is neither mortal nor immortal, neither wise nor ignorant, but a lover of wisdom (*philosophos*). No one who is wise wants to become wise, just as no one who is ignorant wants to become wise. 'For herein is the evil of ignorance, that he who is neither good nor wise is nevertheless satisfied with himself: he has no desire for that of which he feels no want.' The aim of loving beautiful and good things is to possess them, because the possession of beautiful and good things is happiness, and happiness is an end-in-itself.

Diotima then told Socrates of the proper way to learn to love beauty. A youth should first be taught to love one beautiful body so that he comes to realise that this beautiful body shares beauty with other beautiful bodies, and thus that it is foolish to love just one beautiful body. In loving all beautiful bodies, he learns to appreciate that the beauty of the soul is superior to the beauty of the body, and begins to love those who are beautiful in soul regardless of whether they are also beautiful in body. Once he has transcended the physical, he gradually finds that beautiful practices and customs and the various kinds of knowledge also share in a common beauty. Finally, he is able to experience beauty itself, rather than the various apparitions of beauty. By exchanging the various apparitions of virtue for virtue itself, he gains immortality and the love of the gods. This is why love is so important, and why it deserves so much praise.

For Aristotle, happiness involves the exercise of reason because the capacity to reason is the distinctive function of human beings. However, it could be argued that the distinctive function of human beings is not the capacity to reason but the capacity to form meaningful, loving relationships. Plato reconciles these positions by blending desire, friendship, and philosophy into a single total experience that transcends and transforms human existence and that connects it with the timeless and universal truths of the eternal and infinite. For Plato, truth and authenticity are a higher value than either reason or love, which aim at them, and a higher value even than happiness, which is merely the manifestation of their presence.

Neel Burton
Pointe d'Esny, January 2010

By the same author

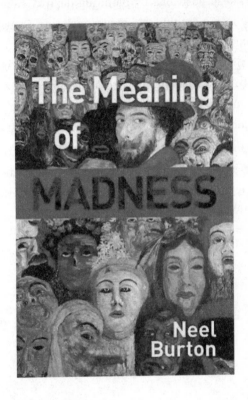

The Meaning of Madness
ISBN 978-0-9560353-0-1
Published November 2008

Winner of the BMA Young Authors' Award

Book Description

This book proposes to open up the debate on mental disorders, to get people interested and talking, and to get them thinking. For example, what is schizophrenia? Why is it so common? Why does it affect human beings and not animals? What might this tell us about our mind and body, language and creativity, music and religion? What are the boundaries between mental disorder and 'normality'? Is there a relationship between mental disorder and genius? These are some of the difficult but important questions that this book confronts, with the overarching aim of exploring what mental disorders can teach us about human nature and the human condition.

Book Reviews

"A riveting read for anyone looking for a window into the world of mental disorder..."

Professor Robert Howard, Dean, Royal College of Psychiatrists

"Most books on mental disorder are either polemical or over-technical. This remarkable book by contrast provides a highly readable and at the same time authoritative account that, by combining literary, philosophical and scientific sources, shows the deep connections between 'madness' and some of our most important attributes as human beings."

Professor Bill Fulford, University of Oxford

"The specific purpose of this young author is to try and demystify the stigma of mental illness. He succeeds brilliantly, not only in explaining different types of mental illness in relatively simple terms, but also in the breadth of understanding he brings to aspects of life outside the mental straightjacket."

British Medical Association.

"This book is a delight... there is no circumlocution or obliqueness, and the surgical efficiency with which the subjects are addressed makes for maximum comprehension... a really accessible and thorough approach to a complex and often impenetrable subject."

British Neuroscience Association

"Burton somehow avoids oversimplification. This is all the more remarkable, since his scope is fairly all-embracing, switching smoothly from side-effects of lithium to the nature of existential anxiety, to the quest for meaning in life... His writing is frequently almost poetic, yet he is capable of being crisply definitive... Ultimately, this is a work of contradictions – an undemanding read that could challenge your view of the world."

Medical Journalists' Association

This book is packed with striking insights... [Burton's] passion and enthusiasm for the subject never slips.

Remedy Magazine

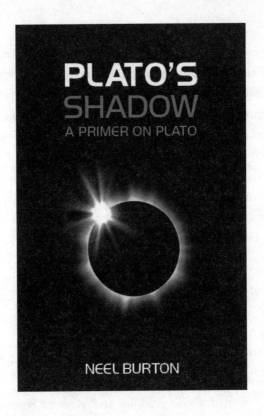

Plato's Shadow – A Primer on Plato
ISBN 978-0-9560353-2-5
Published July 2009

Book Description

Plato thought that only philosophy could bring true understanding, since it alone examines the presuppositions and assumptions that other subjects merely take for granted. He conceived of philosophy as a single discipline defined by a distinctive intellectual method, and capable of carrying human thought far beyond the realms of common sense or everyday experience. The unrivalled scope and incisiveness of his writings as well as their enduring aesthetic and emotional appeal have captured the hearts and minds of generation after generation of readers. Unlike the thinkers who came before him, Plato never spoke with his own voice. Instead, he presented readers with a variety of perspectives to engage with, leaving them free to reach their own, sometimes radically different, conclusions. 'No one,' he said, 'ever teaches well who wants to teach, or governs well who wants to govern.'

This book provides the student and general reader with a comprehensive overview of Plato's thought. It includes an introduction to the life and times of Plato and – for the first time – a précis of each of his dialogues, among which the Apology, Laches, Gorgias, Symposium, Phaedrus, Phaedo, Meno, Timaeus, Theaetetus, Republic, and 17 others.

Book Reviews

"A succinct précis of the work of one of the world's greatest thinkers ... For the newcomer or undergraduate it's a great resource, being both a celebration and an introduction to some of the most remarkable, beautiful, provocative, powerful and vital writings in Western literature."

The Good Web Guide

"This book provides a tremendously useful service to anyone studying Plato, or to the more general reader who might otherwise struggle to make headway unaided ... [It is] an essential addition to the library of any serious student of Plato's philosophy – which, given his undiminished importance, should be every philosopher!"

PhilosophyOnline

"An invaluable, indispensible guide that avoids the usual one-sided approach to Plato."

Dr Alan Cardew, University of Essex

Index

THOMAS COOK
Travellers

BALI, JAVA & LOMBOK

BY
BEN DAVIES

Produced by AA Publishing

Written by Ben Davies

Original photography by Ben Davies

Edited, designed and produced by AA Publishing.
Maps © The Automobile Association 1995.

Distributed in the United Kingdom by AA Publishing, Norfolk
House, Priestley Road, Basingstoke, Hampshire RG24 9NY.

ISBN 0 7495 2028 0

The contents of this publication are believed correct at the
time of printing. Nevertheless, the publishers cannot accept
responsibility for any errors or omissions, or for changes in the
details given in this guide or for the consequences of any
reliance on the information provided by the same. Assessments
of attractions, hotels, restaurants and so forth are based upon
the author's own experience and therefore descriptions given in
this guide necessarily contain an element of subjective opinion which
may not reflect the publisher's opinion or dictate a reader's own
experiences on another occasion.
We have tried to ensure accuracy in this guide, but things do
change and we would be grateful if readers would advise us of any
inaccuracies they may encounter.

First published 1995; Reprinted June 1998; Second revised edition 1999
© The Automobile Association 1995, 1999

A CIP catalogue record for this book is available from the British
Library.

Published by AA Publishing (a trading name of Automobile Association
Developments Limited, whose registered office is Norfolk House,
Priestley Road, Basingstoke, Hampshire RG24 9NY. Registered number
1878835) and the Thomas Cook Group Ltd.

Colour separation: BTB Colour Reproduction, Whitchurch, Hampshire.
Printed by: Edicoes ASA, Oporto, Portugal.

Cover picture: *Lake Braton*; Title page: *Prambanan*; Above: *Balinese
statue*

AA World Travel Guides publish nearly 300 guidebooks to a full
range of cities, countries and regions across the world. Find out
more about AA Publishing and the wide range of services the AA
provides by visiting our Web site at www.theaa.co.uk

Contents

About this Book

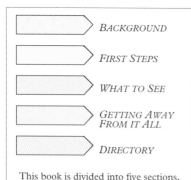

BACKGROUND

FIRST STEPS

WHAT TO SEE

GETTING AWAY
FROM IT ALL

DIRECTORY

This book is divided into five sections, identified by the above colour coding.

Background gives an introduction to Bali, Java and Lombok – their history, geography, politics, culture.

First Steps offers practical advice on arriving and getting around.

What to See is an alphabetical listing of places to visit, interspersed with walks and tours.

Getting Away From it All highlights places off the beaten track where it is possible to relax and enjoy peace and quiet.

Finally, the **Directory** provides practical information – from shopping and entertainment to children and sport, including a section on business matters. Special highly illustrated **features** on specific aspects of Bali, Java and Lombok appear throughout the book.

Magnificent stone carvings are scattered throughout Bali

BACKGROUND

'Hurled onto the shores of Bali, we had, though we knew it not,
reached one of the most fantastic places of the earth.'

VIOLET CLIFTON

Islands of Indonesia (1927)

Introduction

Scattered among the tropical waters of the Indian Ocean, with their palm-fringed beaches and fiery volcanoes, the 13,677 islands that make up the Indonesian archipelago offer visitors some of the most beautiful and exotic destinations in the world – as well as an abundance of culture.

Indonesia has magnificent temples and teeming cities along with thousands of different species of wildlife ranging from orchids to tigers to strawberries.

Ethnically, too, the country is made up of a hugely diverse population, speaking some 300 different languages and drawn from as far afield as India and the Pacific. And whilst some 87 per cent of the people are Muslim, there is room for Hindus, animists and Christians too, amongst others.

Each island, from the legendary Bali, home of the gods, to Sumatra and Irian Jaya with their exotic jungles, is a world of its own offering something a little special. On Lombok, you can climb Mount Rinjani, one of the most spectacular volcanoes in the country, and on Java visit the 1,000-year-old temple of Borobudur. Sun-lovers on Bali can take

The majority of the Indonesian people still earn their living by working the fields

BALI, JAVA & LOMBOK

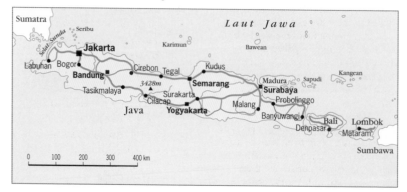

SOUTHEAST ASIA

their pick from a star-studded list of glistening white beaches, as well as luxury hotels and discothèques, and in Jakarta visitors can revel in some of the most chaotic scenes in the world.

Nor is it only the diverse scenery that will delight. In Indonesia you can feast on mouthwatering foods ranging from fresh lobster to *satay* – grilled meat served with peanut sauce. The adventurous can even try Indonesia's *pièce de résistance*, barbecued mutton brain.

Shoppers, too, can take their pick of hand-woven baskets, leather puppets and colourful batiks. And then there are the people: shy, playful, in some areas merely resigned to tourists, in others welcoming them with a ready smile.

THOMAS COOK'S
Bali, Java and Lombok

The first record of a Cook's excursion to Java was in 1909, when it formed part of a three-month personally conducted tour.

At that time the island was known as 'the Garden of the East' and visitors were conveyed there from Singapore by luxurious steamer – a journey taking 40 hours.

History

c700,000–200,000 BC

Fossils discovered in 1891 of the so-called 'Java man' near the village of Trinil prove that Indonesia played host to early *Homo erectus*.

3000–500 BC

Successive waves of migrants arrive from South China and Tonkin.

1st century AD

Indonesia comes under the influence of Indian trade and culture, paving the way for a succession of Indianised kingdoms.

8th–10th century

One of the greatest and most powerful kingdoms is established in Central Java by the Buddhist Sailendra dynasty.

778–856

Construction of the magnificent Borobudur temple by the Sailendras.

8th–11th century

The Hindu Sanjaya dynasty holds sway over parts of Central and East Java, building the famous Prambanan temples.

1222–1292

King Angrok establishes the Singasari dynasty which holds power in East Java, and the Malay Peninsula.

1292

Marco Polo becomes the first European to set foot in Indonesia when he visits Sumatra.

1292–1478

Rise of the powerful Hindu empire of Majapahit, which dominates much of Indonesia and parts of neighbouring Malaysia.

1343

Javanese colony established on Bali.

1400

Islam first introduced to Indonesia. By the end of the 16th century it replaces Hinduism and Buddhism as the dominant religion.

1522

The Portuguese establish trading posts in the Spice Islands and at Sunda Kelapa to control the lucrative spice trade.

1528

Foundation of Jakarta, known as Jayakarta.

1572–1757

The last great Javanese kingdom of Mataram holds sway around Yogyakarta and Surakarta.

1619

The Dutch East India Company takes Jayakarta by force and renames the town Batavia. Gradually they establish trading posts throughout Java.

1628–29

Sultan Agung, the most famous ruler of Mataram, attacks Batavia but fails to dislodge the Dutch.

1811

Following the Napoleonic Wars, the British take control of Batavia under Lieutenant-Governor Sir Thomas Stamford Raffles.

1816

Raffles and the British are ousted by the Dutch.

1825

Prince Diponegoro, son of the Sultan of Yogyakarta, leads a revolt against the Dutch. After five years he is defeated and exiled to Sulawesi.

1894

Dutch military victory on Lombok.

1906

Dutch troops land at Sanur Beach on Bali. The princely families of Badung and Tabanan refuse to surrender and more than 4,000 of them commit *puputan*, or mass suicide.

1911

The Dutch establish control over all the Indonesian islands except East Timor and North Borneo.

1914–1918

World War I. Growing nationalist sentiment takes hold in Indonesia.

1927

Foundation of the Patai Nasional Indonesia, a political party aimed at securing independence.

1942–45

The Japanese occupy Indonesia. Initially they are welcomed as liberators. Later the people turn against them.

1945

Indonesia proclaims its independence, but the Dutch refuse to accept the declaration.

1945

Yogyakarta declared capital of the founding republic.

1948

The Dutch capture Yogyakarta, prompting a guerrilla campaign in rural areas.

1949

The Dutch are ordered to withdraw from Indonesia by the United Nations and a new republic is officially proclaimed.

Soekarno becomes first president of the Republic of Indonesia.

1950–65

Economic and social problems are compounded by domestic unrest and growing support for the communists.

1965

Six army generals are murdered in an attempted *coup d'état* blamed on the communist party. General Suharto, chief of the Army Strategic Reserve Command, takes control.

1967–8

Soekarno is placed under house arrest and Suharto is inaugurated as president. Thousands of alleged communists are killed throughout the country, especially on Bali.

1970–1980

Growing economic prosperity brought about by rising oil prices leads to corruption on a scale almost unparalleled. Continuing unrest in outlying areas.

1989–1992

Suharto liberalises foreign investment regulations and presides over a period of rapid growth. Western observers herald the beginnings of a new economic giant.

1991

Massacre in East Timor.

1993–7

Golkar, the state party, wins sixth consecutive victory, gaining 68 per cent of the vote with Suharto reappointed as president.

1998

May riots in Jakarta result in President Suharto's resignation. Vice-president Habibie takes over.

Medan Merdeka, Jakarta

Geography

*I*ndonesia offers a vast choice of landscape, spread over one of the largest and most diverse areas in the world. In total the country covers almost 10 million sq km, stretching more than 5,500km from its northwestern tip in Sumatra to the coast of Irian Jaya in the south. This equates to one eighth of the circumference of the globe, or 46 degrees of latitude. Furthermore, Indonesia is one of the only countries in the world which has more sea than land; the total area occupied by Indonesia's surrounding seas and oceans is greater than the total area occupied by its 13,677 islands.

Covering the land mass is a wide range of terrain, from steep mountains and rain forests to steaming lowlands and equatorial vegetation. On top of that, Indonesia boasts some 300 volcanoes, 100 of which still rumble and erupt with relentless predictability.

You will find plenty of geological wonders, too, from lakes filled with sulphurous waters to vast calderas, as well as some of the most fertile soil on earth – from the sky, the terraced rice fields on Bali and Java resemble a giant patchwork quilt that stretches as far as the eye can see. Don't expect to see too much wildlife though. Most of the tigers

disappeared many years ago, making way for the endless march of Indonesia's population.

Economy

Potentially one of the richest countries in the world, Indonesia has almost every resource in abundance, from palm oil to rubber, timber, oil, gas, tea, coffee and spices. Its rich soil and abundant workforce produces rice enough to feed the country's 209 million population. These days, with its vast pool of cheap labour, the country also churns out textiles, computer chips and car components.

The one thing that Indonesia doesn't have, however, is evenly distributed wealth. Whilst the rich own huge tracts of land, many of the poor live in shacks and cardboard houses. Indonesia has more than its share of millionaires, but the average income per capita is little more than US$1,000 a year, with 25 per cent of the population on the poverty line.

The arrival of foreign investors rapidly turned Indonesia's economy into one of the fastest moving in the world, growing two or three times faster every year than countries in Europe. The Asian economic

Farming the slopes high up in the hills of the Sarangan

Bali hosts some of the most intricately constructed rice fields in the world

crisis reached its lowest ebb in 1998 resulting in a loss of confidence by overseas investors. While agriculture is likely to dominate the lives of rural inhabitants, people continue to be lured into towns and cities hoping to improve their lot.

Climate

In Indonesia's equatorial climate you are unlikely to suffer from excessive cold, unless you spend the night on top of a mountain, but you may find yourself inundated with tropical rains. This is especially true in the months between November and April when much of the country's 2,000mm annual rainfall occurs. The dry season tends to last from May to October, generally with clear blue skies and only occasional showers. Not surprisingly, this is when most tourists visit the country. Temperatures remain remarkably constant throughout the year, averaging about 26°C. Only in the months before the monsoon is humidity high.

Population

More than 209 million people crowd the teeming islands of Indonesia, making this vast archipelago the fourth most populated country in the world. Nor is the rate of increase slowing down. Every year the population increases by 1.5 per cent and lack of jobs means that millions of school leavers are unable to find work. On Java especially the population has reached frightening proportions and now ranks as one of the densest in the world, with over 850 people per sq km. Bali's total population is estimated at around 3 million, equating to a mere 530 people per sq km, while the total population of Lombok is put at 2.5 million.

PEOPLES OF BALI, JAVA AND LOMBOK

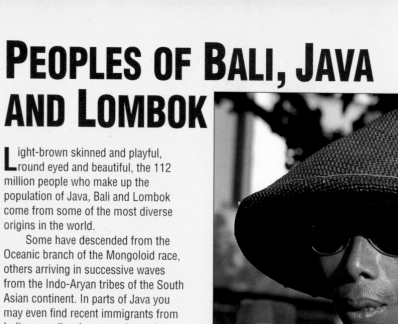

Light-brown skinned and playful, round eyed and beautiful, the 112 million people who make up the population of Java, Bali and Lombok come from some of the most diverse origins in the world.

Some have descended from the Oceanic branch of the Mongoloid race, others arriving in successive waves from the Indo-Aryan tribes of the South Asian continent. In parts of Java you may even find recent immigrants from India, as well as large numbers of Chinese who dominate almost all the large business concerns and who control vast amounts of the country's natural resources.

The Indonesian people not only pride themselves on their different origins, but in many cases have their own distinctive culture, their own language and history. The Badui of West Java have remained aloof from the modern world, recognising no government and forbidding strangers to spend the night in their villages. Others, like the Tenggerese, have intermingled and embraced the Indonesian principles of *Pancasila*, or national unity and social justice. But whatever their origins, these people all share one thing in common: their home is one of the most diverse and fertile countries in the world.

Culture

*F*rom classical dancers to glittering palaces and temples and colourful batiks, Indonesia offers a wealth and breadth of culture almost beyond compare. On Bali alone you will find an estimated 20,000 temples serving the island's 3 million population, while on Java, nearly every town or village has at least one mosque. On top of that are literally thousands of ceremonies, festivals and cremations as well as a complex set of rituals that influence almost every aspect of life throughout the teeming archipelago.

Religions

Islam is the predominant religion in Indonesia. In total, some 87 per cent of the population are Muslim, making this the world's largest Islamic nation. But Indonesia also spawns a variety of other religions from Buddhism to Hinduism and even Christianity.

The largest concentration of Muslims is to be found in Java and on the island of Lombok, home to the Sasak people. Crossing the narrow straits to Bali, you move to a world of good and evil spirits, of rain gods, rice gods and the endless circle of death and rebirth. Hinduism was brought to this island sometime during the 5th century by pilgrims from India. Today the religion has been influenced by Buddhism and animism and absorbed into everyday life.

Daily life

Whatever the religion, ritual plays a crucial role. As well as the greater duties of a pilgrimage to Mecca, all good Muslims must pray five times a day, give alms to the poor, and fast during daylight hours in the holy month of Ramadan. The Balinese Hindus, who worship Tintaya, Brahma the creator, Shiva the destroyer and Vishnu the preserver, must also make daily offerings to, and tend the shrines of, their ancestors, Dewi Sri goddess of rice, Dewi Ratih, goddess of the moon and even Dewi Melanting, goddess of shopkeeping. Together with a host of other spirits, these provide not only the key to their spiritual life but the greater means to ultimate fulfilment.

In Bali and Java, boys and girls marry as young as 14, celebrating their union with feasts and music. Arranged marriages are rare and divorce is almost non-existent. Women, although subservient to their husbands, do have an element of independence.

In the rural villages and towns, where the majority of Indonesians live, the extended family remains the heart of traditional society. Around the house uncles, aunts, brothers and sisters generally live as one unit, eating, working

Religious festivals form an important part of everyday life in Bali

Ancient stone reliefs at Borobudur educate Buddhist pilgrims

and sleeping together. And when the parents are old, it is the duty of the children to provide financial and spiritual support.

Indeed, with the support from family and religion, Indonesians suffer little of the isolation felt by many of their more progressive neighbours, relying on the gods and the community to help them through the ups and downs of everyday life.

The arts

Art is one of the greatest expressions of the sheer *joie de vivre* of the people of Indonesia. It is reflected in the finely carved temples and palaces, the intricate wooden carvings, batiks and colourful paintings. Even the *gamelan* orchestra and the epic Ramayana dance are performed in many towns and villages throughout Bali and Java.

Originally these arts strictly adhered to religious or royal lines. These days they have increasingly been influenced by Western artistry and by more individual interpretations of traditional themes. The result is a sparkling mixture of colour and style that has become one of Indonesia's most celebrated gifts to the world.

Politics

*F*or a country consisting of so many scattered islands and with such ethnic diversity, Indonesia's recent politics have shown remarkable stability – if a poor human rights record. For 30 years until May 1998, the country was ruled by one president. It has a people's consultative assembly made up of 1,000 members, a constitution and elections are held every five years. Furthermore, at grass-roots level, the republic consists of 27 provinces, each of which is headed by a governor appointed for a five-year term.

In 1997 and 1998 the economy was debilitated by the Asian economic crisis, causing rampant inflation, spiralling manufacturing costs and a 400 per cent increase in rice prices. This sparked civil unrest, riots in Jakarta and elsewhere and the downfall of the architect of Indonesia's economic miracle, President Suharto.

Currently there are only three legal

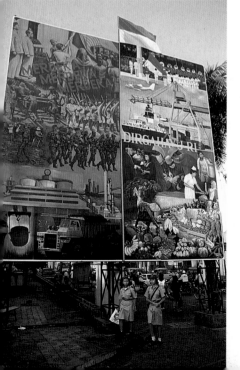

political parties, namely the ruling Golkar party led by Suharto's deputy, President B J Habibie, the Muslim-backed United Development Party and the Indonesian Democratic Party. Each of these parties is restricted in the extent of their opposition.

Ex-President Suharto had plenty of critics, but even the most vocal opponents were forced to applaud his success in holding together this far-flung archipelago as a united nation while presiding over one of the fastest growing economies in the Asian Pacific region. Over the last five years alone, Indonesia has established itself as a key member of the ASEAN (Association of Southeast Asian Nations) group of countries and an increasingly active participant in regional affairs. By the year 2019, ex-President Suharto had even set the goal of achieving the status of a developed nation. Not such a wild target when you consider the rich diversity of Indonesia's natural resources.

The gap between rich and poor continues to widen: a quarter of the population are hungry and bureaucratic corruption is rife. After the 1999 election, government will need to adapt to the needs of its people.

Government poster extolling the virtues of Freedom, Independence and National Unity

FIRST STEPS

'It was a sunrise such as we had
seldom seen, even though here in
the East they are so often almost
terrible in their loveliness.'

JAN POORTENAAR
An Artist in Java (1928)

INTRODUCTION

If you are arriving in Indonesia for the first time, there is no need to panic. Indonesia may be 11,263km from Europe, but it has plenty of comforts to add to its other charms. On Bali there are hotels to match any in the world, as well as all the usual facilities you would expect to find in a city. These days, even the telephones work in Jakarta – mostly. And while cultural and linguistic barriers may throw up a host of new challenges, they will also provide corresponding rewards. Below are a few hints to help you on your way.

AVOIDING OFFENCE

Indonesians have grace, humour and

Bamboo-caged songbirds are a ubiquitous sight throughout Southeast Asia and form an inherent part of Indonesian culture

BARE ESSENTIALS

Lost? Needing directions? Here are a few essential words to help you on your way.

Kamar Kecil Toilet
Bemo Motorised jeep
Becak Tricycle with passenger seats
Bukit Hill
Gunung Mountain
Istanana Palace
Jalan Street
Kali Canal
Merdan Square
Pasar Market
Polisi Police
Stanplatz Bus or taxi station
Stasiun keretapi Train station
Tolong Help

poise in abundance, along with plenty of sensitivities. To avoid causing offence, never touch anyone on the head or point your finger at them; when passing food or shaking hands, always remember to use your right hand, since the left is generally used for bodily ablutions; never insult a religion or make offensive comments about the country's politics, and avoid public displays of affection, which will reduce most locals to uncontrollable fits of laughter. Finally, always treat people with the respect they deserve. Doing so will make your life and theirs immeasurably more pleasant.

BARGAINING

Forget the notion of fixed prices while in Indonesia. You will find that almost everywhere, apart from in hotels and supermarkets, bargaining is the norm and to perfect this art needs neither guile nor aggression, just a little

common sense and a lot of humour. First ask the price of an article, then name a figure considerably lower and somewhat less than the amount you want to pay, and eventually agree on a compromise. If neither party can agree, no damage is done, and it's simply a question of moving on and starting the process all over again.

COPING WITH THE HEAT

When you first arrive in Indonesia the heat will hit you quite forcibly. Whether it be May or November, it is likely to be hot, or if not hot, then wet, and if you come at the wrong time, both. To cope with the heat, allow time to acclimatise, take hats and sun-tan lotion and consume large quantities of bottled water. If you are concerned about your state of health or your ability to cope with the heat, see a doctor before you leave. Don't spend too long in the sun for the first few days – severe sunburn will not only leave you looking like a lobster, but may spoil the remainder of your holiday.

CULTURE SHOCK

In practice culture shock is more a state of mind than a physical debilitation. To cope with it, simply relax, put your preconceptions aside and enjoy the novelty of any given situation. The fact that some people may dine on barbecued dog flavoured with grated coconut in no way reflects any moral inferiority, and although some norms of behaviour may be hard to stomach, always try to reserve judgement. When you return home take careful note of your own country's shortcomings – you may be a little more tolerant.

GREETINGS

Saying *selamat pagi* to an Indonesian is like saying 'good morning' to an Englishman, and everyone will appreciate it. Those with a more advanced linguistic repertoire can show greater refinement. If it's between noon and 3pm, say *selamat siang* (good afternoon); between 3pm and 6pm opt for *selamat sore* (good evening); and between 6pm and midnight, wish people *selamat malam* (good night). Making an effort in this way will not only earn you respect, but occasionally even an invitation to someone's home. Only businessmen need shake hands, although obviously if someone holds their hand out it would be churlish not to respond.

HASSLES

Everyone is likely to be subjected to hassle at some stage during their holiday and the cause may be anything from disagreement over the price of a lurid wooden elephant to a tout becoming angry or a policeman wanting 'baksheesh'. Whatever you do, don't lose your temper as this is greatly frowned upon. If an official wants a bribe, smile and feign ignorance. If someone follows you around in the hope of becoming your tour guide, thank him for his interest, but make it clear that you would prefer to go without. Finally, relax and smile, as this will always prove your most potent weapon. When it comes to theft you should simply leave and report the incident to a higher authority. But take the locals on yourself? Never.

HOSPITALITY

With more than 100,000 temples and mosques and countless gods looking after them, it is little wonder that Indonesians can afford to be happy and hospitable. Don't necessarily expect to find them that way in all the major tourist centres.

Islamic tradition encourages women to cover up in public

Welcome to Indonesia, with a touch of charm

Often the people in these places have got used to the rudities and strangeness of tourists. Outside, however, Indonesians are some of the most delightful people in the world. Often you may be approached by locals just wanting to find out where you come from, and sometimes they may invite you to their homes. For the most part these are acts of friendliness, but always beware as, although most Indonesians have hearts of gold, somewhere along the line you may meet the exception.

INDONESIAN TALK

Visitors wanting to converse with all 210 million inhabitants in Indonesia may have to learn 300 different languages. Less ambitious mortals can limit themselves to just one: Bahasa Indonesia. This national language, based on Bahasa Malaysia, is relatively easy to pick up and has no complicated tenses, genders or articles. On top of that you may also come across Sundanese, Betawi Madurese and Javanese, as well as Dutch and Chinese dialects and occasionally even English. For a handful of basic words and phrases, see pages 182–3. For a greater choice of vocabulary, buy a dictionary or study a language course before you depart.

'Jam Karet'

The Indonesians have a wonderful phrase for 'late'. It is called *Jam Karet*, or rubber time, and in practice it governs everything from train departures to business meetings and even delivery of your breakfast. Before you despair, however, remember that although in the West time is money, in Indonesia time is still a quality to be valued and enjoyed. So if you find yourself having to wait for any length of time, take a deep breath, smell the sweet-scented blossoms, look at the shrines with their offerings for the gods and contain your anger – at least until later.

LAND OF GODS

When on Bali or Lombok, keep an eye out for the small spirit houses or shrines which are built to honour the spirits, the most important inhabitants on the island. These entities live in the trees, in the winds and the rains. If treated with respect, they ensure plentiful rice harvests, good health and happiness. But if overlooked, they will cause drought, death and a thousand traumas. To ensure harmony, good spirits must be thanked with offerings and colourful festivities, and bad spirits appeased by gifts of rice and joss sticks placed on the ground every morning.

AND SPIRITS

Nor is it only the spirits that must be honoured. In every village you will find countless temples and shrines dedicated to the gods Brahma, Shiva and Vishnu, as well as temples for the dead and temples for the founding of the village – indeed, there are so many places of worship that it is little wonder that the island remains an earthly paradise.

There are plenty of temples on Java, too, from the magnificent Buddhist temple of Borobudur to the fine Hindu *candis* at nearby Prambanan and Dieng Plateau. Added to those are statues of the elephant-headed Ganesha and of Kartteya, the six-headed god of war. These days, the island plays host to some 50,000 mosques where more than 80 per cent of the population come to pray, many of them doing so up to five times a day to give thanks to Allah (the prophet Mohammed).

Just to make sure that nobody's been overlooked on Java, Bali or Lombok, there are even holy trout

swimming around in the temple lakes, fed with peanuts and protected by joss sticks and holy water. Religion? In Indonesia it's almost a way of life.

Top, far left: Balinese shrine
Left and above: Borobudur
Top, right: Balinese temple carvings, Ubud

The famous palace of Kertha Gosa in Klungkung, on the island of Bali

A MATTER OF FACE

Maintaining face in Indonesia is as important as wearing underclothes in Europe and those who find themselves deprived of this important commodity tend to lash out accordingly. To avoid undue insult, always pay due respect to senior officials and to members of established families. Never criticise a manager in front of his employees or disagree with a father in front of his children. Remember, too, that the most important person should always stand tallest, which is why you often see the locals desperately craning their necks forward to keep their heads at a low level. While most Indonesians do not expect foreigners to behave in exactly the same way, they will appreciate your deference to their sensitivities.

SAFETY

Petty theft and pick-pocketing may be one of Indonesia's biggest growth industries, but it is certainly no worse than in many other countries. To reduce risks, take a few simple precautions. Buy a money belt in which to place cash and passports, and carry photocopies with details of passport number, air tickets, travellers' cheques and insurance separately. Always check to see that your hotel room is secure and leave valuables in the hotel safe. Beware public buses and trains where robberies are most common. Above all, try not to put temptation in the way of people. A camera may cost just US$200, but to a poor labourer it's worth more than a year's wages for working in the rice fields.

STRAIGHT TALK
Ask five Indonesians the way to the bus stop and you'll probably get five different answers. It's not that they lie or mislead deliberately, but are simply too proud to admit that they don't know. To avoid this problem, ask someone at your hotel to write down directions and take a map.

TEMPLES AND MOSQUES
Whether it is a temple, a spirit house or a mosque filled with prostrate Muslims, treat it as you would any other house of worship. Before entering a Balinese temple, tie a sash around your waist and leave a small donation (generally Rp3,000). Most temples forbid women from entering while they are in menstruation as it is considered unclean; some even forbid women who are pregnant, or insane. On Java and Lombok everyone can enter a mosque,

but always observe the appropriate customs. Remove your shoes before entering and wash your feet in the facilities provided. Women especially should dress conservatively and avoid shorts, singlets or short skirts.

WHAT TO WEAR
There is no need to take thick woollen clothes or anything made from synthetic material unless you are heading up into the hills. Better to stock up on cotton shorts and open shirts, skirts and blouses and a large hat to protect you from the sun. T-shirts, sarongs and shorts can be bought in abundance in many of the tourist areas. If you are staying in a smart hotel, take more formal wear for evening dinner. Only for official calls and formal occasions are a jacket and tie or dresses and blouses a pre-requisite.

Party wear, Balinese style

WHAT'S A CANDI?
The Javanese refer to them as _candi_ and the Balinese as _pura_, but to most people they are simply temples. You may come across other confusing terms too. A _stupa_ is a Buddhist tower, normally in the shape of a bell and a _mandala_ is an elaborate geometric figure used for meditation. Finally the term you are most likely to hear is 'cosmic mountain', which refers to Mount Meru, seat of the gods.

Every village in Bali holds a temple ceremony at least once a year

and, near by, Ujung Kulon National Park, one of the last remaining strongholds of the Java rhinoceros.

Central Java
You will find an abundance of temples, volcanoes and pleasant mountain retreats within easy reach of popular Yogyakarta and Surakarta (Solo). There is plenty of culture here too, from beautiful batiks to shadow puppets, as well as wild coastal seas at Parangtritis.

East Java
Although East Java is the least developed region on the island, visitors will be rewarded with some of the most diverse scenery, ranging from magnificent Mount Bromo to the rarely visited Baluran National Park, and the arid island of Madura, still barely established on the tourist map.

Bali
Surfers flock to Bali, one of the world's most beautiful islands. Alternatively, there are beaches and tranquillity in up-market Sanur or Nusa Dua, as well as temples, festivals and exotic scenery in the countryside beyond. For the perfect getaway, visit Ubud, cultural centre and stepping-stone to the countless villages dotted around the heartlands.

Lombok
Lombok offers many of the attractions of Bali, but without the crowds. For sun, sand and sea, relax on Senggigi Beach or the idyllic Gili islands; for something more energetic, climb Gunung Rinjani, the highest volcano on the island.

EXPLORING JAVA, BALI AND LOMBOK

Once you have got your feet firmly on Indonesian soil, the next step is to organise your itinerary. A glittering choice of attractions awaits you, but don't make the mistake of trying to see everything in one go. It is better to get to know one area well than to rush from one site to another, taking in almost nothing.

Jakarta
Although many people take an instant dislike to this bustling metropolis of 10 million people, Jakarta does have plenty of attractions as well as fine restaurants, nightclubs and five-star accommodation.

West Java
West Java may not play host to many tourists, but it does offer hill resorts, tea plantations and tropical islands. In the far west you will find Krakatau, one of the world's most destructive volcanoes

WHAT TO SEE

'In the whole course of my life, I
have never met with such
stupendous and finished specimens
of human labour.'

CAPTAIN GEORGE BAKER
1810

Java

One of the lushest, most heavily populated and diverse islands on earth, Java literally bristles with colour and fascination. It is an area of beautiful mountains, tea plantations and unspoilt beaches. It is also home to magnificent temples, fertile rice fields – and some very dirty and crowded cities.

Although Java covers only 6 per cent of the country's land mass, it contains 60 per cent of the population with the result that some 107 million people live in one of the most concentrated and crowded areas of the world. Jakarta, the capital, boasts some 10 million of these people, along with more than its fair share of cars, high-rise buildings and slums.

Yet a 2-hour drive to the south of Jakarta will bring you to the unhurried cool of a mountain resort or the famous botanical gardens of Bogor. Take a regular speed boat from Ancol Marina, and you could even find yourself sunbathing on an exotic tropical island surrounded by turquoise seas.

Java also has ancient temples influenced by the great religions of Buddhism and Hinduism which dominated this country before Islam took hold. In addition to Borobudur and Prambanan, there are a host of other lesser-known temples and palaces. Afterwards, you can visit the volcanoes at Mount Meru, Krakatau or Mount Bromo or just wander through the forests in one of the island's national parks.

On returning to the major towns a different world awaits you: a world of factories, busy ports and warehouses, along with endless plantations and the fertile rice fields which produce up to three crops a year. Java is also the administrative centre for Indonesia's sprawling island archipelago and the

JAVA

The beautifully tranquil botanical gardens at Cibodas in West Java

country's economic powerhouse, generating more than 80 per cent of the nation's wealth.

Most people stay on Java for just a few days to acquire a taste of the place, then continue on to Bali and Lombok; however, anyone who opts for a longer stay will be richly rewarded.

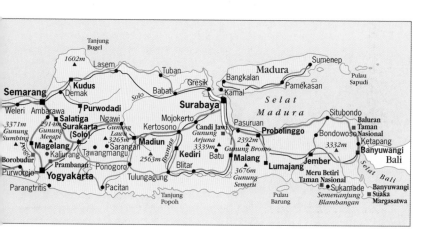

Jakarta

*I*f Indonesia's sprawling capital is your first stop, be prepared for heat, chaos and some of the most interminable traffic jams on earth. Many people take an instant dislike to this bustling metropolis of 10 million people, complaining of the pollution, the poverty and the sheer magnitude of the city. But for those who have the time and the inclination there is plenty of history, culture and even fun to be found, although you may have to search for it.

Founded in the 16th century as a small trading port at the mouth of the Ciliwung River, Jakarta – or Batavia as it was later known – was razed by the Dutch in 1619 and rebuilt as the capital of the Dutch East Indies, sporting canals, grandiose squares and red-tiled houses.

Those somnolent days have long since passed, however, and since independence in 1949 the city has played host not only to the president, but to increasing numbers of high-rise blocks, five-star hotels and glitzy nightclubs.

Don't be put off, though, by these trappings of modernity. Outside the centre Jakarta remains a fascinating city of labyrinthine side streets and crowded markets with plenty to see and do. Around the town you will discover a mind-boggling variety of culinary specialities, as well as shops and bazaars

with a huge collection of arts and crafts from all over the country. Indeed, whilst Jakarta is certainly not the city of the gods, it does offer subtle rewards to those who make the effort.

Getting around

To avoid the ubiquitous traffic jams avoid travelling between 8am and 10am or 5pm and 7pm and to negotiate the one-way streets, overpasses and twisting side streets, take a taxi. If you need a landmark, look for the soaring National Monument in Medan Merdeka which is in the heart of town. To miss the traffic altogether, tour the city on a Sunday.

GLODOK (Chinatown)

For a glimpse of old Chinatown visit the colourful market on Jalan Pancoran, which is intersected by little alleyways and wooden houses. The Chinese moved to this district in 1741 following a massacre and have been making money there ever since. Explore the back streets where you will find little temples and a host of stalls selling glutinous noodle dishes and occasionally even shark's fin soup. Near the shell of the Glodok City Hotel, burnt out in the 1998 riots, the less adventurous can buy grapes and apples. *Jalan Pancoran is situated off Jalan Pintu Besar in the north of the city.*

Jalan Pancoran, Chinatown

ISTANA MERDEKA (Freedom Palace)

This splendid palace was built in 1879 to house the Dutch governors and although the official residence of the president it is now only used on state occasions. At the front of the building is a large portico with Corinthian pillars and the first room, behind the terrace, is the Credential Hall where the president accepts letters from foreign ambassadors.
Northwest corner of Medan Merdeka. Closed to the public.

JALAN JENDRAL SUDIRMAN/ JALAN THAMRIN

This main road which changes its name from Jalan Thamrin to Jalan Jendral Sudirman is Jakarta's equivalent of New York's Wall Street, London's Mayfair and Paris's Champs-Elysées rolled into one. It hosts countless banks, insurance companies, shopping centres and the new Grand Hyatt Hotel, the city's biggest showpiece in luxury accommodation.

Rush hour on Jalan Jendral Sudirman

JAKARTA

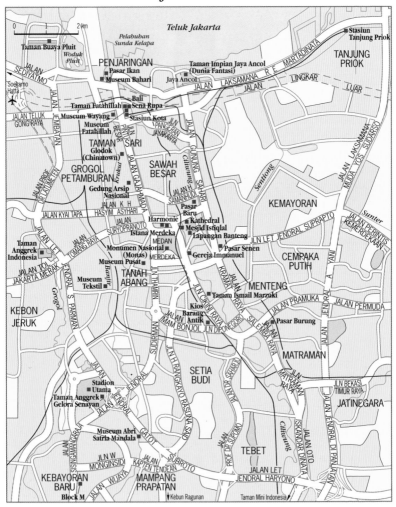

KEBUN RAGUNAN (Ragunan Zoo)

At weekends, thousands of locals invade Indonesia's biggest zoo. Visitors with an interest in wildlife can watch the orang-utans, crocodiles and the famous Komodo dragons, as well as visit a new breeding enclosure for the rare Sumatran tigers. To avoid the crowds, go during the week.

14km south of Jakarta in Ragunan, near

From statues of welcome to concrete columns, Jakarta is littered with monuments

Pasar Minggu (tel: 780 5280). Buses run direct from the centre of town. Open: daily, 8am–6pm. Admission charge.

KIOS BARANG ANTIK

Jakarta's famous flea market is worth a visit for the fun of it, but you may not find much of any real value here. The choice of goods is vast, ranging from brass chandeliers to plastic suitcases. Treat any claims as to age or authenticity with a certain amount of scepticism.
Jalan Surabaya, in Menteng district, to the south of Medan Merdeka. Open: daily, 8am–5pm. Admission free.

A DEADLY CHARM

Jakarta's reputation of being thoroughly unhealthy has more than a little substance. During the 17th century its position on swampland meant it was one of the most disease-ridden cities in the East. Indeed, when Captain Cook put into Jayakarta half his crew died of malaria.

MEDAN MERDEKA (Freedom Square)

You won't be able to miss this giant public square which claims to be one of the largest of its kind in the world. Years ago it was a military parade ground, but now it is a huge park containing state headquarters, the National Monument, the modern parliament building, the national museum and the state palace.
Central Jakarta. Occupies the area between Jalan Thamrin and Jalan Menteng Raya.

MESJID ISTIQLAL (Istiqlal Mosque)

The Istiqlal mosque took more than 10 years to build and is reputed to be the second largest mosque in Southeast Asia, as well as one of the largest in the world. Close up, the edifice is awesome with its six levels, its minarets and its enormous white dome. Visit the mosque on Fridays to see it filled with capacity crowds of up to 200,000, but remember to dress suitably.
Jalan Veteran. Off the northeast corner of Medan Merdeka. Admission free.

COLONIAL ARCHITECTURE

In parts of Java, Dutch architecture is almost as abundant as tulips in spring. It is found in the beautiful old façades that front the narrow alleyways of old Batavia, and in the austere courts of justice and magnificent squares that are scattered around the Kota district. Even murky canals still wind their way through labyrinths of closely packed houses and mounds of garbage.

Of course plenty of the old buildings have been knocked down and replaced by faceless new shopfronts and modern houses, but you'll still find reminders of the days when the Dutch sailed their boats into the harbour and commandeered much of the surrounding archipelago.

In Jakarta's old district of Sunda Kelapa, where the Dutch fort still stands, you could almost be in a European capital with its old warehouses, its Grecian-style museum and distinguished European edifices. Hardly surprising, then, that during the early days the town was known as

'Little Amsterdam'. In Surabaya, Yogyakarta, and Malang – and even high up in the hill resorts – you can still find glimpses of the days when the colonial administrators retreated from the heat of the plains below.

To the interiors of their great buildings the Dutch added fine statues, stained-glass windows and portraits to remind them of home and at night they held great parties with orchestras; the women wore long dresses and the men sported dinner jackets and stiff white collars.

This era ended in 1949, however, and the Dutch, along with their suits and their parasols, departed, leaving behind them an independent Indonesia.

Left: the Mangkunegaran
Palace, Surakarta
Far left: the Bank Indonesia
building, Jakarta
Below: the Museum
Fatahillah, Jakarta
Bottom: detail from the
Surakarta Kraton

The National Monument is Jakarta's most prominent landmark

MUSEUM FATAHILLAH (City Museum)

This fine two-storey building is one of the best examples of Dutch colonial architecture that you are likely to come across in Jakarta. Built in 1710, it became a museum in 1974 and now provides exhibits of Dutch colonial life as well as an insight into the city's 350-year history. From the first-floor balcony you can look down on the square where criminals were executed or severely flogged (see Kota II walk, pages 42–3). *Corner of Taman Fatahillah, across the road from the Wayang Museum. Tel: 692 9101. Open: Tuesday to Thursday, 8am–2.30pm; Friday, 8am–11.30am; and Sunday, 8am–2.30pm. Admission charge.*

This distinguished building houses the delightful Museum Fatahillah

MONUMEN NASIONAL (National Monument)

Towering over the central part of Jakarta and referred to surreptitiously as 'Soekarno's last erection', this vast monument has almost everything except artistic merit. Built out of Italian marble and rising 137m, it was begun in 1961 to commemorate Indonesia's struggle for independence and is topped by a symbolic flame of freedom covered with 35kg of pure gold leaf. For the best photographs, take the elevator up to the platform. Afterwards, visit the museum below and listen to the voice of former President Soekarno broadcasting the declaration of independence. *Medan Merdeka (tel: 384 0451). Open: daily, 9am–5pm. Admission charge.*

MUSEUM PUSAT (National Museum)

Established in 1778 under the auspices of the Batavia Association of Arts and Sciences, this museum has so much to offer that you may find yourself overwhelmed. Allow plenty of time and take a camera, although you must first obtain a permit at the entrance. Some of the most interesting exhibits are to be found in the prehistory section which contains weapons and cooking utensils,

Jakarta's popular Pasar Burung has more than raucous roosters

as well as a skull of the 'Java Man', discovered in the 1890s in East Java and hailed as the 'missing link' between apes and humans. There is also a fine display of pottery and Oriental porcelain as well as treasure rooms, inner courts and an audio-visual room. Conducted tours in English are held on Tuesday, Wednesday and Thursday mornings at 9.30am and last for around 2.5 hours.
Jalan Merdeka Barat 12, on the west side of Medan Merdeka (tel: 381 1551). Open: Tuesday to Thursday, 8.30am–2.30pm; Fridays, 8.30am–11.30am; Saturday, 8.30am–1.30pm; Sundays, 8.30am–2.30pm. Closed Mondays. Admission charge.

MUSEUM TEKSTIL (Textile Museum)

Textile enthusiasts should not miss this museum housed in a 19th-century residence to the southwest of town. The collection contains just about every kind of fabric from the most far-flung areas of the archipelago.
Jalan Satsuit Tuban 4 (tel: 560 6613).

Open: Tuesday to Thursday, and Sunday, 8am–2pm; Friday, 8am–11am; Saturday, 8am–1pm. Admission charge.

PASAR BURUNG (Bird Market)

This market is the place to view *perkutut* song birds as well as colourful parrots and occasionally even the helmeted hornbill. These creatures are piled up in bamboo cages along with roosters and, sadly, rarer breeds that have escaped the eye of conservationists.
A short distance down Jalan Pramuka, in Jatinegara. Open: daily, 9am–5pm. Admission free.

PASAR IKAN (Fish Market)

The old fish market with its auction rooms and colourful stalls occupies an area of narrow alleyways in the old part of town next to the harbour of Sunda Kelapa. Get there early in the morning to see the place at its liveliest (see Kota I walk, pages 40–1).
Pasar Ikan Road, north of Taman Fatahillah. Open: daily.

Old Buginese Makassar schooners still sail the seas with cargos of spices

SUNDA KELAPA

If you only have time to visit one place in Jakarta, choose the magnificent harbour in the old part of town – but allow plenty of time because of the appalling traffic. All along the wharf, which is spread out beside the stinking Ciliwung River, beautiful old Buginese Makassar schooners are loaded up with timber, cartons of Coca Cola and other local commodities destined for the outer islands. For a small fee you can take a short trip around the harbour in a rowing boat, but beware the ropes – and the

MONUMENTAL TASTELESSNESS
From bronze statues to concrete columns and knights charging into battle, Jakarta is littered with monuments to athletes, to the army and even to farmers. Not all have won accolades. The statue of Welcome is nicknamed 'Hansel and Gretel', whilst the famous gentleman holding a flaming dish is simply called 'the mad waiter'.

A mouthful of monuments at Mini-Indonesia

slops which are merrily thrown overboard (see Kota I walk, pages 40–1). *Jalan Krapu, in the north of the city, a short distance from Pasar Ikan. Open: daily, 8am–6pm. Admission charge.*

TAMAN IMPIAN JAYA ANCOL

This vast Western-style amusement park is a must for children and fun-loving adults. There's an oceanarium, a multi-million dollar swimming pool complex with wave-making facilities, as well as bowling alleys, space shuttles, jumping dolphins and even kissing seals. Go during the week for peace and quiet. *2km north of Jakarta at Ancol (tel: 682 417). Bus no 64 runs from Kota Station. Open: Monday to Friday, 3pm–10pm; Saturday and Sunday, 10am–10pm. Admission charge.*

TAMAN ISMAIL MARZUKI

Before dropping by this municipal arts centre, obtain a list of performances from your hotel or the English-language newspapers. Cultural entertainment ranges from Javanese dancing to *gamelan* concerts and batik exhibitions. *Jalan Cikini Raya (tel: 315 4087). Open: Monday to Saturday, 9am–1pm and 5–7pm. Admission charge.*

TAMAN MINI-INDONESIA

Visitors wanting to see the great monuments of Indonesia – with minimum effort – can simply go to the Taman Mini-Indonesia, now billed as Jakarta's top tourist attraction. Among the dazzling number of exhibits spread over 120 hectares are finely crafted houses from each of the 27 provinces of Indonesia, models of the country's major landmarks, as well as theatres, boating lakes, trams, cable-cars and a miniature train. You will find a history museum, acclaimed as the country's best, as well as a wildlife and natural history museum located inside the statue of a Komodo dragon which towers 25m above the ground. There is also an orchid garden containing more than 2,000 varieties of orchid. You would need weeks to see all the sights, but even a day's visit will provide you with a memorable introduction. *20km south of Jakarta, just off the toll expressway to Bogor (tel: 840 9201). Take a bus to Cililitan, then change to a 'mini-Indonesia' bus or, better still, take a tour. Open: daily, 8am–4pm. Admission charge.*

WAYANG MUSEUM, see Kota II walk, pages 42–3.

Kota I

Starting at the delightful old port of Sunda Kelapa, this walk will take you through an area known as 'Little Amsterdam'. It is made up of fetid canals, old Dutch warehouses, European-style bridges and colourful markets. *Allow 3 hours.*

Get up at dawn to avoid the traffic and take a bus or taxi to the entrance of Sunda Kelapa which lies to the north of the city in the old Kota district.

1 SUNDA KELAPA

Centuries ago, this magnificent wharf was Jakarta's only major link with the outside world. These days it is still the departure point for ancient vessels laden with sugar and spices and you can watch the old Bugis schooners with their towering wooden masts being loaded up for their next voyage. For a small sum you can take a rowing boat around the harbour.
Return to the entrance gate and continue for 200m. Turn right over the bridge on to Jalan Pakin and you will see the Uitkijk.

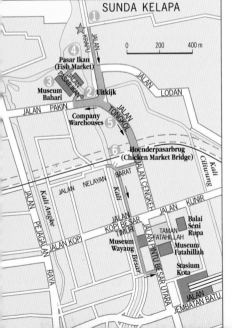

2 UITKIJK (LOOK-OUT TOWER)

Built by the Dutch in 1839, this old look-out tower was used both to signal to incoming ships and as a vantage point. Climb up to the top for excellent photo opportunities. Note, too, the cannons pointing towards Sunda Kelapa.
Turn right down Jalan Pasar Ikan and almost immediately you will see the Museum Bahari on your left.

3 MUSEUM BAHARI

These two old warehouses were originally used to store tea, coffee, tin and spices. These days they have not only been restored, but transformed into a maritime museum with models of various fishing boats and other navigational items. In front of the museum are the last remnants of the wall which surrounded old Batavia in the 17th and 18th centuries.
Continue down Jalan Pasar Ikan until you

reach the fish market, a short distance further on.

OPENING DETAILS
Museum Bahari (tel: 669 3406 or 669 2476). open Tuesday to Friday 8.30am–3pm; Saturday and Sunday, 8.30am–1.30pm.

---

4 PASAR IKAN (FISH MARKET)

The time to see this fish market is at dawn when piles of freshly caught barramundi and tuna line the stalls and the auction halls are crowded with buyers. You can explore the maze of small alleyways which run parallel with the waterfront and buy exotic fruits, clothes, hardware or delicious *nasi goreng* (fried rice).
Retrace your steps over the bridge and turn right down Jalan Tongkol. After a few hundred metres you will see the old warehouses on your right.

5 COMPANY WAREHOUSES

These dilapidated 19th-century warehouses with their corrugated roofs and flag poles were used to store grain and spices. The area is now mainly used as a car park, although you may see the odd goat nibbling on grass near the entrance. *Continue along Jalan Tongkol until you reach the main intersection with Jalan Nelayan Barat. Turn right and on your right you will see the Hoenderpasarbrug.*

6 HOENDERPASARBRUG (CHICKEN MARKET BRIDGE)

This charming red-painted drawbridge which crosses the Kali Besar Canal was built in the 17th century and marks the southwest corner of the old Dutch fort. It is also the last of its kind in the city, and a reminder of the days when boats used to sail all the way up to Ciliwung River. On the nearby road bridge you may find a small market where you can refresh yourself with cool drinks, and occasionally even a slice of *durian*. *Continue south parallel to the Kali Besar, past some run-down old colonial buildings. At the second junction, turn left and left again on to Jalan Pintu Besar Utara where you will find Taman Fatahillah (Fatahillah Square; see Kota II walk, pages 42–3). Alternatively, catch a taxi back to your hotel.*

Shopping at Pasar Ikan

Kota II: Fatahillah Square

Starting out in the heart of the old Dutch city, this walk takes you to some of the finest museums in Jakarta. You can explore the old square before taking a short walk past the Bank of Indonesia to the Portuguese Sion Church. *Allow 2.5 hours.*

Catch a bus or taxi to Taman Fatahillah, which lies in the Kota district, a short distance south of Sunda Kelapa.

1 TAMAN FATAHILLAH
Although this square has been extensively renovated, it still gives a delightful sense of Batavia's past with its old colonial buildings, its fountains and nearby canals. The square was built in the 17th century and designed by the Dutch Governor-General, Jan Pieterzoon Coen.
Standing in the centre of Taman Fatahillah, the Museum Fatahillah is directly in front.

2 MUSEUM FATAHILLAH
This distinguished old building, which dominates the square, was at various times both a military headquarters and the city hall. Inside the museum is a fine selection of Dutch memorabilia ranging from antique furniture to busts and portraits of former governors. Outside, you can explore the dungeons now filled with old cannon balls. (See also page 36.)
Leave the Museum Fatahillah and a short distance to your right you will see the Balai Seni Rupa.

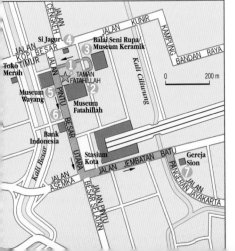

3 BALAI SENI RUPA (FINE ARTS MUSEUM)
Formerly the palace of justice, this fine little museum, built in the 1870s, now plays host to famous paintings by prominent Indonesian artists such as

Raden Saleh, as well as to a selection of ceramics, terracotta and Javanese water jugs. Note, too, the rare Ming pieces gathered together by Adam Malik.

From the Fine Arts Museum, cross back into the square and on your right you will see a large bronze cannon.

4 SI JAGUR

Legend tells that this bronze cannon was brought to Batavia in 1641 by the Dutch after the fall of Malacca. These days, it has established itself as the city's pre-eminent fertility symbol and you may occasionally see women sitting astride the cannon in the hope of conceiving children. Behind the cannon is a lively market selling clothes, fruits and other items.

Leave the square and cross over on to Jalan Pintu Besar Utara. Turn left and the Museum Wayang is on your right.

5 MUSEUM WAYANG

This two-storey building, which originally served as the museum of Old Batavia, now contains a collection of puppets from all over the world, including magnificent Chinese hand-puppets and the intricate buffalo-hide shadow puppets known as Wayang Kulit.

Walk out of the museum and turn right down Jalan Pintu Besar Utara. After a short distance the Bank Indonesia is passed on the right.

6 BANK INDONESIA

This grand-looking edifice houses one of the most important financial institutions in the country. The Bank of Indonesia, which is the country's central bank, sets the exchange rate, monitors the 160 different banking companies and advises the government on economic policy.

OPENING DETAILS
Museum Fatahillah. See page 36.
Balai Seni Rupa (tel: 690 7062).
Open: Tuesday to Friday,
8.30am–3pm; Saturday and
Sunday, 8.30am–1.30pm;
closed Monday.
Museum Wayang (tel: 692 9560).
Open: Tuesday to Sunday,
8.30am–3pm.
Wayang performances every
Sunday at 10am.

From Bank Indonesia, continue until you reach the main square in front of the station. Turn left on to Jalan Jembatan Batu and then third right to Gereja Sion.

7 GEREJA SION (SION CHURCH)

This incongruous little church, which dates from 1695, not only has a charming interior with copper chandeliers and a baroque pulpit, but is listed in the history books as the oldest church in Jakarta. It was originally built by the Portuguese, although it has since been renovated several times.

Catch a bus or taxi back to your hotel.

Fine leather shadow puppets are found throughout Indonesia's archipeligo

West Java

Stretching from the Selat Sunda (Sunda Straits) in the west to the border of Central Java, this province gives you a choice of lush rain forests, beautiful hill resorts, tea plantations and dazzling islands. Here you can rest amidst tropical splendour at the Pulau Seribu (Thousand Islands), visit the botanical gardens of Bogor or catch a boat out to Krakatau, one of the world's most destructive volcanoes. All these destinations can either make a perfect break from the bustle of Jakarta, or be used as stepping-stones on the way to Central Java and to Bali which lies further to the east.

BANDUNG

A 3-hour drive from the heat and hassle of Jakarta will bring you to Java's third largest city, situated on a plateau to the southeast. Bandung is the cultural centre of West Java, home to some of its best-known universities and to some of its most modern architecture. During the 1930s it was known as the Paris of Java, although these days you will find precious few noteworthy buildings and little reason to spend much time here. *Location: 180km southeast of Jakarta.*

Regular buses run from the Kampung Rambutan terminal on the Pasar Rebo interchange (tel: 840 0062). Trains depart from Jakarta Gambir, situated on Jalan Medan Merdeka Timur (tel: 384 2777). Also served by Merpati flights.

Dago Hill Tea House

For the finest views that Bandung has to offer, visit this little tea house situated to

The overwhelming formality of Bandung's Gedung Sate

the north of the city, beyond the Sheraton Hotel. Get there at sunset to see the place at its best, but be prepared for the bar/restaurant to be closed.
Jalan Juanda, 6km north of town. Admission charge.

Gedung Merdeka

Unless you are particularly interested in the history of the non-aligned movement, there is little reason to visit this building which hosted the Afro-Asia conference in 1955. All that's on offer is a small museum and occasionally a film of the event.
Jalan Asia Africa. Open: Tuesday to Friday, 8am–1pm. Admission charge.

Gedung Sate

Bandung's most imposing building has everything from lush green lawns to well-clipped hedges. You can't go inside though, as these days it has become the province's main administrative and telecommunications centre.
Jalan Diponegoro, a short distance to the north of town. Closed to the public.

BOGOR

The name of Bogor is almost synonymous with botanical gardens and few visitors come to this hill town without visiting them. There are, however, several other sites to see, including the imposing presidential palace known as Istana Bogor and the Zoological Museum. To avoid the crowds, visit on a weekday.
Location: 60km south of Jakarta. Regular buses run from the Kampung Rambutan on the Pasar Rebo interchange. Trains take 90 minutes from Jakarta's Gambir Station on Jalan Medan Merdeka Timur.

Botanical Gardens

These magnificent gardens have not

Sir Stamford Raffles sowed the seeds for the Bogor Botanical Gardens

become one of West Java's finest showcases without good reason. In all they extend over 87 hectares, boasting more than 15,000 specimens of exotic native plants, trees and bushes along with lakes and shady walkways. The gardens were founded in 1817 by Sir Stamford Raffles, and were subsequently tended by the then Dutch Governor-General van der Capellan. Since then numerous other new species have been added, including African water lilies and the famous Rafflesia, which is claimed to be the biggest flower in the world.
The entrance to the gardens is on Jalan Empang, on the south side. Open: daily, 8am–4pm. Closed Friday between 11am and 1pm. Admission charge.

Zoological Museum

This little museum boasts more than 250,000 specimens of birds, reptiles, insects and mammals, as well as the last rhinoceros from Tasikmalaya – stuffed.
Jalan Empang. Next to the botanical gardens. Open: daily, 8am–4pm. Admission charge.

CIBODAS

Although the botanical gardens of Bogor are better known, this high-altitude extension is beautifully tranquil, set away from the crowds near the slopes of Gunung Gede and Gunung Pangrango. In all there are some 80 hectares of gardens, planted in 1889 and still sprouting prolifically. Most visitors simply take walks in the park or shop for tropical plants and dazzling flowers in the 'nurseries' that line the street outside. Those in search of more energetic recreation can climb nearby Mount Gede, a 10-hour hike there and back, with the help of a guide.

Location: situated off the main road from Bogor to Bandung, near the town of Cipanas. Ask to be dropped off by the bus and catch a bemo for the last 5km to Cibodas. To climb Mount Gede, first obtain a permit from the PHPA office next to the entrance to the botanical gardens.

KRAKATAU

The world's most active volcano in reality blew itself to smithereens just over a century ago, but in its place you will find its offspring, Anak Krakatau (son of Krakatau), which is gradually rising out of the sea. If you want to explore the volcano a boat can be hired from Labuhan or Carita for the 4-6-hour trip, but only when seas are low and conditions permit. A better and safer alternative is to take an organised tour. During the monsoon season, between November and March, high seas mean that trips can be extremely hazardous.

Location: 50km off the west coast of Java. Charter a boat from Labuhan, Anyer or Carita, or make arrangements at the Carita Krakatau Beach Hotel. Tours can

UP IN SMOKE

When Krakatau erupted on the morning of 27 August, 1883, the noise could be heard as far afield as Sri Lanka, Burma and Australia. Great piles of volcanic debris landed in Madagascar and tons of rocks were hurled more than 20km into the sky. In all, some 295 villages in West Java and South Lampung on Sumatra were destroyed and an estimated 36,000 people killed. These days only a small cone remains, known as Anak Krakatau; occasionally it rumbles, producing ash, smoke and a lot of fear.

also be organised through travel agents in Jakarta.

MERAK

There's precious little reason to visit this sprawling town unless you are catching the ferry to Sumatra. Boats take 1.5 hours to reach Bakauheni and 4 to 6 hours to Strengsem. Enquire at travel agents for current departure times.

Location: 140km west of Jakarta. Trains arrive and depart twice daily for Jakarta's Tanah Abang Railway Station on Jalan J Jati Baru. Regular buses take 3 hours from Jakarta's Kalideres Terminal.

PANGANDARAN

This gem of a little fishing village is rapidly becoming West Java's most popular resort area, offering fine beaches as well as access to the nearby nature reserve at Pananjung Pangandaran. Keen swimmers head out to the west side of the peninsula, but check on local conditions and beware of

Above: enjoy Pangandaran's fishermen, but
beware its dangerous tides and currents
Right: take the pick of the catch at the morning
market

dangerous currents which take their toll
every year. A safer option is to walk to
the headland reserve, reached by
crossing the narrow isthmus. For a
pleasant morning's hiking, hire a guide
at the entrance. You are bound to catch
sight of monkeys and deer and if you are
lucky you may even find the rare
Rafflesia lotus flower which smells like
rotting garbage and resembles a bloated
pink cabbage.

*Location: 400km southeast of Jakarta.
Buses run from Bandung, Jakarta or
Yogyakarta to the town of Banjar, from
where you must catch another bus or bemo.
Crowded boats also leave in the morning
from the town of Cilacap, taking 4 hours.*

Tea plantations cover the rolling hills around Puncak Pass

PANTAI CARITA

This 3km sweep of sand lined with coconut groves is a popular weekend haunt of expatriates and Jakartans, who leave the city in swarms. There is reasonable accommodation here and on clear days fine views of the distant Krakatau can be had. For information on trips to the volcano, call in at the Carita Krakatau Beach Hotel. Otherwise, spend the time snorkelling, surfing or taking lazy strolls into the nearby paddy fields.

Location: 150km west of Jakarta. Regular buses run from Jakarta's Kalideres Terminal to Labuhan, from where you must take the short minibus ride. Avoid at weekends.

PULAU SERIBU (Thousand Islands)

Weary city dwellers flock to the beautiful islands known as Pulau Seribu, or Thousand Islands, to laze under palm trees, swim in clear turquoise water and relax in a perfect hideaway just 2 to 4 hours by boat from the capital. Many of the islands are surrounded by sparkling white beaches; others are better known for their coral. Only a handful of them, however, have been fully developed as tourist destinations. For bungalows and cottages try Pulau Putri and Pulau Pelangi, though you should book in advance. To avoid the crowds go during the week and remember to take a sun hat, sun-tan lotion and heaps of mosquito repellent.

Location: 70km from Jakarta's waterfront. Boats run from Ancol Dreamland Marina in the north of the city, leaving every morning at around 7am and taking between 2 and 4 hours. Make an advance booking if you intend to stay the night. Alternatively, contact Panorama Tours (tel: 630 8105).

PUNCAK PASS

You could travel to beautiful Puncak Pass (2,900m) for the views alone. It sits

high up in the heart of the tea-growing area east of Bogor, offering magnificent vistas of the surrounding area. Stop by the Gunung Mas tea estates (3km to the west) for photographs of the workers picking tea leaves and stacking them in giant wicker baskets. Tours of the plantation can be arranged on arrival. Afterwards, for a touch of tropical splendour, continue to the botanical gardens at Cibodas (10km to the east).
Location: 25km southeast of Bogor, on the road to Bandung or Cianjur. Catch one of the regular buses and ask to be dropped off at Puncak Pass.

TANGKUBAN PRAHU

The popular Tangkuban Prahu (2,081m) cannot compare with the awesome scenery around Mount Bromo or Mount Batur on Bali, but it can provide a pleasant excursion from Bandung. Legend has it that the crater is part of a giant upturned boat that an eccentric young prince built after he fell in love with his own mother. Pleasant walks can

be taken around the main crater and to a series of 11 craters in the vicinity, which are signposted. For ease of transport, take a tour.
Location: 32km north of Bandung, near the village of Lembang. From the park entrance it is 6km to the crater. Admission charge.

UJUNG KULON NATIONAL PARK

Java's finest national park makes up for its lack of tourist facilities with the largest concentration of wildlife on the island. There are plenty of colourful birds, deer, wild ox and crocodiles; park officials even claim that 50 protected rhinoceros live in the vicinity. Unless you have sufficient time, it is best to take a tour organised in Carita or Labuhan since access is difficult and expensive (see Getting Away From it All, pages 140–1).
Location: southwestern tip of Java. Reached by a 6–8-hour boat trip from Labuhan, which is situated midway along the coast. You must obtain an entry permit and, ideally, a guide

The inner crater at Tangkuban Prahu

Central Java

Central Java, stretching from Pangandaran east to Tawangmangu, offers a dazzling choice of destinations from rugged beaches to cool hill resorts, volcanoes and some of the most magnificent ruins on earth. This is the cultural heart of Indonesia, home to the great cities of Yogyakarta and Surakarta (Solo). It is also the region where you will find the temples of Borobudur and Prambanan, and the awesome Mount Merapi, along with some of the most colourful batiks and shadow puppets in the country. Buses and trains connect major towns with East Java and West Java.

YOGYAKARTA

Almost everybody who visits Central Java will spend some time in Yogyakarta, for this vibrant metropolis of 500,000 people oozes with history, culture and sheer exuberance.

Founded by the rebel prince Mangkubumi in 1755 following the division of the kingdom of Mataram, the town became one of the most powerful Javanese states until it was sacked by the British in 1812. At the end of World War II the city once again rose to prominence as the rebel capital of the new republic of Indonesia in its struggle for independence from the Dutch.

Those efforts did not go unnoticed and in 1949 the city was granted status as a special region, and the only one on Java to retain a functioning sultanate.

Yogyakarta (better known as Yogya) has plenty of attractions. You can explore the ancient ruins of the Taman Sari or the Kraton in the morning, shop for shadow puppets or traditional batiks in the afternoon and afterwards take a delightful tricycle ride to the artists' quarter or to the colourful bird market.

When the city's spell is finally broken, there are trips to the magnificent temples of Borobudur and Prambanan which, although easily done in a day, deserve longer.

Location: 565km east of Jakarta. Trains take 10 hours from Jakarta's Kota Station on Jalan Station 1 (tel: 679 194). Buses take 12 hours from the Pulo Gadung Terminal on the corner of Jalan Perintis Kemerdekaan and Jalan Bekasi Timur Raya. Garuda, Merpati, Bouraq and Sempati offer air connections to Adisucipto Airport, 8km east of town.

A stone guard at Yogyakarta's Kraton

Yogyakarta prides itself for its role in achieving national independence

Kraton (Sultan's Palace)

Yogya's most popular tourist site may lack immediate charm, but it will certainly reward more than a passing visit. Founded in 1755 to house Yogyakarta's sultans, the area around the Kraton has become the veritable heart of the city, home to countless shops, markets and private residences.

Modelled on the cosmos, the palace has a symbolic value aimed at ensuring harmony between the court and the divine forces of the universe. Even the inner courtyards mirror the oceans which surround the cosmic mountain of the deities. The present Sultan, Hamengkubuwono X, lives here, waited upon by several hundred loyal retainers and worshipped by the people.

To view the centrepiece of the palace situated within the old walls visit the Bangsal Kencono (Golden Pavilion) with its four teak pillars and its peaked roof that represents Mount Merapi. To the south you will also find two 14th-century *gamelan* orchestras. To round off the tour, drop into the nearby Museum Kereta Kraton on Jalan Rotowijayan with its royal brass gongs and horse-drawn carriages, the most impressive of which is the Kereta Kyai Garuda Yeksa, built in the Netherlands in 1861 out of 18-carat gold. *Enter from the west gate off Jalan Rotowijayan. Open: Saturday to Thursday, 8am–2pm; Friday, 8am–11am. Admission charge includes a guided tour.* Gamelan *rehearsals held on Mondays and Wednesdays, 10am–noon.*

SHADOW PUPPETS

Made from leather, beautifully carved by hand and painted with gilt or even gold, the sacred Wayang Kulit puppets are not only some of Indonesia's greatest works of art, but also one of the country's most beloved forms of entertainment.

Dating back more than 1,000 years, these frail figures supported on posts of wood are seen as instruments of the gods, and the very symbols of the struggle between good and evil.

Typically, the puppets enact a host of different and often well-known stories. Some feature epic events from the Indian *Ramayana*, others heroic deeds or tales of ferocious

battles between the gods and mortals. Often the age-old performances are spiced with local political and historical references, punctuated by comedy and accompanied by the sounds of a four-piece *gamelan* orchestra.

For up to 8 hours at a time the puppet master, known as the *dalang*, sits cross-legged behind a screen lit up by the flame of an ancient oil lamp. During the entire performance he alone manipulates the puppets, chanting in up to 50 different narrative voices and beating the tiny cymbal with his feet in a unique display of drama and passion. Only at the end of the show is there silence when the left side of the screen is empty and the power of good symbolically vanquishes the power of evil.

You may occasionally come across full-length versions of the Wayang Kulit, held at temple festivals or as part of a local celebration. Shorter versions are also held at tourist venues in Yogyakarta or Ubud. Elsewhere, you will find plenty of factories producing the beautiful hand-made puppets, reminders of the frailty of man who is little more than a puppet on the bigger stage of life.

(WAYANG KULIT)

Shadow puppets have passed on stories from one generation to the next in a region of the world where the written word was not available to the vast majority of the populace

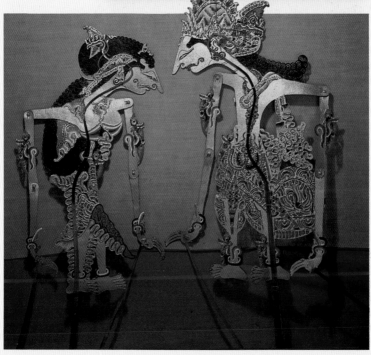

Gembira Loka Zoo

One of the highlights of Yogya's zoo is the famous Komodo dragon which comes from the Lesser Sunda Islands and is reported to be the oldest living species of lizard, dating back almost 60 million years. There are plenty of other animals, too, as well as 22 hectares of garden, an orchid nursery and a children's park.

Jalan Gembira Loca, to the east of town, beyond Kali Gajah Wong. Open: daily, 7am–6pm. Admission charge.

Jalan Malioboro (Marlboro Street)

Yogya's most colourful shopping district has everything from leather and batik shops to underwear stalls presided over by dozens of grinning *becak* (tricycle) drivers. To get to Pasar Beringharjo, the city's largest covered market, continue to the southern end where the road changes its name to Jalan Jend A Yani. Otherwise just wander through the district, especially in the early evening when the shops do a roaring trade.

Painters' Colony

Aspiring batik makers took a liking to the area around Taman Sari years ago, transforming the network of little alleyways into a veritable batik painters' colony. Many of the older residents still specialise in traditional scenes from the *Ramayana*, but others have opted for a more surrealist style aimed at pleasing the growing Western clientele. Wander from gallery to gallery just watching the artists at work. There's plenty on sale, but standards are variable, so bargain hard.

North of Taman Sari, off Jalan Ngasem. Admission free.

Pasar Ngasem (Bird Market)

In this lively little market birds literally go for a song. Homing pigeons are snapped up for as little as Rp25,000; prize-winning turtle doves for more than Rp2 million. Occasionally you may come across yellow-crested parrots, fighting cocks or even baby Komodo dragons which are kept in buckets and used as a backdrop for less-than-exotic photographs.

Jalan Ngasem, north of Taman Sari. Admission free.

Sono Budoyo Museum, see Yogyakarta walk, pages 64–5.

Taman Sari (Fragrant Garden)

This famous little water palace, totally dedicated to pleasure with its sunken baths and underwater tunnels, was where the Sultan Hamengkubuwono I, his family and harem could escape from the cares of the world. Designed by a Portuguese architect and built in 1758, its idyllic existence was to prove short-lived, however, and following the sultan's death it was abandoned and subsequently destroyed by an earthquake. Guided tours take in the ruined gardens and underwater mosque,

---

WATER PALACES

Between 1765 and 1946, when king Gusti Bagus constructed the last of them, Balinese and Javanese kings and sultans were responsible for an abundance of water palaces and pleasure parks. Some had domes, others follies and pagoda-like thrones for the gods. So well planned was the Taman Sari in Yogyakarta, that it even provided water baths for the royal concubines.

ASPIRING ARTISANS

Impressed by the beautiful cloth painted with wax and dyed in dazzling colours known as batik? Most tourists are content merely to buy an example or two, but those who are sufficiently intrigued can attend day or week courses in the craft which are now advertised in several shops. There is even a Batik Research Centre on Jalan Sultan Agung.

but these days there is little else left of those happier times.

Jalan Taman, a 10-minute walk south of the Kraton. Open: daily, 7am–5pm. Admission charge.

Excursions

For a delightful tour of Yogya's neighbouring handicraft villages, either rent a taxi from outside your hotel, or better still hire an *Andong* (horse-drawn cart). First stop should be Kasongan (7km south), which is best known for its pottery and its copies of Javanese wooden dolls. Afterwards visit Kota Gede (6km southeast) with its fine silver jewellery. Finally, drop by the small village of Bantul, home to Pak Warno Waskito, one of the most famous living mask-makers of Yogya.

The famous Taman Sari was a favourite retreat of the sultan and his harem

Borobudur, one of the world's most impressive Buddhist monuments

BOROBUDUR

One of the great wonders of the ancient world, the magnificent Borobudur complex lies just a short distance from Yogyakarta, rising up from the fertile Kedu Plain. You can see it from below, a doughnut-shaped structure made up of intricate reliefs, spired domes and serene Buddha images.

Built during the reign of the Sailendra dynasty between AD778 and 856, Borobudur predates even the great Angkor Wat in Cambodia by nearly 300 years. Little is known of its early history, however, and shortly after its completion, Mount Merapi, the neighbouring volcano, erupted and Borobudur along with much of Central Java was mysteriously abandoned.

It was only in 1814 that the British Lieutenant-Governor of Java, Sir Thomas Stamford Raffles, was informed of the existence of the ruined temple and dispatched 200 men to uncover what was left. In 1907 restoration work got under way, but it took two world wars and another 76 years before the task was finally completed at a cost of US$25 million.

Location: 42km northwest of Yogyakarta. Buses run from the Umbulharjo terminal on Jalan Kemerdekan to Muntilan, from where you must catch another bus to the village of Borobudur. Most visitors simply take a tour. Open: daily, 6am–5pm. Admission charge.

Touring the site

Most tours begin at the east gate, gradually working their way around the panels in an anti-clockwise fashion just as the many pilgrims did 10 centuries ago. By keeping the panels on your right, the journey will take you through 5km of corridors, past 72 *stupas* weighing as much as 600kg and containing more than 500 stone Buddhas.

Each level marks a gradual transition from *khamadhatu*, the world of desires, to *rupadhatu*, the sphere of form, and *arupadhatu* or *nirvana*, the ultimate perfection. Each terrace offers a different and richer perspective and the *mandala* shape of the monument is believed to symbolise the wheel of life and the infinite cycle of birth, death and rebirth.

As you reach the highest level, marked by circular terraces, you enter an area of formlessness with only a few *stupas* and dramatic views of distant mountains, a fitting end to the journey into the realms of perfection.

Etchings of perfection

There is no need to look at all 1,400 relief panels as even a cursory glance at the 8,000 sq m of sculpting will provide rewards. The first series around the base

Stone reliefs at Borobudur depict scenes from the life of the Buddha

depicts the transitory pleasures of worldly existence. Later panels show the birth of the Buddha and his journey from the confines of the palace to the valleys of the Ganges and his final enlightenment and release from suffering. You will find plenty of other reliefs, too, from the former lives of the Buddha as depicted in the Jataka Tales to depictions of the Buddhist cosmos, all executed with delicate and beautifully intricate detail.

The best time to view the reliefs is at dawn or dusk during the week. Opt for luxury accommodation at the Amanjiwo Hotel or the cheaper but beautiful Taman Borobudur Guest House. Avoid weekends when the place is over-run.

Other temples

If you have seen Borobudur and have the time, drop by the nearby temple complexes of Candi Mendut and Candi Pawon. While they cannot compare in scale, they do offer elaborate carvings from the Jataka Tales as well as a pleasant respite from the crowds.

3km east of Borobudur. Open: daily, 6am–5pm. Admission charge.

Sulphur springs at sunset on Dieng Plateau

DIENG PLATEAU

A stunning stretch of road that passes steep gorges and mountains will bring you to another of Central Java's great hideaways, Dieng Plateau. Known as the 'abode of the gods', it is cooler than the plains and commands a magnificent setting amid sulphur springs, volcanic lakes and ruined temples. Don't expect up-market accommodation, though, or many tour groups for that matter.

Location: 117km northwest of Yogyakarta. Buses run from Yogya's Umbunharjo Terminal on Jalan Kemerdekan to Magelang, from where you must catch another bus to Wonoboso (25km) and then a minibus to Dieng.

Temples

To appreciate Dieng's temples at their finest, view them at dawn when the simple ruins are still shrouded in early-morning mist. In all there are more than 100 of them, built between the 7th and 9th centuries by the Sailendra dynasty and scattered over the northern part of the valley. Eight temples have since been restored. They are named after the famed characters of the *Mahabarata* epic: Arjuna, Srikandi, Semar, Puntadewa, Sembadro and Gatot. All of them are dedicated to Shiva.

The entrance to the central plateau is a short distance east of Dieng village. Admission charge.

Other excursions

From the guesthouses in Dieng, guides will take you to the Telega Warna coloured lake (2km) and the awesome Sikidang Crater (3km), as well as to a nearby mountain-top from where to view sunrise. Alternatively, get a map and just wander among the sloping fields where the locals cultivate cabbages and potatoes against a backdrop of ruined temples.

GUNUNG MERAPI (Mount Merapi)

On a clear day, Mount Merapi can be seen in all its glory and there are magnificent views over the surrounding region. But this 2,950m-high mountain is also one of the world's most destructive volcanoes, with six observation posts now monitoring its activity 24 hours a day. Enthusiastic climbers scale the mountain in 6 hours; less fit mortals take considerably longer. The best approach is from the village of Selo, which can be reached from Muntilan, and a guide is strongly recommended. (See Getting Away From it All, pages 134–5.)

KALIURANG

This delightful mountain resort on the slopes of Mount Merapi is just a 1-hour

Join the locals on a horse-and-cart tour of Parangtritis's beaches

ride from Yogyakarta, yet it offers spectacular panoramas, fine walks and cool mountain air as well as several enchanting waterfalls. Stay away at weekends.
Location: 24km north of Yogyakarta. Regular buses leave from the main Umbunharjo terminal on Jalan Kemerdekan, taking 1 hour.

PARANGTRITIS

For a glimpse of blue ocean and crashing waves, take this route south past rice fields and banana plantations to the beach resort of Parangtritis nestling among spectacular cliffs and fringed by sand dunes. Apart from taking a ride in a horse-drawn cart, nibbling on fried squid in one of the handful of drink stalls, or taking long walks along the beach, there isn't a lot to do here. You can paddle in the sea, but don't swim in the vicious undercurrents that take their toll every year.
Location: 28km south of Yogyakarta. Regular buses run from Umbunharjo terminal on Jalan Kemerdekan, taking 50 minutes.

ENIGMATIC GODDESS

It is unwise to wear green in the vicinity of Parangtritis's beach, or indeed at Pangandaran or any of the other neighbouring coastal areas, for legend has it that this is the favourite colour of the beloved Kangjeng Ratu Kidul, Queen of the Southern Seas. Swimmers who defy the warnings risk being taken to the beautiful goddess's underwater palace – on a one-way ticket.

More than 220 temples make up the Prambanan complex

PRAMBANAN

Experts may consider Borobudur larger and more beautiful than Prambanan, but locals claim these imposing Hindu temples are among the finest in Asia. Built between the 9th and 10th centuries, and covering a vast area of undulating plains and rice fields, the great monuments were abandoned when the Sanjaya dynasty mysteriously moved to Eastern Java.

Following a great earthquake in the middle of the 16th century many of the temples fell into rack and ruin. Only over the last 40 years has extensive restoration taken place, with the main complex of temples being restored to its former glory.

Location: 17km northeast of Yogyakarta. Regular buses run from the Umbunharjo Terminal on Jalan Kemerdekan to Prambanan town, taking 45 minutes. From the bus stop, it is a short walk to the entrance to the historical park. Open: daily, 6am–6pm. Admission charge.

The Shiva Complex

The centrepiece of the Prambanan complex is not just another temple, but a veritable work of art carved with stone monkeys and heavenly parrots that soars 47m high. It is dedicated to Shiva the Destroyer.

To appreciate the full sequence of narrative reliefs, start to the left of the eastern stairway and proceed clockwise. Each of the panels shows a scene from the Hindu epic, the *Ramayana*, beginning at the palace of Rama's father and recounting the story of Rama's marriage to Sita, her kidnapping by the Demon King of Lanka and rescue by Hanuman, King of the monkeys.

Nor are bas-reliefs the only attraction. If you continue to the main eastern chamber you will find a 3m-tall, four-armed statue of Shiva standing on a huge lotus pedestal, covered in flowers left by devotees. Adjacent rooms contain other surprises, with the statues of the sage Agastya, his son Ganesh and Loro

Jonggrang, a formidable young virgin who was turned into stone for refusing to marry a love-struck giant.

Flanking the Shiva temple are two smaller temples dedicated to Vishnu the Protector and Brahma the Creator. Although these cannot compare in stature, they also contain fine reliefs from the *Ramayana* and the *Mahabharata*, as well as carvings of heavenly nymphs trying to seduce the gods.

Further around the complex you can take your pick of another 224 smaller shrines, some of them renovated, others just piles of stone and broken memories. While most coach tours arrive in the late morning or afternoon, the best times to visit Prambanan are dawn and dusk when the temples are bathed in golden rays and infused with the silent power of times gone by: real enthusiasts should spend the night in one of the small guesthouses outside the park and experience both.

Candi Plaosan, Prambanan

Around Prambanan
Within a short distance of the main Prambanan complex are countless other temples, some of them undergoing restoration, others still in ruins. Candi Sewu, Candi Plaosan, Candi Kalasan and Candi Sari are all worth a visit. Ask a local guide to take you there, or better still take a bicycle or motorbike (see Prambanan drive, pages 66–7).

Ramayana performances
Visitors in the vicinity of Prambanan between May and October on the nights of the full moon should not miss the performance of the *Ramayana*. This spectacle, set against the background of Candi Prambanan, brings together one of the leading dance groups on Java and provides one of the island's most memorable experiences. For information, call (0274) 496404 or ask at a travel agent in Yogyakarta.

SURAKARTA (SOLO)

Lovers of this bustling city of half a million inhabitants claim that Surakarta's charms are not only greater than those of neighbouring Yogyakarta, but that its attractions, which range from art galleries to the Sultan's Palace, are equally invigorating.

Known more often as Solo, this royal city also claims its place in history. During the 17th century the district was the seat of the Mataram Kingdom, the last of the great kingdoms in Central Java. Only in 1755 was the kingdom divided by the Dutch and a rival court established in neighbouring Yogyakarta.

These days there's still a Kraton to remind you of the grand old days, as well as wide, tree-lined streets, lively little markets and an air of relative calm.

Most visitors explore the town in a

Pakubuwono X (1893–1939) was responsible for the main decoration of Kraton Surakarta

day, but Solo also makes a good base from which to explore the surrounding region with its hills and lush mountain resorts.

Location: 65km northeast of Yogyakarta. Buses leave from Yogya's Umbunharjo Terminal on Jalan Kemerdekan to Solo, taking 90 minutes. Trains run from the station on Jalan Pasar Kembang. Garuda has direct flights to Adisumarmo Airport, 10km from Solo.

Kraton Surakarta

Legend has it that this palace, known as the Susuhunan's Palace, which means 'royal foot placed on the head of vassals paying homage', burnt down in January 1985 because its sultan did not pay sufficient attention to the powerful spirits. To make amends, the head of a tiger, a buffalo and a snake were offered up to the offended spirits, along with 30 truckloads of ashes, by throwing them into the sea at Parangtritis. The offerings appear to have done the trick and since then the newly rebuilt palace, along with its museum and richly gilded audience hall, have continued to thrive – as have the fortunes of Pakubuwono XII, the sultan who occupies it.

Alun-Alun Square, south of Jalan Slamet Riyadi. Open: Monday to Thursday and Saturday, 8am–2pm; Sunday, 8am–3pm; closed Friday. Note that visitors are requested to wear a gold and red tassel as a mark of respect. Admission charge.

Mesjid Besar, see Surakarta walk, pages 68–9.

PURA MANGKUNEGARAN (Mangkunegaran Palace)

This 200-year-old palace, which was built for a junior line of the ruling house of Surakarta, contains a vast and

Surakarta's sultans are still revered despite their fall from power

intricately decorated pavilion, a shady garden divided in two – one side for women, the other for men – and a museum filled with ancient coins, masks, jewellery and even a chastity belt for the queen. On Saturday mornings, at 10am, you may be serenaded by musicians playing the palace's 200-year-old *gamelan*, known as 'the drifting of smiles'.
At the end of Jalan Diponegoro. Open: Monday to Saturday, 8am–2pm; Sunday, 8am–1pm. Admission charge includes guided tour.

Pasar Klewar, see Surakarta walk, pages 68–9.

THR Sriwedari Amusement Park
The perfect spot for relaxation. Visit a selection of animals from Central Java, nibble on sticks of pork *satay* under shady trees – and enjoy carnival rides and a children's playground. Next door you can

find the Museum Radya Pustaka which has a collection of *gamelan* instruments and shadow puppets.
Jalan Slamet Riyadi, to the west of the Kraton. Open: daily, 8am–10pm. Admission charge.

Excursions around Solo
For delightful scenery with fine walks and waterfalls, leave Solo and catch a bus to the hill resort of Sarangan (53km) or the busier Tawangmangu (40km), situated on the slopes of Mount Lawu. Keen archaeologists can also explore the 15th-century Candi Sukuh (36km) with its ancient phallic objects hewn into the rock. For details of Sarangan and Tawangmangu see Getting Away From it All, pages 142–3.

Some large sections of Kraton Surakarta escaped the fire of 1985

Yogyakarta

Starting out at the busy central market, this walk will take you past the old Dutch fort and presidential palace to the royal mosque and the Sultan's Palace. Afterwards, you can explore the colourful bird market. *Allow 3 hours.*

Begin at the central market known as Pasar Beringharjo on Jalan Jen A Yani.

1 PASAR BERINGHARJO

This is not only the biggest covered market in Yogyakarta, but by far the most intriguing with its dimly lit stalls selling every kind of tropical fruit as well as beautiful fabrics, baskets and motorbike spare parts. Beware of pick-pockets though, and persuasive touts who will take a commission on whatever you buy.

Walk south down Jalan Jend A Yani for 250m and on your left you will find the Benteng Budaya.

2 BENTENG BUDAYA

Locals call this fine old building Fort Vredeburgh, after the Dutch garrison which was built here in 1765 to house 500 troops; it also served as the local gaol. The government has since turned the place into a museum containing exhibits of Yogyakarta's history, featuring especially its exploits in the war for independence.

Leave the museum and almost directly opposite you will see the Gedung Agung.

3 GEDUNG AGUNG (STATE GUESTHOUSE)

This elegant building set amid lush gardens and fruit trees was built in 1823 as the Dutch president's mansion and rebuilt in 1869 following an earthquake. Between 1946 and 1949, when Yogyakarta was declared capital of the

founding republic, it served as the presidential palace. Today it is closed to the public.

Continue straight over the main road (Jalan P Senopati) to Alun-Alun Utara and on your right you will see the Museum Sono Budoyo.

4 MUSEUM SONO BUDOYO (NATIONAL ART MUSEUM)

You will find some of the best Javanese, Balinese and Madurese art in this fine little museum as well as stone carvings and the shadow puppets known as Wayang Kulit. Keep an eye open for the famous statue of the monkey god Hanuman, and a bridal suite dedicated to the goddess of rice and fertility.

Leave the museum and continue along Jalan Alun-Alun until you see the Mesjid Besar a short distance ahead on your right.

5 MESJID BESAR (GRAND MOSQUE)

Despite its rather ordinary appearance the royal mosque, which was built in 1773 under Sultan Hamengkubuwono I, has an unusual triple-layered roof as well as some striking engraved gold doors. Every September, during the colourful Gunungan procession, hundreds of believers walk to the mosque carrying mounds of rice, peanuts and chillies which they leave as offerings.

Continue south along Jalan Alun-Alun until you reach the entrance to the Kraton on your left.

6 KRATON

This building is the veritable seat of power in Yogyakarta and is inhabited by the revered Sultan Hamengkubuwono X. It was built in 1755 during the reign of Hamengkubuwono I and is largely symbolic of Mount Merapi, centre of the

A retainer of the sultan, Kraton Yogyakarta

cosmos. A short distance behind the Kraton, on Jalan Rotowijayan, you will find the ancient royal stables.

From the Kraton walk down Jalan Rotowijayan and turn left at the intersection with Jalan Ngasem. At the end of the road either catch a tricycle back to your hotel or continue to the Pasar Ngasem Bird Market (see pages 54–5).

OPENING DETAILS

Benteng Budaya. Open: Tuesday to Thursday and Sunday, 8am–4pm; Friday, 8am–11am; Saturday, 8am–1pm.

Museum Sono Budoyo. Open: Tuesday to Thursday and Sunday, 8am–1.30pm; Friday, 8am–11am; Saturday, 8am–noon.

Kraton. Open: Saturday to Thursday, 8am–2pm; Friday, 9am–1pm. Stables are open daily, 8am–4pm. Admission charge.

Prambanan

Jakarta
JAVA
Prambanan · Surabaya
Yogyakarta · Surakarta

Starting from the recently discovered Candi Sambisari, this tour will take you to the magnificent Candi Prambanan as well as to several smaller and lesser-known temples near by. You will need to arrange transport before you go. *Allow a full day.*

Take the main road east from Yogyakarta towards Prambanan and at the 12.5km marker turn left and drive 2km north to Candi Sambisari.

1 CANDI SAMBISARI

Although this small *candi* was only discovered in 1966 by a local farmer, it has since been excavated along with three smaller temples dedicated to Shiva. Inside are several fine carvings of Ganesh as well as some unfinished reliefs which may have been abandoned following a sudden volcanic eruption.

From Candi Sambisari, return to the main road and continue for 3km until you see a signpost for Candi Kalasan on the right.

2 CANDI KALASAN

One of the oldest Buddhist shrines in the area, Candi Kalasan may date back as far as AD778, although restoration has since taken place. Next to the southern doorway you will see beautifully decorated stone reliefs. The temple also contains one large and three small chambers inhabited by great numbers of bats.

Continue along the road towards Prambanan and after 200m turn

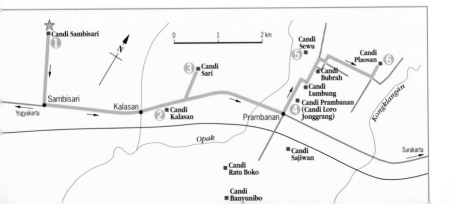

*left to Candi Sari, signposted a short
distance off the main road.*

3 CANDI SARI

Set in delightful scenery of banana and
coconut groves, this square temple was
once a Buddhist sanctuary and contains
36 panels of dancing goddesses,
musicians and Buddhist deities. It was
built some time during the 9th century,
although extensively restored in 1929.
Around the windows you will find small
niches overlooked by stern *kala* heads.
*From Candi Sari return to the main road,
turn left and head towards Prambanan
village. Turn left at the crossroads for Candi
Prambanan.*

4 CANDI PRAMBANAN

This magnificent complex is one of the
finest single monuments in all Indonesia
and is the biggest and best-known Hindu
candi in the country. It was completed
during the 10th century to
commemorate the victory of the Sanjaya
dynasty over the Buddhist Sailendra
kings of Central Java, but was deserted a
few years later. Explore the great Shiva
temple, which is 47m tall, and the two
smaller shrines dedicated to Vishnu and
Brahma.
*From Prambanan Temple follow the
signpost for Candi Sewu, which lies 1.5km
to the north.*

5 CANDI SEWU

This complex, known as the 'thousand
temples', contains just 240 shrines and
was built around AD850. Renovation was
completed in 1993 and you can now
admire finely carved galleries, the main
temple and the two large statues
brandishing clubs which guard the
entrance from evil spirits.
From Candi Sewu drive 1.5km to the east

The carved reliefs of celestrial beings on Candi
Sari were originally painted in bright colours

*along the main road and you will find
Candi Plaosan on your left.*

6 CANDI PLAOSAN

This delightful complex consists of a
large rectangular temple surrounded by a
number of shrines and *stupas* believed to
date from the 9th century. Inside the
main temple you will find six beautiful
stone statues of Buddha along with
reliefs of worshippers. A short walk south
will bring you to the Plaosan Kidul,
made up of a ruined complex currently
undergoing extensive restoration work.
*From Candi Plaosan either continue to the
small temples of Candi Sajiwan and Candi
Ratu Boko, which lie further south, or head
back to Yogyakarta.*

Surakarta (Solo)

Starting at the Kraton Surakarta, this walk will take you from ancient pavilions and audience halls to the local batik market and the royal mosque. From here it is a pleasant stroll to the city's other famous landmark, the Mangkunegaran Palace. *Allow 3 hours.*

Begin at the Kraton Surakarta Hadiningrat, situated off Jalan Kratonan in the south of town.

1 KRATON SURAKARTA HADININGRAT

The centrepiece of Solo was built in 1745 by King Pakubuwana II and contains several pavilions and an elegant marble

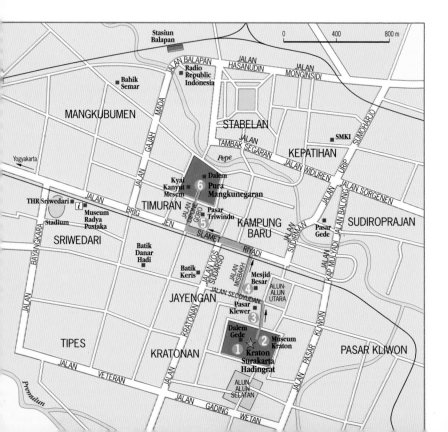

audience hall. Although much of the Kraton was burnt down in January 1985, Susuhunan's private residence and meditation chamber have since been restored.

Next door to the Kraton you will find the Museum Kraton.

2 MUSEUM KRATON

Housed in this museum built around a courtyard you will find a collection of 200 to 300-year-old royal carriages as well as fine bronze statues, ceremonial outfits and demonic figureheads. If you want to take photographs, remember to obtain a special ticket at the entrance.

Leave the museum and on your left, on Jalan Secoyudan, you will find Pasar Klewer.

3 PASAR KLEWER

Inside this two-storey concrete block is one of the largest batik markets in Indonesia. You can buy anything from best silk to flamboyant western boxer shorts. Remember to bargain.

Leave Pasar Klewer and almost directly opposite, on Jalan Secoyudan, you will see the Mesjid Besar.

4 MESJID BESAR (GRAND MOSQUE)

The most impressive aspect of this incongruous looking mosque is its sheer size. Pakubuwana III built the original structure in 1750 although it has since been enlarged by various Sultans to occupy an area of 3.5 hectares. There are plenty of other points of interest too, from its Middle Eastern-style minaret to its Javanese-style traditional peaked roofs. Visitors are welcome, but dress neatly and wash your hands and feet before entering the mosque.

Exit the mosque and follow the road around until you reach Jalan Brig Jen Slamet Riyadi. Turn left and 800m further on turn right on to Jalan Diponegoro. You will find Pasar Triwindu on your right.

5 PASAR TRIWINDU (ANTIQUE MARKET)

This delightful little flea market offers almost everything you can dream of from ancient paintings and masks to puppets and an abundance of fake antiques and curios.

Leave Pasar Triwindu and continue along Jalan Diponegoro. At the end of the road you will see the Pura Mangkunegaran.

6 PURA MANGKUNEGARAN

Although smaller and less well known than the Kraton Surakarta, this palace built by a branch of the Surakarta royal family has beautiful gardens, birds and European-style fountains as well as a vast audience pavilion which was until recently the largest on Java. The palace was begun by Mangkunegoro I at the end of the 18th century and completed in 1866. Behind the audience pavilion is the museum with a collection of antique jewellery, coins and chastity belts.

Leave the palace and walk to the main road, Jalan Brig Jend Slamet Riyadi, from where you will be able to catch a tricycle back to your hotel.

OPENING DETAILS

Kraton Surakarta Hadiningrat. See page 62 for opening times.

Museum Kraton. See Kraton opening times. Admission included in price of entry to Kraton..

Pura Mangkunegaran. Open: Monday to Saturday, 8am–2pm; Sunday, 8am–1pm.

East Java

*E*ast Java, stretching narrowly down from Ngawi to the port of Ketapang, is the least visited part of Java, offering national parks and volcanoes along with hill resorts and a staggering lunar landscape. If you are travelling overland to Bali, it's easy to visit Mount Bromo or the lesser-known Baluran National Park. Buses travel between all the major towns, and trains connect Surabaya with Jakarta, Surakarta, Probolinggo and Banyuwangi. For an easy hop, you can take the plane to Surabaya from Jakarta or Denpasar on Bali.

SURABAYA

Most visitors tend to miss out Surabaya, the big busy industrial town which lies a short distance from the coast, but the provincial capital of East Java does offer reasonable hotels and a tourist office, as well as some of the friendliest inhabitants in the whole of Java. It is also a good stopping point before visiting Mount Bromo or the nearby island of Madura.

During the struggle for Indonesia's independence, Surabaya was a major centre of resistance against the Dutch. At one stage, in 1945, it was even bombed by the British who led an assault on the city in which thousands of Indonesians were killed. Today, the heroes' monument, situated in the centre of town, stands as a proud reminder of Surabaya's contribution to the nation's founding.

Location: 780km east of Jakarta. Buses leave for all the major towns and cities from the main bus terminal on the corner of Jalan Yani and Jalan Sutoyo. Trains take 15 hours to Jakarta and 4.5 hours to Surakarta. There are also flights to Bali, Lombok and major destinations on Java from Juanda Airport, 18km to the south of town.

Jembatan Merah (Red Bridge)

For a glimpse of the old Dutch commercial district with its run-down warehouses and turn-of-the-century office buildings, visit

Monument recalling Surabaya's role in the struggle for independence

The charming but dilapidated backstreets around Jembatan Merah, Surabaya

the area around this famous bridge which was the scene of heavy fighting during the battle for Surabaya in 1945. Hire a tricyclist to take you to such famous buildings as Grahadi, the former residence of the Dutch governor, as well as the Majapahit Hotel – or just explore the labyrinth of little alleyways to the west of the bridge.
Jalan Rajawali, in the northern part of town, a short distance from Tugu Pahlawan.

Kebun Binatang (Surabaya Zoo)
More than 500 species of animals and exotic birds are crammed into the Surabaya Zoo along with flying squirrels, dolphins, dwarf buffalo and the biggest attraction of all, a Komodo dragon. Don't expect to see the animals accommodated with many comforts though. The cages are small and the place crowded for much of the time.
Jalan Raya Diponegoro, in the south of town. Open: daily, 9am–5pm. Admission charge.

Pasar Sore
Between 6pm and 9pm this little street is a solid row of stalls selling anything from T-shirts to antique alarm clocks .
Jalan Pandegiling.

Tanjung Perak Harbour
Although not officially a tourist spot, the harbour does play host to several delightful wooden Schooners. Frequent boats also leave from the adjacent quay to the island of Madura at regular intervals, 24 hours a day.
Jalan Kalimas Baru, in the north of the city. Ask the taxi driver to take you to Pelabuhan Tanjung Perak.

Tugu Pahlawan (Heroes' Monument)
This rather uninspiring monument in the centre of the main square was built to commemorate the valiant struggle of the Surabaya people against the Dutch, and especially for the thousands who died when British troops attacked the city on 10 November 1945.
Jalan Pahlawan.

Crossing the sand sea at spectacular Mount Bromo

BALURAN TAMAN NASIONAL (Baluran National Park)

You can't go further east than Baluran National Park, unless you cross over into Bali, but this 240 sq km game reserve set amid arid savannah and surrounded on three sides by the sea has no shortage of attractions. If you visit the park between the months of June and November, when wildlife is more plentiful, you may well catch rare glimpses of wild pigs and barking deer, as well as countless birds, monkeys and huge wild oxen. Make sure that you contact the PHPA office at the park entrance to obtain a permit and organise accommodation, and take food if you intend to stay overnight. Guides are available to take you on walks.
Location: 280km east of Surabaya (tel: 0333 24119). Buses run from Surabaya and from Ketapang (37km), the arrival and departure point for ferries to Bali. Ask to be dropped off at the park headquarters. Admission charge.

BATU/SELEKTA

These neighbouring towns with their fine views of Mount Arjuna make popular weekend retreats from the plains below. Batu is larger and more suburban, but with fine walks and lively markets. Selekta is more up-market, with bubbling streams, orchards and pine trees.
Location: 23km northwest of Malang. Irregular buses leave from Malang's Dinoyo station on Jalan Haryono. Alternatively, agree a price and take a taxi.

GUNUNG BROMO (Mount Bromo)

The jewel in the crown of East Java's tourist industry lies about an hour's drive from Probolinggo, high up in the Tengger mountains, surrounded by volcanic peaks and craters. Mount Bromo offers awesome views and a desolate landscape that is not easy to find elsewhere in Indonesia.

As you take the spectacular road up to Cemara Lawang you will see

TEMPESTUOUS LOVE
Were it not for a love-struck ogre and a beautiful princess, Bromo might have looked like any other volcano. But when, according to legend, the unsightly lover was rejected he flung a half coconut shell on to the ground – which turned into Mount Batok – then leapt into the fiery crater.

Tenggerese guides

magnificent vistas of rice fields and cabbage fields clutching on to almost sheer mountainsides, every little area cultivated. Some visitors come here for the journey alone, but the majority arrive at dawn to watch the sun come up over the vast sea of sand and all the big hotels and package tours now run these early-morning trips from Surabaya. A cheaper and more adventurous way though is to take a *bemo* from the nearby town of Probolinggo (40km) and spend the night in one of the small hotels or guesthouses in Cemara Lawang. Remember to take warm clothes and a torch.
Location: 3-hour drive southeast of Surabaya. Buses run from Surabaya to the town of Probolinggo. From here you must take a crowded minibus to Ngadisari (40km) and then another minibus 3km further to Cemara Lawang, the departure point for Bromo. Alternatively, for a touch of comfort, simply charter a minibus from Probolinggo.

Climbing the summit
You won't need a guide to take you up to the summit. These days literally hundreds of tourists make the pre-dawn trek, and locals are on hand with horses to carry you to the foot of the mountain. Allow an hour if you are walking from the village of Cemara Lawang. As you cross the sand

sea and begin climbing the 250 steps that lead up the rim of the volcano you will be able to smell the sulphur like some malodorous form of methane gas. Bromo, however, though live, has not erupted for many years and is considered to be one of the safest volcanoes on Java. After watching the dawn come up, some people then walk the entire way round the vast crater. Be warned, however; the rim is extremely narrow in some parts and accidents are by no means unheard of.

Exploring the area
The majority of visitors simply bus into Bromo from Probolinggo, watch the sunrise and bus out again. A better alternative is to spend the day exploring the area. Visit Mount Penanjakan (6km away) with its magnificent views of Bromo and Gunung Semeru, one of the most active volcanoes in the whole of Indonesia. To arrange a jeep, visitors staying at the Bromo Permai I Hotel can simply contact the manager. Failing that, negotiate a price with any of the *bemo* drivers in the village. It is also possible to trek from Cemoro Lawang to Ngadas (8km) on the southern rim of the Tengger crater, although you should allow a full day and seek information locally.

Distant Gunung Semeru viewed from Mount Penanjakan

GUNUNG SEMERU (Mount Semeru)

One of the most beautiful and highest peaks on Java, this mountain, known as Mehameru (great mountain), reaches 3,600m. You can climb it in two days with camping equipment and a guide but make sure you enquire about conditions locally since volcanic eruptions have become something of a Semeru speciality.

Location: access is from the small village of Ranu Pani, to the east of Malang. Buses run via Tumpang, Gubug Klakah and Ngadas. Accommodation consists of one rest house.

MADURA ISLAND

Legend has it that the best lovers in the whole of Indonesia come from the poor and arid island of Madura, along with the swiftest running bulls. To see them both, visit the island between August and October when the famous races are held in several of the major towns and villages. Make sure that you get the precise dates from the regional tourist office in Surabaya (tel: 828 8410) as the timing of the event changes from year to year.

Location: 1-hour boat trip from Surabaya. Boats leave regularly 24 hours a day from Tanjung Perak Harbour on Jalan Kalimas Baru to Kamal, on the southwest coast of Madura. Jeeps circulate the island at regular intervals, but tourist services are almost non-existent.

MALANG

Situated on the banks of the Sungai Brantas River, the busy town of Malang boasts numerous parks, tree-lined streets and villas. Only 150 years ago, the Dutch turned it into a centre for the production of coffee and tobacco, and these days they return in vast numbers to admire its colonial architecture and spotlessly clean streets. For something special, visit the famous Candi Singosari (10km north), built by the Singosari dynasty at the turn of the 13th century, or the 13th-century Candi Jawi (49km north).

Location: 90km south of Surabaya. Buses to Surabaya, Probolinggo and Jakarta leave from the Arjosari terminal on Jalan Intan. Trains for Surabaya and Jakarta depart from the station on Jalan Kerta Negara.

A diet of beer helps turn Madura's fleet-footed bulls into winners

BOISTEROUS BULLS

Beginning with the wave of a red flag and ending 9 seconds later with screams from the crowd, the famous bull races of Madura have become known as one of the major attractions of the island. Specially trained bulls dressed in fine colours parade before the crowds to the fortifying sounds of *gamelan* music. The winners of the 100m races bring fame not only to their owners, but to entire villages, while the top bulls merrily retire to father the next generation of champions.

Bali

*I*ndonesia's favourite tropical hideaway nestles just 2km from the eastern tip of Java, surrounded by lush paddies and shimmering white beaches. On Bali, the flowers appear to be always in bloom and every day is a celebration of the beneficence of the gods. Temples dot the towns and villages whilst thousands of spirit houses watch over the well-being of the island's 3 million inhabitants.

When the first European sailors came across this earthly paradise, they simply jumped ship and it took the captain more than two years to round them all back up. Later, artists settled in Ubud, enchanted by the people and their Hindu culture.

These days almost a million tourists arrive on Bali every year, swamping its

beaches, piling into its temples and turning parts of the island into the Torremolinos of Asia.

Sun, sea and religion, Bali's recipe for success is epitomised at Candi Dasa

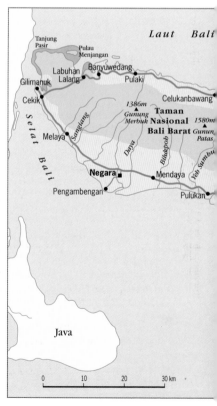

But although Kuta and some of the other popular tourist destinations have inevitably declined, it's easy to escape the crowds by going into the rice fields around Ubud or the unspoiled coastline of the east. From the peak of Mount Batur you can witness the magnificent sunrise over the lake and elsewhere view more than 20,000 temples built to honour the gods and lovingly tended by the Hindu people.

Nor should anyone miss the opportunity to attend a cremation or a temple festival.

Above all, however, it is the culture that most impresses visitors; the fleeting sense of spiritual calm and the Balinese religion which, despite the pervading air of commercialism, somehow continues to survive and thrive.

Although tours now operate excursions to almost every major site on the island, it is just as easy to arrange your own transport.

BALI

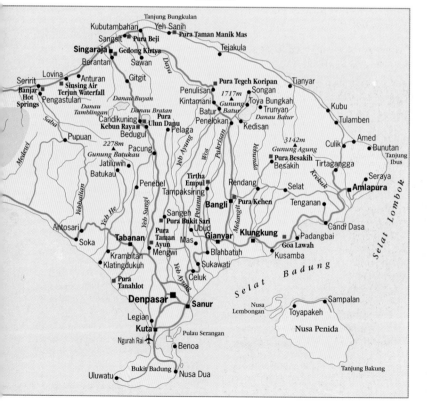

Coastal Bali

*A*lmost everyone will, at some stage, visit Bali's tropical beaches. Most tourists opt for Kuta or the more up-market Sanur or Nusa Dua, but beyond these well-known resorts there are plenty of less highly developed areas, not necessarily as beautiful, but having the charm of relative isolation. Getting around from one resort to the other is easy. *Bemos* (minibuses) run regularly and for trips further afield buses, motorbikes, jeeps or (for the fit) bicycles are all good alternatives.

KUTA BEACH

Sun-tanned Australians don't travel to Kuta Beach without good reason, for this 10km stretch of sand has not only become the island's best-known surfers' paradise, but its most crowded and flamboyant Western playground.

From the moment you set foot in the place you will be sucked into a world that has no comparison. From the crowds of topless sunbathers to the surfers, masseurs and hustlers, Kuta literally seethes with life. Modern-day lotus-eaters can take their pick of a host of elderly masseurs who, for a price, will pummel every part of your anatomy with coconut oil. You can also get your hair plaited, buy a wooden 'antique' elephant and drink a Fosters beer – almost simultaneously.

Inland, beyond the beach, you'll find restaurants, markets selling hippie gear and literally hundreds of tour agencies, money-changers, motorbike rentals, *losmen* (guesthouses), and a growing number of classy hotels. And while the old hands may lament the demise of dreamy Kuta, there are plenty of newcomers who have no wish to go any further.

To find accommodation, simply wander along the *gangs* (alleyways) or take a taxi. There's something for just about every taste. Indeed, the only thing

there isn't much of here is tranquillity, so if that is what you are after, try Sanur or Nusa Dua.

Location: 9km south of Denpasar. Taxis run from Ngurah Rai International Airport to Kuta Beach, taking 15 minutes. Regular bemos *ply the roads between Kuta and Tegal terminal in Denpasar. Buses to most tourist destinations can be booked through any travel agent.*

Watersports, waves and adventure

For a touch of excitement, hire a surfboard and hit the water with a splash. Almost every shop rents them out by the day. The best surf is between March and July, but at virtually any time of the year you'll find ample-sized waves. Make sure, however, that you swim between the signposted water towers and red flags, which are patrolled by Australian-trained Balinese life savers, as dangerous rip-tides lead to regular drownings.

You could also try your hand at bungee jumping or white-water rafting. For gentler activity with just as much thrill, visit the pools and waterslides at the Waterbom Park and Spa (tel: 755676). For an escape from hustlers peddling vulgar wood carvings, head north past Legian to Seminyak.

After dark

At night, everything you could think of is

Choose your wave on Bali's best-known surfing beach, Kuta Beach

on offer in Kuta, from tranquil restaurants on lotus ponds to cafés and pizzerias. Pubs, discos and bars line the roads serving food and drink to the sound of a unique cocktail of heavy rock, reggae, or even *gamelan* music, and you can have a game of darts, enter a beer-drinking competition or simply attend one of the dance shows specially laid on for tourists in the big hotels.

Tours from Kuta

Kuta's band of tour agencies offers packages to suit every taste, from the shoestring to the luxurious. Popular sights in the vicinity include Uluwatu Temple (20km), Pantai Suluban (22km) and Tanahlot (40km).

One of the many luxury hotels that are the life and soul of Nusa Dua

NUSA DUA

Rising up from the Bukit Peninsula amid
mangroves and dazzling tropical lawns,
Nusa Dua (where the Reagans stayed)
has become Bali's showcase resort, home
not only to the most exclusive hotels on
the island, but to its biggest convention
centres. Here the roads are perfectly
tarmacked and clipped hedges, fountains

and beautiful sculptures abound.

Started in the mid-1970s with loans
granted by the World Bank, this vast
complex now comprises more than
3,000 luxury rooms with magnificent
views and white sand, with the bonus of
being able to stroll along the sea front
without being hounded by vendors and
masseurs. Enthusiastic sportsmen have

a choice of tennis, health clubs, horse riding or an 18-hole international golf course. In addition, each hotel offers fine restaurants decked out with exotic tropical plants and palm trees where you can feast yourself on delicious, if expensive, seafood while watching a display of Balinese dancing.

Don't expect to get a feel for the real Bali here, however; the security guards who stop 'undesirable' local elements from entering the grounds also isolate you from a culture that predates the Hyatt and Sheraton Hotels by thousands of years. *Location: 25km south of Denpasar. Taxis take 20 minutes from Ngurah Rai International Airport, although many hotels lay on minibuses. Regular bemos connect Nusa Dua with Denpasar's Tegal Terminal and with Kuta Beach.*

Benoa Village

Watersports lovers don't bother too much with Nusa Dua these days. After all, with Benoa village just a short distance to the north, there is little reason to. Here you'll find windsurfing, parasailing, scuba diving and jet skiing. Less energetic visitors can hire a boat to nearby Turtle Island (Pulau Serangan), or sit at expensive cafés on the beach feasting on fresh fish and prawns caught by local fishermen.
5km north of Nusa Dua. Most hotels run minibuses at any time of day.

SOUTHERN BALI

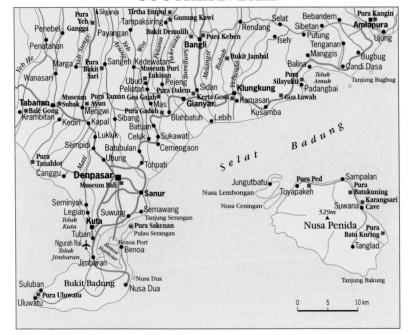

Enchanting paintings and sculpture at the Museum le Mayeur

pools, amphitheatre and restaurants.

The beach stretches for about 3km and there is a fine lagoon with a coral reef where, at dawn and dusk, you can see fishermen hard at work. Here, too, you can catch one of the colourful *prahu* fishing boats that ply the shores sailing to Turtle Island, or go further afield to the less visited islands of Nusa Lembongan and Nusa Penida. Note, however, that at low tide sea urchins can abound along Sanur Beach and swimming can be poor.

In the evening there is plenty of entertainment to be had, ranging from leafy restaurants to Balinese dances, and, for those of modern heart, discos.
Location: 7km east of Denpasar. Taxis run from Ngurah Rai International Airport (15 minutes). Regular bemos *operate between Sanur and Kreneng Terminal in Denpasar.*

Museum le Mayeur

This museum set in charming gardens contains some fine sculptures and paintings. The house was originally inhabited by Belgian artist Le Mayeur, who moved here in 1932 and resided in Sanur for more than 25 years. Le

SANUR

With one of the most beautiful stretches of beach on the island, plus a fleet of fishing boats and a touch of culture, Sanur offers something for everyone. You won't find many hippies here, either, or too much cheap accommodation, but you will find a scene that is considerably more relaxed than Kuta Beach and more natural than Nusa Dua.

During the 1930s the great Belgian artist Adrien Le Mayeur settled at Sanur, attracted by its pristine waters and exotic location. More recently the beach front has played host to growing numbers of hotel developments, including the Bali Festival Park (tel: 289211), a huge theme park containing crocodiles and komodo dragons, roller-coasters, rides, swimming

A TOUCH OF HISTORY

Sanur may be better known for its beaches than its history, but in fact the village is not without the latter. In 1906 the Dutch fought a pitched battle along the sea front, then in 1943 it was the turn of the Japanese who landed here. In 1946 the Dutch retook Sanur, with the tranquil beaches only regaining their sparkle with independence some three years later.

Above: early morning on Sanur Beach
Right: fishermen take tours to Turtle Island

Mayeur died in 1958, a decade before the opening of the first big tourist hotel, but the house remains and is looked after by his widow Ni Polok, formerly one of Bali's greatest Legong dancers. Explore the interior with its works of art from Africa, Europe and the South Pacific, as well as Bali, and afterwards relax in the luxuriant little garden with its diminutive pond sporting goldfish.
Next to the Bali Beach Hotel. Open: Tuesday, Thursday and Sunday, 8am–2pm; Friday and Saturday, 8am–11am. Admission charge.

Pulau Serangan (Turtle Island)

Although the appealing sounding Turtle Island is promoted in Sanur as one of the great trips, most visitors find the place considerably overrated; it is full of crowds of tourists who stream over to buy expensive shells and to stare at miserable-looking green-back turtles in a muddy pond. Besides the highly revered temple of Pura Sakenan situated to the north of the island, the chief attraction is

the beaches on the east coast. Even these are hard to get to though, and visitors constantly complain of the hassle and cost.
Public boats leave from Suwung, 1km south of Sanur. Boats can also be rented in Sanur or from Nusa Dua and Benoa. Day tours can be booked at any of the hotels.

Around the Coast

AMED

This little fishing village with its black sandy beaches and fine views of Mount Agung makes a perfect break either on the journey north or as part of a more extended island circuit. Currently there is no accommodation in Amed itself, but visitors wanting to stay the night will find cottages in neighbouring Bunutan (4km). As a pleasant side-trip, take the winding road along the coast to Ujung and Amlapura (see the Amlapura drive, pages 94–5).

Location: 22km north of Amlapura. Irregular bemos run via Culik, although private transport is recommended

Mount Agung viewed from Amed

BALI BARAT NATIONAL PARK, see Getting Away From it All, page 141.

BALINA BEACH

Diving enthusiasts can explore some of the richest marine life on Bali from this little fishing village situated halfway up the eastern coast. Resorts organise diving trips to Nusa Penida, Nusa Lembongan and Pulau Menjangan and also rent out diving equipment. Although there is now plenty of accommodation, the feeling of relative isolation remains.

Location: 5km west of Candi Dasa. Bemos run from Klungkung and Candi Dasa. You will have to walk the short distance from the main road to the beach.

BENOA PORT

Cruise ships, yachts and oil tankers anchor at this harbour that juts out east of the airport. There's little other reason to come here, though, except to visit the Bali International Yacht Club.

Location: 9km south of Denpasar.

CANDI DASA

Visitors wanting to avoid the big, brassy beach resorts of the south coast thought they had discovered a pleasant alternative when they came across this sleepy little village. But in the years since it was established, Candi Dasa (pronounced Chandi Dasa) has rapidly joined the ranks of crowded resort areas and much of the beach has now been washed away along with the outlying reef. There are, however, plenty of bungalows squeezed into lush gardens with views of the breaking waves and the hills across the bay. You can take brightly coloured fishing boats to Nusa Penida, explore the beautiful lagoon at the eastern end of the beach and take your pick of countless bars and restaurants famed for their fresh fish and chocolate cake.

Location: 69km northeast of Denpasar. Bemos run from the Batubulan terminal, 6km to the northeast of town. Nearby destinations: Padangbai (15km), Tenganan Village (3km) and Balina (5km).

Candi Dasa's rapid ascent to resortdom has triggered the erosion of its beaches

GILIMANUK

Situated on the western tip of Bali, a 3–4-hour trip from Kuta, this busy little port links Bali with East Java and the town of Ketapang. Ferries run regularly, day and night, taking just 30 minutes to cross the narrow strait. It's a pleasant enough trip with few hassles and reasonable bus connections on either side.

Location: 128km northwest of Denpasar. Regular buses run from Denpasar's Ubung terminal on Jalan Cokroaminoto, taking 3 hours. Nearby attractions include the Bali Barat National Park, which lies 3km south (see Getting Away From it All, page 140).

GOA LAWAH

Thousands of squeaking bats pack the entrance to Goa Lawah Cave and temple. They hang upside-down and deposit large amounts of droppings on even larger amounts of visitors. Legend has it that the bats provide sustenance for the legendary giant snake, Naga Basuki, which resides somewhere in the gloomy depths beyond.

The cave can even boast a little history: earlier this century, in 1904, the kings of Bali held a conference here to plan an attack against the Dutch armies.

Location: 9km east of Klungkung on the route to Padangbai. Ask to be dropped off at the entrance. Admission to the temple is by donation.

Goa Lawah and its colony of bats

FISHERMEN

At dusk, as the first oil lamps begin to flicker in the small village of Kusamba which lies under the shadow of distant Mount Agung, the fishermen push out their colourful outriggers, known as *prahus*, on to the sand and from there into the sea. By the time darkness falls the bay is bespeckled with white sails hovering a few hundred metres from the shore, their nets submerged in the darkened swell.

These fishermen go out every night, regardless of whether the sea is stormy or calm, earning little more than Rp5,000 for their back-breaking labour. For up to 10 hours at a stretch they remain out in the bay, rocked by the ebbing of the tide as they cast their nets in the hope of a good catch.

Apart from calling on the goodwill of the deities, they also make offerings to Batter Braun, god of the sea, and paint the bows of their vessels with a large pair of eyes so that the boats can find their way.

The boats themselves consist of little more than a carved-out tree trunk propped up by large bamboo poles on either side. But the rickety appearance is misleading, for these boats not only catch barramundi and sea perch, but occasionally shark.

By dawn the first fishermen are back on shore, some of them carrying piles of freshly caught tuna, others with little to show for their efforts. A few women wait on the sand, ready to sell the morning's catch.

Left: fresh catch
Above: fishermen at dawn
Right: after the trawl

Salt farming provides an important source of income in the Kusamba area

KUSAMBA

It's just a short distance from the bat cave of Goa Lawah to the fishing village of Kusamba with its black sandy beaches, its colourful boats and straggling groups of salt-panners. Most people come here to take the uncomfortable 2- or 3-hour boat trip to the island of Nusa Penida, but a better alternative is to continue to neighbouring Padangbai (9km) where there is accommodation and a more regular service.

Location: 8km east of Klungkung. Regular bemos run on route for Padangbai and Amlapura. Nearby attractions include the Goa Lawah Bat Cave (3km).

LEBIH

The best time to visit this little coastal village is during one of the famed ritual purification ceremonies. At other times of the year there are only black-sand beaches and fishing boats, plus a few other tourists to share them with.

Location: 8km south of Gianyar. Catch an irregular bemo.

LOVINA BEACH

If you are looking for white sparkling beaches and tropical palms, then give Lovina a miss. Visitors who are happy with black sand and a relaxed atmosphere can, however, find plenty of consolation. Small bungalows and more up-market developments now line the coastline almost as far as Singaraja, and you can take your pick of the bunch. There are plenty of opportunities, too, for snorkelling, fishing or boat trips out to the nearby reef. Perhaps the highlight, though, is the dolphin tour at dawn when leaping fish can be seen silhouetted against the rising sun. Almost every guesthouse or hotel will either organise the trip or point you in the direction of someone who will. Day trips can easily be made to the Sinsing Air Terjun Waterfall (6km), the hot springs of Banjar (12km) or the beautiful Pura Beji temple beyond Singaraja (16 km).

Location: 10km west of Singaraja. Buses run from Denpasar's Ubung terminal, on Jalan Cokroaminoto, to Singaraja, from where there are regular bemos to Lovina and the neighbouring villages.

NUSA PENIDA AND NUSA LEMBONGAN

Years ago, the island of Nusa Penida was a penitentiary for criminals and other undesirable subjects. These days, visitors wanting to get away from it all have taken a liking to the place, although much of the island is poor and arid and the place renowned for the power of its demons. Several sites are worth visiting though. Stop by the Pura Ped temple complex (4km east of Toyapakeh) to see the dwelling place of the evil monster Ratu Gede Macaling, or visit the Karangsari limestone cave 6km south of Sampalan.

From Nusa Penida, a 30-minute ride by boat will take you to Nusa Lembongan, the smaller and more popular sister island with beautiful beaches, turquoise water and some of the best opportunities for snorkelling in the area.

Location: irregular boats leave for Nusa Penida and Nusa Lembongan from Padangbai, taking between 2 and 3 hours. Travel agencies in Kuta and Sanur now offer package tours, and will arrange accommodation.

PADANGBAI

This charming little fishing village, although best known as the departure point for the island of Lombok, has plenty to recommend it, including fine snorkelling and boat trips to the island of Nusa Penida (2 hours), plus a host of cheap and cheerful bungalows. At night you will see the lights of the colourful fishing fleet heading out to sea and at dawn the sun rising from behind the distant hills near Mount Agung. There are now several restaurants, too, set around the crescent-shaped bay and renowned for their delicious fresh seafood.

Location: 56km north of Denpasar, off the main road to Klungkung and Amlapura. Buses run from Denpasar's Batubulan terminal. Car and passenger ferries to Lombok leave regularly throughout the day.

A shrimp fisherman sifts his way through the waters of Lovina Beach with a scissor net

The dramatic sea cliffs at Pantai Suluban, eroded by the powerful rollers treasured by the surfers

PANTAI SULUBAN (Uluwatu Beach)

Surfers flock to this magnificent spot at the base of steep cliffs to take on some of the most testing waves on the whole of the island. Most surfers bring their own boards and colourful regalia, but amateurs can hire all the equipment from nearby stalls. Beware dangerous currents though, especially at high tide, and if in doubt, just watch.

Location: 22km south of Kuta, on the Bukit Peninsula. To get to the surfing point, take the signposted path to the right, a short distance before you reach Uluwatu Temple. Motorbike drivers will take you along the 2km dirt track for a small charge – or else you can walk.

PURA ULUWATU (Uluwatu Temple)

The most staggering thing about the Uluwatu Temple is its setting on the edge of sheer cliffs overlooking the Indian Ocean. Built in the 11th century in grey volcanic stone, this revered edifice also houses a troop of monkeys known to run riot among unsuspecting tourists and locals. To appease them, buy peanuts in the nearby car park and hold on tightly to cameras, sunglasses and other valuables lest they take more of a mouthful than you bargained for. (See the Badung drive, pages 92–3.)

Location: 20km south of Kuta. Buses run from Denpasar's Tegal terminal, next to the intersection of Jalan Imam Bonjol and Jalan G Willis. For direct transport, take one of the minibuses organised by most travel agents. Open: daily, 7am–5pm. Admission charge.

TANAHLOT

Every travel agent runs trips to this 16th-century temple perched out at sea on a rocky outcrop and neither the afternoon crowds of tourists nor the markets selling over-priced trinkets can detract from the

glorious moment when its five shrines are silhouetted against the setting sun. For the best photographs, station yourself on the cliff directly opposite the temple. Early arrivals get best seats, others find their views obscured by the lines of tripods. At low tide it is possible to walk over the rocks to the temple, although access is only permitted at festival time.
Location: 31km northwest of Denpasar. Bemos run from Denpasar's Ubung terminal on Jalan Cokroaminoto to Kediri, where you must change for the 12km ride to Tanahlot. To avoid returning at night, a better alternative is to take a tour. Open: daily. Admission by donation (so long as it is more than Rp500).

TULAMBEN

If it wasn't for a US cargo boat that was torpedoed during World War II, this little village on the east coast might have remained off the beaten track for ever. However, the beaching of the ship and its cargo at Tulamben led to an influx of interest that has continued ever since. You can still see the wreck of the S S *Liberty* some 50–60m offshore and enjoy some of the finest diving on Bali here. There's not a lot else to the place, however, except black-pebbled shores, a few charming bungalows and a feeling of being remote from mainstream Bali.
Location: 27km north of Amlapura, beyond the village of Culik. Irregular bemos run from Amlapura. Better still, take your own transport.

YEH SANIH

This tranquil little spot has cool freshwater springs as well as picturesque gardens. It makes a good spot to spend the night if you are continuing further up the coast.
Location: 18km east of Singaraja. Bemos run from Singaraja's Kampung Tinggi terminal, taking 40 minutes. Nearby sites include the Pura Beji at Sangsit (10km).

The holy temple at Tanahlot

Coastal Bali

Starting out from Sanur, this drive takes you to Benoa village and from here to some of the most beautiful beaches on Bali. Along the way you will see the spectacular Uluwatu Temple, and a few other interesting sights besides. *Allow 1 day.*

Begin at Sanur Beach which lies on the east coast, some 8km from Denpasar, and take breakfast on the patio of the Hyatt – or any other hotel of your choice.

1 SANUR BEACH

For decades a charming little backwater, this bay has now been transformed into a complex of up-market hotels, leafy

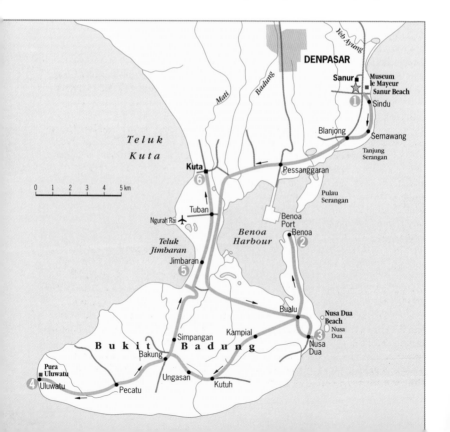

bungalows and tropical restaurants. For a reminder of the old days, visit the Museum le Mayeur next to the Bali Beach Hotel, or take a short trip out to sea in one of the local fishing boats.

From Sanur, drive 20km south on the road to Nusa Dua. Shortly before you arrive, you will see a signpost on your left for Benoa village, which lies 5km further on.

2 BENOA VILLAGE

During the late 19th century, the area around this fishing village on the Bukit Peninsula was the hunting ground for Denpasar's rajas. These days it has become popular with tourists who come here to water-ski, to paraglide or take boat trips to nearby Pulau Serangan (Turtle Island).

From Benoa village, backtrack 5km to the turn-off and follow the signpost to Nusa Dua. Park next to any of the hotels and wander down to the beach.

3 NUSA DUA

Residents of Nusa Dua swear that this vast and isolated peninsula offers the best of all worlds. It has a beautiful bay, luxurious hotels tucked away in tropical splendour – and there are no masseurs or vendors. Beware excessive eating or drinking though as prices are sky-high.

Leave Nusa Dua and keep going for 9km until you see a left-hand turning to Uluwatu. Follow the signposts for 9km until you reach Pura Uluwatu.

4 PURA ULUWATU (ULUWATU TEMPLE)

You will find this temple hanging on for dear life to a cliff that drops sheer into the sea 100m below. It's flanked by statues of Ganesh and guarded by a platoon of monkeys that bounce around with great ferocity, begging for peanuts

With its fine beaches, no wonder Sanur's inhabitants smile

and stealing cameras. Make sure you hold on to all your belongings tightly.

From Uluwatu Temple return to the main road and backtrack, following signs to Denpasar. After about 15km you will reach the village of Jimbaran.

5 JIMBARAN

At the end of a stunning stretch of road that offers fine views of the coastline is this little fishing village nestling close to a crescent of white sand and turquoise sea. The luxury Four Seasons and Ritz Carlton hotels have an established foothold here, while excellent fish restaurants compete with cheap food stalls on the beach.

Follow signs for Denpasar until you see a signpost to the left for Kuta Beach. Park anywhere near the seafront.

6 KUTA BEACH

The antithesis of Nusa Dua and Sanur, Kuta literally seethes with crowds and sheer excitement (see also pages 78–9). Take a stroll past outrageously semi-clad sun-bathers or hit the surf on a board, always making sure that it is in an area patrolled by lifeguards. Afterwards revel in the magnificent sunsets for which Kuta is renowned, but make sure that you don't leave it too late before heading back to Sanur or Denpasar.

Eastern Bali

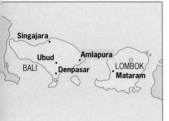

Starting out from the popular little beach resort of Candi Dasa, this pleasant drive will take you to ancient temples, magnificent rice fields and beaches. Those captivated by the scenery can even spend the night along the way. *Allow a whole day.*

Begin at the beach resort of Candi Dasa which lies on the eastern coast of Bali, a 2-hour drive from Denpasar.

1 CANDI DASA

Although it cannot compare with Kuta in terms of its beaches or its nightlife, Candi Dasa does have lots of pretty fishing boats as well as opportunities for walking and swimming. Its biggest attraction is the beautiful lagoon that lies at the eastern end of the beach.

From Candi Dasa drive north along the main road to Amlapura, which lies 13km further on.

2 AMLAPURA

Originally called Karangasem, this sleepy provincial town was renamed after it almost went up in smoke when Mount Agung erupted in 1963, killing several hundred inhabitants. To see what survived visit the 19th-century Puri Agung (puri Kanginan) on Jalan Teuku Umar, with its sculptured panels, its dilapidated courtyard used for royal tooth-filing ceremonies and its floating pavilion.

From Puri Agung, follow the one-way system around until you re-cross the bridge at the entrance of town. Turn right for Tirtagangga, which is signposted 7km further north.

3 TIRTAGANGGA

Surrounded by some of the most staggering rice terraces in the whole of Bali, this area also plays host to the famous Tirtagangga water palace which was built in 1948 by King Gusti Bagus

and damaged 15 years later by the eruption of Mount Agung. There are shady gardens and fountains for picnickers, plus a swimming pool.
From Tirtagangga continue north for 11km until you reach the village of Culik.

4 CULIK

At the end of another fine stretch of road which winds its way past spectacular rice terraces you will reach the village of Culik, overshadowed by distant Mount Agung. Enthusiastic divers can continue straight on to the town of Tulamben (see page 91), scene of one of Bali's most famous shipwrecks.
Leave the village of Culik and turn almost immediately right to Amed, which is situated 3km further on.

5 AMED

This sleepy Muslim fishing village with its black sand and colourful fishing boats offers magnificent views of Mount Agung, especially at sunset. For a short trip out to sea, pay the locals to take you out in their boats. Those wanting to keep their feet on land can simply walk along the beach and watch salt-panners hard at work.
Continue along the road for a further 4km until you reach the small village of Bunutan.

6 BUNUTAN

This quiet fishing village is a perfect retreat from the crowds and you will find several charming places serving food and refreshments. If it's late spend the night, as the last section of the journey is the

Fishermen along the east coast

most difficult and time consuming.
From Bunutan continue for 27km along a steep, winding and poorly surfaced road until you reach Puri Taman Ujung.

7 PURI TAMAN UJUNG (UJUNG WATER PALACE)

Although little remains of the grand water palace constructed by Anak Agung Anglurah in 1921, visitors can still explore the area once graced by moats and fountains. That glorious chapter came to an end with the eruption of Mount Agung, which left only a few sculptures and portals since worn down by the wind and the rain.
From Puri Taman Ujung, continue 3km north to Amlapura from where you can retrace your steps to Candi Dasa or take the road to Selat and Besakih.

OPENING DETAILS
Puri Agung (Amlapura). Open: daily, 8am–5pm. Admission charge.

Inland Bali

*B*eyond the touristy beaches of Kuta, Sanur and Nusa Dua lies a different face of Bali, a richly textured canvas of intricate rice terraces, volcanoes and dreamy villages. Here you will discover the temples of Besakih, beautiful Danau Batur (Lake Batur) and the fast-growing cultural centre of Ubud, as well as countless other attractions which remain further off the beaten track.

Visits to these towns and sites can easily be arranged by any hotel or tour agent, but it is better to hire a jeep or a motorbike, or even a bicycle, and go where your fancy takes you.

DENPASAR

Bali's capital of 300,000 people has traffic jams, banks and shops by the dozen, but besides a museum and a colourful market few real places of interest. Visit the tourist authority on Jalan Surapati 7 (tel: 0361 223602) to get details of any festivals that are being held during your stay, and explore the shops and restaurants on Jalan Gajah Mada.

Apart from this, there is little reason to spend much time here, except perhaps to take a horse and cart around the city.

Getting there
Denpasar's Ngurah Rai International Airport, which lies 12km south of town, has connections with Europe, Asia and North America and regular flights serve all domestic destinations. Overnight buses run from major cities on Java to Ubung Terminal on Jalan Cokroaminoto and generally include the price of the ferry ticket from Ketapang to Gilimanuk. All major travel agencies will organise tickets.

Island transport
Getting in and out of Denpasar can be a less than wonderful experience with *bemos* (minibuses) arriving and departing from several different terminals. For the west of Bali, North Bali and Java, go to the Ubung terminal on Jalan Cokroaminoto. For Sanur, go to the Kereneng terminal off Jalan Kamboja, and for the east, go to Batubulan terminal 6km to the northeast of town, near the village of Batubulan. *Bemos* also leave for Kuta, Legian and Nusa Dua

The Bali Museum complex is an amalgamation of palace and temple architecture from the Tegal terminal, next to the intersection of Jalan Imam Bonjol and Jalan G Willis. There are also metered taxis and delightful horse-drawn carts known as *dokars* for hire.

Bali Museum

Art lovers will have a field day at the Bali Museum with its selection of pieces ranging from prehistoric times to the early 20th century. Items include fine masks, paintings and woodcarvings, along with several less easily identifiable implements. Note, too, the beautiful stone sculptures, gateways and pavilions, best seen by climbing the steps in the far corner.

Next door to the museum you will find the state temple of Pura Jagatnatha, devoted to the supreme god Sanghyang Widi, and containing a famous statue of a turtle and two *naga* snakes, symbolising the founding of the world.
Jalan Wishnu, near Puputan Square in the centre of town. Open: Tuesday to Thursday Saturday and Sunday, 7.30am–2.30pm; Friday, 7.30am–11.30pm. Admission charge.

Werdi Budaya (New Arts Centre)

Most visitors bypass this delightful arts centre in their haste to get to the Bali Museum, but it offers not only paintings, sculptures and fine examples of Balinese architecture, but also lush gardens with lotus ponds. Exhibits on show include work from famous artists such as Affandi and Ida Bagus. On most evenings, there is traditional Legong or mask dancing performed by the island's famous academy of Indonesian dance on the open-air stage. Enquire locally for details.
Jalan Nusa Indah, 3km east of the Bali Museum. Open: daily, 8am–4pm. Admission charge.

Alun-Alun Puputan monument commemorates the mass suicide of Bali's nobility in 1906

ROYAL SUICIDE
When Dutch troops surrounded Denpasar's royal palace on 20 September 1906, Bali's nobility dressed up in all their finery, flung open the gates and committed mass suicide by rushing headlong at the attacking forces or stabbing each other with ceremonial knives and spears. Several hundred people died in all, and a monument has since been built in their honour, called Alun-Alun Puputan (Suicide Square).

VILLAGE CREMATION

As the midday sun beats down on the small village of Pejeng, in Central Bali, a line of villagers rushes headlong down the main street carrying great wooden towers covered in tinsel and glitter. At every intersection the wooden towers are shaken

Now that the celebrations are under way, the souls of the deceased may finally begin a new life as they are reborn in a different and possibly better form as part of the endless cycle

and spun to the sound of cheers and laughter and the music of the *gamelan*.

This festive occasion is not, however, a wedding or a temple anniversary, but a Balinese cremation for seven members of a family, some of whom died more than two years ago.

Like many families they have waited many years to save sufficient money to pay for the lavish send-off. Predictably, they have also awaited a suitably auspicious date.

of birth and death.

After the Brahman priest, or *pedanda*, has murmured prayers and placed offerings of rice and sweetmeats

to the gods, the decomposed bodies are dug up, dressed in white cloth and anointed in sweet-smelling perfume and oils. They are then given money and goods for their long journey to the next world and a sprig of jasmine flower for their nose. Finally, each body is placed in a tower, whirled around so the spirits will not be able to find their way back home, and torched by flames.

By the time dusk falls, the ashes have been taken to the nearby river, the locals are celebrating the new beginnings with rice wine, and the Balinese heavens have gained a new addition to their smiling ranks.

Far left: a decorated cremation tower
Far left (main): village funeral procession
Left: a *Gamelan* band
Top and above: burning the body

Some of Bali's finest stone carvings are found at Batubulan

AROUND DENPASAR

Dotted along the main roads that lead out of Denpasar are hundreds of little villages each specialising in a different form of artistry. Some make the most colourful shrines, others are renowned for mythical animals, carved wooden demons or even kitsch garden gnomes. *Bemos* leave from the various different terminals around the city (see pages 96–7), or, alternatively, take your own transport – but be prepared for very heavy and congested traffic around here.

Batubulan

The sound of workers chipping away on stone is the first noise you are likely to hear at Batubulan, a small town which has become famous for its stone sculpture. Here you will find rows of temple guardians, mythical animals, demons and other sculptures of every shape and size. The name Batubulan itself means 'moon stone' and the whole area offers abundant supplies of the stuff. There are also several shops sporting antiques, ceramics and woodcarvings.

Prices rise every morning when tour groups arrive for the *barong*, *kecak* and *kris* dancing and return to normal after their departure. Nature lovers, photographers and young families can spend half a day at the new Bali Bird and Reptile Park and see hundreds of species, including the rare Bali Mynah (see page 161).
10km northeast of Denpasar, on the road to Ubud and Gianyar.

Celuk

Best known as a prolific producer of silver, this little village sells almost every type of jewellery you can think of, and bracelets and earrings can be made to order. In some of the shops and vast air-conditioned galleries you can watch craftsmen hammering away on ornate silver and gold designs destined to be exported to Europe and Japan. Before buying, remember to shop around, as easy money has led to inflated prices.
12km northeast of Denpasar on the road to Ubud and Gianyar.

Kapal

This little village has two claims to fame. Not only is it the sculpture capital of Bali and a prolific manufacturer of shrines, but it is also home to the Pura Sada, one of the oldest temples on the island. Dating from the 12th century and set back a short distance from the main road, it was destroyed by an earthquake in 1917 and only restored in 1949. You will still find some fine stone carvings though, as well as statues of the nine lords of directions. Just in case these deities are not enough to safeguard the inhabitants from another earthquake, you will find a spirit house outside set in the midst of a huge tangled banyan tree.
12km northwest of Denpasar, on the road to Mengwi.

Lukluk

Take a left turn off the main road at the village of Lukluk to see the charming Pura Dalem Temple. You may have to ask the guardian to open the gates, but if you do you will be rewarded by fine stone carvings and pleasant leafy surroundings which you will probably have to yourself.
10km northwest of Denpasar, on the road to Mengwi.

Sukawati

Situated almost midway between Denpasar and Ubud, this bustling market town is the producer of one of Bali's most pleasing commodities – those wind chimes which tinkle in the wind, sounding like the music of the gods. There's little other reason to come here except to visit the 'Sukawati art market', a vast complex of overpriced and often poorly made handicrafts ranging from woodcarvings to *krises* and baskets made of palm leaf.
13km northeast of Denpasar, on the road to Ubud and Gianyar.

Visitors are welcome in Celuk

Pura Kehen Temple near the ancient town of Bangli

AMLAPURA, see Amlapura drive, pages 94–5.

BANGLI

The highlight of this ancient little town which is situated in the cool rice fields of Central Bali is a visit to the Pura Kehen Temple with its magnificent staircase, terraced courtyards and fine stone relief carvings. Locals claim that the 11 tapering roofs and inner shrine with thrones for Brahma, Shiva and Vishnu have made it the holiest of all resting places for visiting gods. According to early inscriptions, it may have been constructed in the 9th century. It is one of Bali's loveliest temples and is open daily 8.30am–5pm.
Location: 40km northeast of Denpasar. Regular bemos *run from Denpasar's Batubulan terminal to Bangli. Pura Kehen*

is 1km north of town, on the road to Besakih and Penelokan. Admission charge.

BEDUGUL

A short drive from Bedugul will bring you to delightful Lake Bratan. Not only are there fine walks around the lakeside, speed boats and pedal boats for hire, but one of the most serene temples in the whole of Bali – Pura Ulun Danu. The temple, which is dedicated to the goddess of water, was built in 1633 by the king of Mengwi. Although it nearly sank in the mid-1970s when the waters in the lake began to rise, today it can be seen in all its simple glory. Get there at dusk to see the temple at its best and stay in one of the nearby bungalows which have panoramic views.
Location: 48km north of Denpasar. Regular

bemos *run from Denpasar's Ubung terminal on Jalan Cokroaminoto. Ask to be dropped off at Bedugul or, better still, at Lake Bratan, 2km further on. Pura Ulu Danu is open daily, 8am–4pm. Admission charge.*

Bukit Mungsu (Central Market)

Flowers, vegetables and a dazzling display of spices, along with orchid seeds and occasionally even carrots, are neatly stacked up in this little market
Candikuning: 500m north of Pura Ulu Danu on the road to Bedugul.

Handara Kosaido Country Club

Voted one of the world's 50 most beautiful golf courses, this impressive 18-hole course offers world-class-standard greens. Telephone 0361 288944 for reservations.
2km north of Lake Bratan.

Kebun Raya (Botanical Gardens)

These gardens cover 130 hectares and contain more than 1,000 different trees, plants and flowers. They were established in 1959 as an offshoot of the national botanical gardens at Bogor and today are prized above all for their wild orchids.
Next to the market. Open: daily, 8am–4pm. Admission charge.

BESAKIH

When the sacred Gunung Agung (Mount Agung) volcano erupted on 17 March 1963 it literally engulfed Bali's 'mother temple', killing several hundred priests who leapt into the flames while trying to appease the angry gods. The 11th-century complex has since been rebuilt in all its magnificence, with 22 different temples spread over an area of more than 1 sq km.

For the majority of the time visitors can't actually explore Pura Agung, the most important single shrine, as regulations prohibit non-Hindus from entering the inner courtyards. Guides will, however, take you to a panoramic viewpoint from where you can see the profusion of *puras* scattered over the slopes below. Enthusiasts can even climb Mount Agung (3,142m) from here, although you should make sure you take a guide and allow at least 5 hours to get to the summit (see Getting Away From it All, page 134).
Location: 60km northeast of Denpasar. Bemos run from Denpasar's Batubulan terminal to Klungkung. From here catch another bemo to Besakih. Open: daily, 8am–5pm. Admission charge.

Sacred temples at Besakih

Multi-tiered shrines, or *merus*, at Pura Taman Ayun, the main temple of the Mengwi kingdom

GUNUNG AGUNG (Mount Agung), see page 134.

GUNUNG BATUR (Mount Batur)
Rising up from Lake Batur, strewn with rocks and boulders, this dramatic mountain is one of the best and most accessible peaks on Bali from where to view the sunrise. Guides can be rented at many of the bungalows and guesthouses in the small village of Kedisan, a short distance from Penelokan. (See Getting Away From it All, page 134.)

KINTAMANI
This scruffy little town offers fine views of Lake Batur below. There's little reason to stay here, however, except to visit two temples in the near vicinity.
Location: 68km north of Denpasar, beyond the town of Penelokan.

Pura Batur
When Mount Batur erupted for the second time in 1926, the locals simply dismantled what was left of the temple, moved it to safer ground near the crater rim and dedicated it to the goddess of the crater lake. The result is not only one of the island's most revered nine-tiered *merus*, but one of its most important directional temples.
A short distance south of Kintamani. Open: daily. Admission charge.

Pura Tegeh Koripan
Temple buffs rank the Pura Tegeh Koripan as one of the oldest and holiest on Bali, but unless you relish the thought of climbing 300 steps, you'd be well advised to give the place a miss. At the topmost shrine are some rather ordinary-looking statues, and some portraits of Balinese kings, queens and divinities said

Intricately terraced rice fields near Pupuan in northern Bali

to date back to the 11th century.
8km north of Kintamani at the town of Penulisan. Open: daily. Admission charge.

KLUNGKUNG

Until the Dutch attacked Bali's most important principality in 1908, Klungkung was home to the powerful Gelgel dynasty and a flourishing centre for the arts. These days it is a pleasant little handicraft town best known for its royal palace and its traditional style of painting.
Location: 40km east of Denpasar. Bemos leave from Denpasar's Batubulan terminal.

Kertha Gosa

This famous little palace contains a beautiful pavilion surrounded by a moat and a hall of justice, with fine Klungkung-style paintings on the ceiling. The most vivid of them show women being boiled alive or having their heads sawn in two – the punishment for the guilty. Adjoining the court of justice is the Bale Kambang, or 'floating pavilion'. Further round, there is a small museum with ancient ceramics, paintings and a collection of weaving looms.
The Kertha Gosa lies at the main intersection on Jalan Untung Surapati. Open: daily. Admission charge.

MENGWI

This town's most popular temple, Pura Taman Ayun, has a number of impressive shrines with slender-tiered roofs as well as a pleasant courtyard surrounded by a moat filled with lotus flowers. The temple was originally constructed in the mid-18th century, but renovated in the 1930s.
Location: 18km north of Denpasar. Buses run from Denpasar's Ubung terminal. Other attractions in the vicinity: Tanah Lot (12km) and the monkey forest at Sangeh (9km).

Amlapura's ornamental gardens at Tirtagangga

PENELOKAN

From the crater rim at Penelokan it is easy to see why the locals call Bali the island of gods, for the views that can be had of Mount Batur and the turquoise lake below are among the finest on offer. There are plenty of other attractions within easy reach, too. While enthusiastic walkers leave every morning to climb the peak of Mount Batur, less energetic individuals simply relax by the lake in the village of Kedisan (4km).
Location: 60km north of Denpasar. Bemos run from Denpasar's Batubulan terminal to Bangli, from where you must catch another bemo for Penelokan. There is also a regular coach service. For the best places to stay, take the road east to Kedisan (4km).

PUPUAN

The real joy of visiting Pupuan is the journey there through spectacular rice terraces with distant views of Gunung Batukau (Mount Batukau). For a pleasant day's excursion, take the winding route from Seririt (west of Singaraja) or travel all the way north from Pulukan, but whichever way you

go, take your time. This is a journey for connoisseurs, and if you are in a hurry, don't even dream of it.
Location: 42km southwest of Singaraja. Buses occasionally travel the road, but it is best appreciated with your own transport.

SANGEH

An intrepid band of monkeys inhabits this sacred temple (Pura Bukit Sari) and the surrounding forest planted with nutmeg trees. Bring a camera and a handful of peanuts, but hold on tight to all your belongings.
Location: 9km northeast of Mengwi, via the town of Kedampal. Use private transport.

SINGARAJA

When the Dutch occupied northern Bali in the 19th century, they chose this little town as their capital. Although most tourists now hurry through on their way to the beaches of Lovina, you will still find a handful of old colonial buildings on Jalan Ngurah Rai as well as tree-lined avenues and rows of Chinese shops.
Location: 78km north of Denpasar. Regular buses leave from Kuta Beach and from Denpasar. Bemos *leave from Denpasar's Ubung terminal on Jalan Cokroaminoto.*

Pura Beji

This delightful little temple has a fine gateway of *naga* snakes and some of the most detailed stone carvings on Bali. It is built in the northern style and dedicated to the goddess of agriculture.
7km east of Singaraja in the village of Sangsit.

TENGANAN

A brand new stretch of road leads through lush countryside to this Bali Aga village, home to some original Balinese and to a host of colourful customs, boxing contests and mating dances dating back hundreds of years. However, the real world has arrived in this beautiful little village with a vengeance. Outside the courtyard, with its rows of diminutive houses and stalls selling famous Ikat cloth made from silk, woven and dyed by hand, there is now a car park large enough to handle coach tours and inside the village one of the first things you see is a concrete public convenience.

Location: 4km north of Candi Dasa. Motorbike taxis will take you from the signposted turn-off. Donation requested.

TIRTAGANGGA

Many visitors travel to Tirtagangga simply to admire the rice terraces, but the place has another attraction: the water

Bali Aga woman, Tenganan

Fine stone carvings at Pura Beji, Singaraja

palace built by Amlapura's last raja which features fountains, ornamental gardens and a swimming pool. Locals come here with picnics and sit on the green lawns. Tourists can take their pick of several restaurants, with panoramic views of the gardens. (See the Amlapura drive, page 94.)

Location: 85km from Denpasar. Bemos run via the town of Amlapura. The water palace is open daily. Admission charge.

TRUNYAN

Unless you relish the idea of being hassled by some of the pushiest inhabitants on the whole of Bali, you'd be well advised to stay clear of this Bali Aga village, which is inhabited by descendants of the original Balinese. The only real attractions of the place are a 4m-high statue of a guardian spirit and a cemetery where the people are left to decompose.

Location: catch a fixed-price boat from the village of Kedisan, 4km east of Penelokan, which will take you on a round-trip to Trunyan. Boats leave daily at regular intervals between 8.30am and 3.30pm.

RICE FARMING

In the beautiful heartlands that make up Central Bali, the first light of day reveals farmers already out in their lush paddy fields, knee-deep among the glistening green shoots that stretch to a distant horizon.

Some of these people have worked in the fields for an entire lifetime, others only do so during the harvest, but almost everyone on this fertile island in some way contributes to the annual crop of rice which exceeds 900,000 tons.

Nor is it only Bali where the production of rice is the single most important commodity. Almost four out of five Javanese work the soil, each consuming an average of 180kg of rice every year and making Java both one of the biggest producers and consumers in the world. Even on Lombok, around the delightful village of Tetebatu, you will see workers thrashing out husks beneath the shadow of Mount Rinjani.

Generally the rice is planted by hand and the terraced paddies are then flooded by a complex system of irrigation channels leading from nearby rivers and streams. Within a matter of weeks the young green shoots appear. As soon as the rice has ripened and turned to a golden brown, men and

women from the surrounding area gather to cut the crop, remove the husks and store the grain to feed their families in the months to come.

Far left: rice fields at Pupuan
Left: central Bali
Bottom left: planting the rice seedlings
Above: terraces in northern Bali
Below: harvesting the crop

In the past the harvest benefited from the extremely rich volcanic soil, with farmers often harvesting two crops a year. With the introduction of new high yield, insect-resistant strains, however, the output will soon be even higher and the rice gods recipients of even greater praise.

UBUD

This delightful town surrounded by rice fields is undoubtedly the most popular inland destination on Bali as well as the most rewarding. Ubud is not only cooler than the coastal areas, but has a wealth of cultural activities and opportunities for walking, shopping or just relaxing. You can feast on *babi guling* (roasted pig), shop for paintings and woodcarvings, or take gentle strolls in the surrounding countryside. Ubud also makes the perfect stepping-stone for trips to the north.
Location: 25km north of Denpasar. Tourist buses run from Kuta and Sanur to Ubud. Bemos *run from Denpasar's Batubulan terminal, taking 1 hour.*

Orientation

There are only two roads of any significance in Ubud. Running east to west you'll find Jalan Raya, where the central market and dozens of shops and restaurants are located; running north to south is Monkey Forest Road, with art shops, stalls and charming little bungalows. Good restaurants and a range of accommodation can be found everywhere, so just wander until you find something that takes your fancy.

Museum Neka

A fine collection of paintings ranging from work by famous local artists such as Ida Bagus and Anak Agung to collections by western artists which include Le Mayeur, Walter Spies and Antonio Blanco is on display at this museum. Set up in 1982 by Suteja Neka, it provides a wonderful insight into the transition from traditional to modern Balinese style. Paintings by local artists are in the first gallery arranged in chronological order. To see paintings by Western artists, visit the second and third galleries.
1.5km west of Ubud past the village of Campuhan. Open: daily, 9am–noon and 2pm–5pm. Admission charge.

Museum Puri Lukisan (Palace of Fine Arts)

This little museum is a must for anyone interested in the development of modern art on Bali. Set up in the mid 1950s, it

The rice fields of Ubud

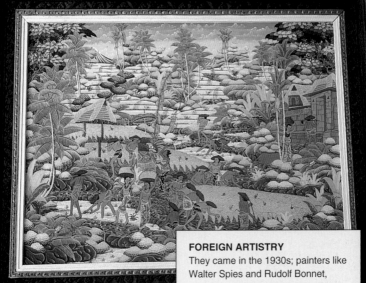

Ubud's paintings combine traditional subjects with a modern style of artistry

has an excellent display of paintings and sculptures, and an idyllic little garden. *Jalan Raya, just west of the market. Open: daily, 8am–4pm. Admission charge.*

FOREIGN ARTISTRY

They came in the 1930s; painters like Walter Spies and Rudolf Bonnet, drawn to Ubud by the beauty of the countryside and the charm of the people. Over the years they were joined by a host of other local and foreign artists. And the result? An intriguing mix of styles and colours that provides yet a new perspective on the island, its religions and its inhabitants.

Shopping

Art galleries, studios and souvenir stalls have sprung up all over Ubud, selling every form of painting, antique or wooden carving imaginable, as well as a host of shirts and tie-dye bed covers. Some of them are real artistic pieces, but most are mass produced.

Temples and shrines

Several temples can be found along Jalan Raya, including the Pura Saren and the delightful Puri Saraswati, situated behind the Lotus Café Restaurant. For other temples and countless shrines, just keep your eyes open – you won't be able to miss them.

Wayang Kulit and dances

If you haven't already seen the Wayang Kulit shadow puppets or the mask dance, or even the Legong and Kecak dance, Ubud is the place to put this right. Performances take place almost every night either at the Pura Dalem or the Puri Saren. Check your guesthouse for details, and get there early to reserve a seat.

UBUD

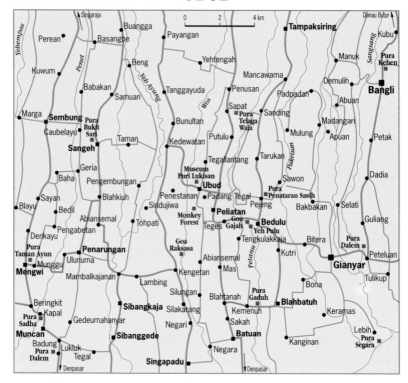

AROUND UBUD

For a glimpse of handicrafts and beautiful countryside, go to any of these villages which lie within a 10km radius of Ubud. Most of them can be reached by *bemos* which leave regularly from the market place on the corner of Monkey Forest Road and Jalan Raya. Alternatively, just walk out into the countryside and make up your own route. You're unlikely to be disappointed.

Batuan

Some of Bali's finest ink drawings are to be found in this village, along with plenty of second-rate imitations. Much of the work is said to be influenced by the great Made Nyana who was born here in 1948, while other paintings are by Nyoman Lempad. You may find the Batuan style to be moodier than the Ubud style, but purists claim it to be just as good.

7km south of Ubud.

Bedulu

This little village might have gone by an altogether different name if it hadn't

been for the ability of a former king with two heads to switch them at will, which led to the term Bedulu (he who changed heads). Walk east of the junction to see the town's most important site, the Pura Samuan Tiga. It was built in the 11th century when the town was capital of the Pejeng kingdom, and every year, on the full moon of the tenth month, hosts one of the island's most important festivals, Odalan.
5km east of Ubud.

Campuan

This little village, which was once the proud home of Dutch artist Arie Smit, still plays host to American artist Antonio Blanco, as well as several delightful *losmen* (bungalows) and the charming Hotel Tjampuhan, former home of artist Walter Spies. Leave the main road to enjoy beautiful strolls in the

Stone demons perched over the town of Gianyar

rice fields.
1km west of Ubud (see the Ubud to Campuan walk, pages 118–9).

Gianyar

You would be hard pushed to spend more than a morning in this bustling modern town, renowned for its textiles and its *babi guling* (roast pig). Having said this, you can visit the factories to watch sarongs being woven and catch a glimpse of the old palace of the Gianyar royal family, which is a fine example of traditional Balinese architecture. The palace on Jalan Ngurah Rai is still inhabited though, so you can only inspect it from the outside.
10km southeast of Ubud.

Carvings at Pura Samuan Tiga (Temple of the Meeting of the Three), Bedulu

Mas has a high reputation for producing quality carvings and masks

days they are accompanied by a wealthier and less discerning clientele with the result that some of the most intricate woodcarvings on Bali lie alongside some of the nastiest and most expensive examples. Check out several of the showrooms, and remember that the smarter the place, the higher the prices.
4km south of Ubud. Showrooms generally open 9am–6pm. Admission free.

Pejeng

A vast drum measuring over 3m long is the highlight of Pejeng's old state temple known as Pura Panataran Sasih. Legend tells that this was formerly the thirteenth moon which fell to earth when a thief urinated on it. Nearby temples have equally catching names and stories. You'll find the 14th-century Pura Pusering Jagat (Navel of the World) a short distance south and next door the Pura Kebo Edan (Crazy Buffalo Temple) with a demonic statue bearing six penises.
4km east of Ubud.

Goa Gajah (Elephant Cave)

A fantastically carved rock and a cave full of phallic symbols are the chief attractions of this popular tourist site which lies a short distance from Ubud. You can explore the dimly lit interior of this 11th-century hermitage, although you must walk through the mouth of a Kala head to enter. Inside is a statue of the elephant-headed god Ganesh, as well as various symbols of the Hindu god Shiva. Excavations outside the cave have also uncovered two bathing pools with six statues of nymphs holding waterspouts.
4km east of Ubud. Open: daily. Admission charge. Most trips combine Goa Gajah with a visit to nearby Yeh Pulu (1km).

Jalan Monkey Forest (Monkey Forest Road), see the Ubud to Nyuh Kuning walk, pages 116–17.

Mas

Shrewd art collectors have been visiting this village for decades to get their hands on the beautiful wooden carvings, including fruit bowls and mythical birds, which are displayed in its galleries. These

Wooden carvings can be made to order by the artisans of Mas

In the late afternoon Petulu is suddenly inundated with white egrets returning from a day's feeding

Peliatan

Peliatan's biggest claim to fame is that it plays host to one of Bali's best-known dance troupes, which performs regularly at the Puri Agung and the Pura Dalem Puri in Peliatan. So highly thought of was the troupe that during the 1950s they were used in a Hollywood film co-starring Bing Crosby and Bob Hope. Check out times at the tourist office on Jalan Raya.

1.5km southeast of Ubud.

Petulu

Although you will find plenty of proficient woodcarvers in the vicinity, this small village is above all associated with white egrets which come in their thousands to nest in the surrounding trees for much of the year. In the late afternoon photographers with powerful lenses can have a field day, but watch out for bird droppings, which can be quite prolific.

4km northeast of Ubud. Turn left where you see a sign with a large heron.

Tampaksiring

Travel north of Pejeng village to see the monumental hermitage known as Gunung Kawi set in a deep ravine and surrounded by spectacular rice terraces. The memorial shrines carved into the rock face are believed to honour an 11th-century royal family and their concubines. Other sites in the vicinity include the famous springs of Tirta Empul, 2km further north.

15km north of Ubud. Turn right on the outskirts of Tampaksiring. Open: daily. Admission charge.

Yeh Pulu

According to legend, Kebo Iwa, the great giant, carved these 14th-century rock carvings in one night with his fingernails. You will find other attractions about the place too, with its nearby rice fields and sacred well. Best to combine a trip to Yeh Pulu with a visit to nearby Goa Gajah.

Signposted 1.5km southeast of Goa Gajah. Open daily. Donation required.

Ubud to Nyuh Kuning

Starting at the charming little gallery of Gusti Nyoman Lempad, this popular walk takes you past the central market down bustling Monkey Forest Road to the Pura Dalem Temple. From here it is a pleasant amble to the village of Nyuh Kuning. *Allow 2 hours.*

The walk begins at Gusti Nyoman Lempad's gallery on Jalan Raya.

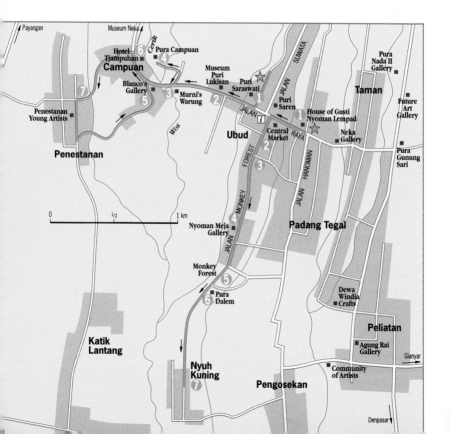

1 HOUSE OF GUSTI NYOMAN LEMPAD

This little red-brick gallery which is open to the public was formerly home to one of Bali's best-known artists, Gusti Nyoman Lempad, who died in 1978. He was responsible for a fine collection of ink drawings as well as stone carvings and Barong heads.

Leave the gallery and turn right. A short distance further along you will see the central market.

2 CENTRAL MARKET

The best time to see Ubud's main vegetable and food market is at dawn when the place is packed with locals buying exotic fruits and meats. At other times, visit the small spirit shrines next door with their clutch of offerings and joss sticks.

Leave the market and continue along Jalan Raya. After a short distance, turn left down Jalan Monkey Forest.

3 JALAN MONKEY FOREST (MONKEY FOREST ROAD)

Ten years ago rice fields stretched out on both sides of Monkey Forest Road. These days they have been replaced by silversmiths, galleries and stalls selling hand-woven cottons, batiks, paintings and woodcarvings. Walk in and inspect any of the goods, but remember that the prices on Monkey Forest Road may be a little higher than in the villages outside Ubud.

Continue down Monkey Forest Road for about 800m and on your right, just before you descend the hill, you will see the gallery of Nyoman Meja.

4 NYOMAN MEDJA GALLERY

This spacious gallery contains pictures by Nyoman Meja who is famous for painting traditional scenes in a post-modern style. You are under no obligation to purchase any of the works, but you should certainly appreciate them.

Continue to the entrance of the Monkey Forest 150m further on, sign your name in the book, and leave a donation. Rp2,000 should suffice, although the people will press you to give more.

5 MONKEY FOREST

This small but dense forest is inhabited by a band of exuberant monkeys who hang out high up in the trees, swinging from branch to branch and leaping around in search of food. Keep your hands on your cameras, sunglasses or any other valuables since they have become famous for taking more than just bananas or peanuts.

From the ticket office follow the path into the forest and on your left, after about 100m, you will find the Pura Dalem.

6 PURA DALEM (TEMPLE OF THE DEAD)

You will find this forest temple poking out of lush vegetation and over-run with monkeys. Keep your eyes open at the entrance of the inner temple for the stone carvings of *rangda* figures devouring children.

Continue down the steps to the right of the temple and follow the path. After 400m you will reach Nyuh Kuning village.

7 NYUH KUNING

This little village set amidst rice fields makes a perfect end to the tour, with its friendly woodcarvers and delightfully unhurried air of days gone by.

From Nyuh Kuning, you can either head east to Pengosekan, where there is a community of artists, or retrace your steps back to Ubud.

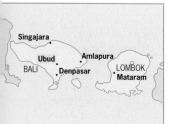

Ubud to Campuan

Starting out from the delightful little Saraswati temple near the centre of Ubud, this walk will take you to the Museum Puri Lukisan and from there to the surrounding villages where a number of great artists settled down to enjoy a taste of paradise. For the route see the Ubud to Nyuh Kuning walk map on page 116. *Allow 3 hours.*

Begin at the Puri Saraswati on Jalan Raya, situated behind the Lotus Café.

1 PURI SARASWATI

This little temple situated behind a lotus pond contains several

fine stone carvings by the famous local artist Gusti Nyoman Lempad, as well as a magnificent stone lotus throne which is upheld as one of Ubud's great examples of artistry. Before entering, make sure you put a sash around your waist and leave a small donation.
Continue a short distance west down Jalan Raya. On your right, you will see a signpost for the Museum Puri Lukisan.

2 MUSEUM PURI LUKISAN

Built by the Noble Aspiration Foundation, which was founded by the late King of Ubud together with German artist Walter Spies and Dutch artist Rudolf Bonnet, this charming museum contains traditional and modern paintings along with a collection of wooden carvings (open: daily, 8am–4pm).
From Puri Lukisan continue west down Jalan Raya towards the village of Campuan.

3 CAMPUAN VILLAGE

Marking the spot where the Wos and

Cerik rivers converge, Campuan is a bustling little village that has become closely associated with foreign artists like Antonio Blanco and Walter Spies. You will find several craft shops, the popular Murni's Warung and, near by, pleasant walks into the rice fields.

A hundred metres before you reach the bridge follow a sign to your right for Pura Campuan and descend the steps to the temple.

4 PURA CAMPUAN (GUNUNG LEBAH)

This secluded little temple, which lies far below the bridge, is thought to date back as far as the 8th or 9th century, although it has since been thoroughly renovated. Near by is a cave believed to play host to Goa Raksasa, a local devil.

Retrace your steps to the junction and after crossing the suspension bridge over the Wos River you will find Blanco's Gallery signposted immediately on your left.

5 BLANCO'S GALLERY

This delightful edifice, set in magnificent gardens, is home to American artist Antonio Blanco who has resided here for more than 40 years. While most Balinese artists concentrate on brightly coloured rural scenes, Blanco's speciality is erotic art. If you are lucky, you may even find the great artist at work.

Continue 150m up the road and on the right you will see Hotel Tjampuhan.

6 HOTEL TJAMPUHAN

Until 1944 this exquisite establishment overlooking the river was the residence of Walter Spies, one of the European painters who settled on the island. It is now a hotel, but you can still wander in the exotic gardens and for a fee use the swimming pool.

Above and far left: the secluded temple of Pura Campuan

From Hotel Tjampuhan, walk 100m further up the road and turn left up the stone steps, signposted to Penestanan Bungalows. After following the path through rice fields for about 800m you will reach the village of Penestanan.

7 PENESTANAN

This little village has thrived as the centre of a native art movement which was inspired by the Dutch artist Arie Smit in the 1950s. Today it is full of galleries, bead centres and silver workshops as well as some delightful houses. Watch the artists at work and remember to bargain hard if you buy anything.

From Penestanan follow the road around until you arrive back at the suspension bridge. From here, it is a short walk back to Ubud.

Lombok

Only a 4-hour boat journey away from Bali, yet three decades away in development, the island of Lombok remains an oasis of calm lapped by the warm waters of the Indian Ocean.

In this newly discovered tourist destination, that measures 80km by 70km, you'll find every kind of scenery from the vast arid landscape of the south to the lush rice fields of Tetebatu and the magnificent beaches and islands that dot the western coast.

Historically, too, this is a world of contrasting cultures. During the 17th century armies from East Bali invaded Lombok, seizing many of its coastal towns from the ethnic Sasaks. Even today, although the majority of the island's 2.5 million population are Muslim, some 80,000 Balinese still live in the western districts, holding ceremonies and festivals to honour the gods.

Don't expect to find another Bali though. Lombok may have rice terraces that match those in Ubud, as well as an unspoiled coastline, but it is poorer than its western neighbour and does not have the serene, sweet-smiling inhabitants, nor the rich artistry and the countless temple festivities and celebrations.

For a short tour, most visitors head straight to up-market Senggigi Beach or the gem-like islands of Gili Air and Gili Trawangan. Better, though, to take your

Lombok's most spectacular landmark: Mount Rinjani viewed from Tetebatu

LOMBOK

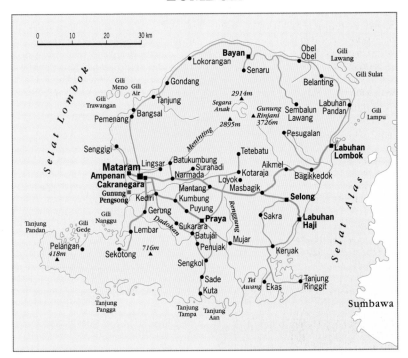

time and enjoy while you can the quieter charms of what will undoubtedly become Indonesia's next major tourist destination.

Getting there

Regular flights leave from Denpasar's Ngurah Rai Airport for Selaparang Mataram Airport on Lombok. There is also a ferry service which runs regularly from Padangbai to Lembar, taking between 4 and 5 hours, depending on the weather. The Mabua-Express, an air-conditioned catamaran, leaves Benoa Harbour twice a day and arrives in Lembar 2½ hours later.

Travelling around

Although the Balinese will tell you that transport is undeveloped and dangerous, roads on Lombok are for the most part of an extremely good standard and, with the recent completion of a road link on the northeast coast, you can now drive right around the island. Countless visitors rent jeeps and motorbikes on Bali and transport them over on the ferry from Padangbai. Those without their own transport can take crowded public *bemos* or charter their own. For shorter trips, there is the ubiquitous horse and cart, known as a *cidomo*.

MAJOR TOWNS

Lombok's three major towns lie on the
west coast, a short distance from one
another. Few tourists stay here, but there
are a couple of sites to visit, as well as the
main transportation hub at the Bertais
bus terminal, 2km east of Cakranegara.

MATARAM

There is precious little reason to spend
time in Lombok's capital unless it is the
Bank of Indonesia or the immigration
office that you are after. Besides these
and a few other government offices, the
place is simply a modern administrative
town with an airport and a couple of
rather ordinary hotels.
*Location: west of Lombok. Regular bemos
(minibuses) travel the short distance between
Mataram, Ampenan, Cakranegara and the
main bus station at Bertais, a short distance
further east.*

AMPENAN

A delightful way to explore this
dilapidated old fishing town is to catch
one of the popular bell-jingling horse and
carts known as *cidomos* which potter
around town. Ask the driver to take you
to see some of the local antique shops. A
pleasant side trip can be made to the
Provincial Museum of Nusa Tenggara
Barat, on Jalan Banjar Tilar Negara
(open: Tuesday to Thursday, Saturday
and Sunday, 8am–4pm; Friday,
8am–11am), which contains a collection
of textiles from around the region. Keep
your eyes open for the few old Dutch
buildings still remaining, and for the
small but lively Chinese and Arab
quarters. (See the Lombok coastal drive,
pages 130–1.)
Location: 3km west of Mataram.

CAKRANEGARA

You may be hard pushed to find the
exact point where Mataram ends and
Cakranegara begins, but the latter is
considerably busier than its neighbour, if
somewhat lacking in charm. During the
17th century Cakranegara was the capital
of Lombok. Today there are plenty of
shops selling sarongs, baskets and silver
trinkets, especially around the bazaar on
Jalan Selaparang. Also keep your eyes
open for stalls dispensing Lombok's
gastronomic delicacy known as *ayam
taliwang*, a delicious, if incongruous,
flattened and heavily spiced barbecued
chicken.
Location: 1km east of Mataram.

Mayura Water Palace

Built in 1744 as part of the former
Balinese empire on Lombok, this palace

The Mayura Water Palace was once the hub of
Cakranegara

Balinese-style temples are a feature of Lombok's Pura Meru

marks the spot where, a century later, the Balinese routed the Dutch army. You will find several old cannons as well as a delightful little shrine to the east. In the middle of the lake is an open-sided hall of justice, known as the floating pavilion.
North of Jalan Selaparang. Open: daily, 8am–5pm. Admission charge.

Pura Meru (Meru Temple)

Cross the street from the Mayura Water Palace to see Pura Meru, which is one of the largest Balinese temples on Lombok. Prince Agung Made Karang built it in 1720 as an attempt to unify the island. Although his efforts failed, the temple, with its three courtyards and 33 shrines, lives on – dedicated to the Hindu trinity of Shiva, Brahma and Vishnu.
East of the Mayura Water Palace, off Jalan Selaparang. Open: daily, 8am–5pm. Admission charge.

SWEET REVENGE

When the Dutch demanded payment from Lombok in 1882, the occupying Balinese armies simply attacked their forces, killing 100 soldiers. The Dutch responded by calling up reinforcements and, supported by the Sasaks, captured Cakranegara in 1894. Shortly afterwards the island formally became a part of the Dutch East Indies.

Gunung Pengsong

Three hundred metres and an awful lot of steps up the hillside have to be tackled to reach this little temple shrine commanding magnificent views. At the end of March or April, locals sacrifice a water buffalo here to celebrate the end of the harvest. At other times, it is a place for die-hard fitness fanatics and those with an appreciation of fine vistas.
9km south of Mataram. Charter a bemo and ask the caretaker to open the gates. Donations appreciated.

REST OF LOMBOK

GILI ISLANDS

The three little island pearls known as
Gili Trawangan, Gili Air and Gili Meno,
all with magnificent beaches, fine coral
and dazzling turquoise seas, lie 30
minutes away by boat off Lombok's
northwest coast. There are no big hotels
here, but plenty of travellers nevertheless
come here to laze away the days, to feast
on freshly caught fish and to watch
wonderful sunsets over Gunung Agung
(Mount Agung) on Bali and sunrises
over Gunung Rinjani (Mount Rinjani).
For the best snorkelling and the liveliest
entertainment go to Gili Trawangan, and
for a quieter alternative, to Gili Air.
Note, however, that during high season
(June–September) accommodation can
be extremely hard to come by, especially
if you arrive in the late afternoon.
Location: Bangsal, the departure point for
the Gili Islands, lies 25km north of
Ampenan and can be reached by bemo *via*
Pemenang. Public boats leave at irregular
intervals for the islands, taking 30–45
minutes. Failing that, charter a boat.

Around Gili

Continue further up the coast from
Pemenang to beautiful Tanjung Sirah.
Currently there is nowhere to stay, but
you will find good snorkelling
opportunities and it is one of the most
tranquil spots on the island.
3km north of Pemenang.

GUNUNG RINJANI (Mount Rinjani)

Unless you hire a guide and are in
reasonably good physical shape, you
would be ill advised to climb this
magnificent mountain. During the dry
season, however, you can catch fantastic
views of the summit (3,726m), typically
shrouded in mist and towering over the
entire island. Its enormous crater,
reached by a difficult 2-day trek from the
town of Bayan, is filled with emerald-
green water and its steep slopes covered
in forest. Twice a year the Balinese make
a pilgrimage here to throw offerings to
the goddess of the mountain. For the rest
of the year, it remains quiet and

Bangsal is the departure point for the Gili
Islands

unspoiled and indescribably beautiful.
You will experience some of the finest
views, without the effort, from the village
of Tetebatu (see pages 128–9) and from
the Gili Islands (see page 124), but from
almost anywhere on the island this
awesome mountain is visible.
*Location: northern Lombok. Best approaches
are from the town of Bayan to the north or
Sembulan Lawang to the east. (See Getting
Away From it All, pages 134–5.)*

KUTA BEACH
This beautiful stretch of beach is nothing
like its namesake on Bali. The luxurious
Novotel is the first hotel to form part of a
plan to develop the coastline into a Nusa
Dua-type destination, yet the place
remains off the beaten track. Here
backpackers mingle with fishermen and
locals against a backdrop of simple
bungalows nestling a short distance from
the sea front. Only when the winds are
high and large amounts of stinging
seaweed have been washed ashore does
the place lose some of its inherent
charms.
*Location: 60km south of Mataram. Public
bemos run from the Bertais terminal to*

Irregular and crowded ferry boats convey
visitors to and from the Gili Islands

*Praya, where you have to catch another
bemo to Sengkol and change again for
Kuta. A simpler alternative is to take your
own transport.*

Excursions from Kuta
For a pleasant excursion, head 1.5km east
to Segara Beach and take a signposted
right turn over the bridge. From the top
of the nearby hill you will get fine views of
Mount Rinjani and a series of bays.
Continue a further 3km along the main
road to the beach at Tanjung Aan, but get
here soon though, as even in this tranquil
area the talk is of new hotels and big
exclusive developments.

Kuta Market
Kuta's Sunday beach market is a sensory
delight of exotic fruits, live chickens,
woven baskets and smiling locals – and
well worth an excursion, even if beaches
are not your thing. Arrive early and be
sure to have a camera handy and vast
amounts of film.
Kuta Beach. Sundays only.

Guarding the shrine at Lingsar, sacred to both the Hindu and Islamic religions

Location: 15km east of Mataram. Open: daily, 8am–6pm. Admission charge. Bemos *run from the Bertais bus terminal in Cakranegara to Narmada, where you must catch another* bemo *to Lingsar.*

NARMADA

When King Anak Gede Karangasem of Mataram was too frail to climb to the summit of Mount Rinjani, he simply built an imitation of the lake and made offerings to the gods from his luxuriant gardens instead. Besides a pool which is open to the public and a small Hindu Balinese temple built in 1805, the place is run down now, with few real attractions.

Location: 10km east of Cakranegara. Bemos *run from Cakranegara's Bertais terminal. Open: daily, 8am–6pm. Admission charge.*

PENUJAK

Water pots and storage jars made from coils of clay are the speciality of this little village, situated a short distance from Praya. There is a promotion centre and plenty of locals prepared both to show off and sell their work.

Location: 5km south of Praya on the road to

LEMBAR

Lombok's main port is little more than an arrival and departure point for ferries to Bali. You will be met by dozens of *bemos* which will transport you to Ampenan, Mataram, Cakranegara and the Bertais bus terminal for onward connections.

Location: 22km south of Mataram.

LINGSAR

Legend has it that when the Balinese first arrived on Lombok, a holy spring gushed out of the earth at Lingsar. Four Hindu shrines mark the spot along with a Muslim shrine, and in the adjacent Wektu Telu temple there are numerous baby eels. From stalls in the car park buy a hard-boiled egg to feed the sacred creatures, although you will have to break it in half as the fishes' spiritual skills do not extend to swallowing the egg yolks whole.

TERRACOTTA AHOY

When travelling around Lombok keep your eyes open for the beautiful terracotta pots made by Sasak potters. These beautiful storage jars, water jugs and vases are sculptured by hand, dried in the sun and fired in open-air kilns. They can be bought all over the island.

Above: the rarely visited gardens at Narmada
Right: Sasak traditions in Sade. Other Sasak
villages in the area are less changed by tourism

Kuta. Take a bemo *from Praya. Also
included on many day tours.*

SADE

For a glimpse of traditional Sasak life,
visit this delightful little village set
incongruously between rice fields and a
tarmacked main road, a short distance
from Kuta. Be prepared though for a
barrage of women selling woven rugs and
girls as young as five demonstrating the
art of weaving. English-speaking guides
will explain the various Sasak rituals,
point you in the best direction for taking
photographs and negotiate for purchases.
Get here early to avoid the crowds.
*Location: 6km north of Kuta and included
on many day tours. A donation is requested
on entry to the village.*

In practice, Senggigi Beach extends for more than 6km

weavers in this little Sasak town, for Sukarara has established a reputation for producing some of the best hand-woven cloth in the area. Watch the people weaving patterned sarongs and exquisite *kain songket*, a richly coloured cloth interwoven with gold thread. For a price you can even buy woven bags, although they may be cheaper in the market in Cakranegara. If you have the time, explore the surrounding countryside with its thatched villages, its rice fields and its merry inhabitants trotting around in horse-carts.

Location: 26km south of Mataram, off the Kediri to Praya Road. Catch a bemo to Puyung and hire a cidomo (horse and cart).

SURANADI

Whilst in a trance, a fervent Hindu saint supposedly founded this little village in the foothills east of Mataram and to celebrate the great event a Balinese temple was built at the source of a mountain spring. Inside the Pura Suranadi are some ornate carvings, several mischievous monkeys and lots of exceedingly holy eels. You can take walks in the vicinity and admire fine views of the hills and rice fields. Visitors wanting a longer stay can reside in a comfortable hotel with a restaurant and swimming pool opposite the temple.

Location: 18km east of Mataram. Bemos run from the Bertais bus terminal in Cakranegara to Narmada, from where you must take another bemo to Surana.i.

TETEBATU

This mountain retreat at the foot of Gunung Rinjani is the place to relax

SENGGIGI BEACH

Lombok's best-known beaches cannot compare with those at Nusa Dua or Sanur, but they do offer sheltered bays for swimming, white sands and, further up the coast, magnificent countryside with palm trees and rugged cliffs. Until a few years ago you might have found yourself almost entirely alone here, but these days a dearth of holiday bungalows, shopping complexes, bars and restaurants have sprung up within walking distance of the Sheraton and Holiday Inn. During the day most people lie out on the beaches or relax by hotel swimming pools and in the late afternoon crowds gather by the nearby temple of Batu Bolong (see the Lombok coastal drive, pages 130–1) to watch the sunset.

Location: Senggigi Beach covers an area 12–18km north of Mataram. Bemos run from Jalan Salah Singkar in Ampenan to Senggigi, taking 40 minutes. Occasionally, you may be able to charter a bemo at Lembar.

SUKARARA

Don't be surprised to find hundreds of

amid tropical rice fields. There are expansive views over southern Lombok as well as fine walks to the surrounding waterfalls and forests. Self-appointed guides will lead you through the rice fields to small Sasak communities, or simply get a map and go yourself. Make sure you get up early though as by lunchtime the mountain has generally clouded over and the village is covered in a thin veil of mist.

Location: 50km east of Mataram. Bemos *depart from Cakranegara's Bertais terminal to the town of Pomotong, from where you must take a* bemo *to Kotaraja and then another* bemo *or* cidomo *to Tetebatu. Better to use your own transport.*

Excursions
Almost everyone who stays in Tetebatu will visit the beautiful Jekut waterfalls situated in the Mount Rinjani National Park, 6km east of town. Either hire a guide for the pleasant 5-hour walk there and back, or follow the road and ask directions at the entrance to the park. Make sure you take water to drink and swimming clothes. Other villages in the vicinity include Kotaraja (4km), Loyok (8km) and Pomotong (12km). Alternatively, follow any of the roads out of Tetebatu and admire some of Lombok's most magnificent countryside.

Children from the rural community of Suranadi

Lombok Coastal Drive

Starting out from the run-down old fishing port of Ampenan, this drive takes you along the beautiful coast to Bangsal and to the tranquil Gili Islands. Spend a day relaxing on Gili Air or take the circular route back via panoramic Baun Pusak. *Allow one day.*

Begin in the town of Ampenan on the west coast of Lombok, a short distance from Mataram.

1 AMPENAN

This old port was once the commercial heart of Lombok and still offers small markets, dusty alleyways and colourful fishing boats as a reminder of happier days. On Jalan Yos Sudarso you will find a Chinese quarter, and further to the north an intriguing little Arab quarter.

From Ampenan take the coastal road which heads north to Senggigi. After 1km, turn left down the small alley next to Dewi Sri Murni Tours. Pura Segara lies 0.5km further on.

2 PURA SEGARA

This little beachside temple looks as if it has come straight out of Bali, with its spirit houses, shrines and joss sticks, but the colourful fishing boats, the decayed shacks and the shy inhabitants are all Lombok.

From Pura Segara, return to the main road and continue north for 7km along the coast. Shortly before you reach Senggigi you will find the Batu Bolong temple situated on a small headland to your left.

3 BATU BOLONG

If you had come to this temple a century ago you might have seen beautiful

Spectacular views over Bangsal from the island of Gili Air

virgins being thrown into the water as offerings for the gods. These days there is only a large hole in the rock (presumably through which they leapt) and the temple jutting out to sea from where there are fine views, especially at sunset.

From Batu Bolong, continue 2km north to Senggigi Beach. You can park outside any of the hotels and wander down to the beach.

4 SENGGIGI

This series of sweeping bays has become Lombok's best-known stretch of coastline, and recently home to countless major hotel chains including a Sheraton and Holiday Inn. Further along the road, however, are several just as magnificent and unspoiled beaches fringed by palm trees and overlooked by steep cliffs.

From Senggigi, continue a further 20km through impressive scenery to Pemenang and then take the left turning to Bangsal.

5 BANGSAL

This little village marks the departure point for the three idyllic offshore islands of Gili Air, Gili Meno and Gili Trawangan. Charter a boat for a quick tour of the islands, or take one of the public boats and spend the night in relative tropical splendour.

From Bangsal, head back to the crossroads at Pemenang and continue straight on the road to Mataram. After 10km you will reach Baun Pusak, situated at the highest point of the road.

6 BAUN PUSAK

Set in magnificent scenery at the end of a stretch of road that climbs past rice fields and lush trees inhabited by monkeys, this mountain pass offers one of the finest panoramas in the whole of Lombok. Climb up the steps next to the coffee shop from where, on a clear day, you can see the coastline and, occasionally, even the distant Gili Islands.

From Baun Pusak continue south for 13km along another fine stretch of road. At the main crossroads turn left for Mataram or continue for 2km to Ampenan.

THE SASAK PEOPLE

Small, dark skinned and clad in sarongs made of beautiful cloth, the Sasaks inhabit some 270 towns and villages throughout the island of Lombok. Like the Balinese, they are mainly farmers, but they also have their own mosques and their own set of rituals.

These days many of the inhabitants produce textiles for the burgeoning tourist industry; others have moved into the larger towns. You can still see glimpses of the old way of life, however, in the beautiful village of Sade and the nearby weaving community of Sukarara.

Left: working the fields
Below: Sasak woman at Kuta Beach market day

Outwardly these people are more reserved than the Balinese. They wear different clothes, drink rice wine and practise weaving. Traditionally, too, the houses are distinct, built square or rectangular from bamboo and wood.

According to the most recent census, Lombok's Sasaks make up some 80 per cent of the island's 2.5 million population. They are also Lombok's original inhabitants, practising a form of Islam that is based on animism and ancestor worship.

GETTING AWAY FROM IT ALL

'Life is so simple and primitive in the warmth of the tropics. A bunch of bananas, a basket of steamed rice, and a leaf full of betel comprise the necessaries and luxuries of daily living.'

E.R. SCIDMORE,
Java, The Garden of the East (1899)

INTRODUCTION
Java, Bali and Lombok offer some wonderful places to escape to, and there are plenty of opportunities to explore islands further afield as well. Many of the trips can be done with minimal planning, others demand a little more time and effort but can be equally rewarding. Before deciding what you want to do, check on weather conditions and availability of transport. If in doubt seek advice from the tourist office in Jakarta (tel: (021) 314 2067) or Denpasar (tel: (0361) 222 387).

MOUNTAINS AND VOLCANOES
Indonesia has mountains and volcanoes to suit every taste, from gentle inclines to erupting giants. To check on conditions, always consult the locals before you go. Be sure to take warm clothes and on the tougher approaches a guide as well. Finally, if it is clear views that you are after, it is imperative to get to the summit at dawn, which means climbing at night with the use of torches.

Gunung Agung
This giant peak, soaring 3,142m high, is the tallest mountain on Bali and offers fantastic views. You will have to be fit to get to the top though as the tough 5-hour hike involves a series of steep paths, slippery slopes and narrow ridges. Make sure you take a guide as paths lead off in all directions, plus a thick sweater, food, water and bags of enthusiasm.
Location: approach from Pura Besakih, 60km northeast of Denpasar. Bemos operate via KlungKung (22km). Simple accommodation is available near the temple. Enquire locally for guides.

Gunung Batur
Towering over beautiful Lake Batur is Bali's fourth highest mountain and one of the most spectacular points from which to view sunrise. You can climb it in 2 hours with good shoes (take a torch if you attempt it at night), and ideally a guide who will take along breakfast. By setting off at around 3am from the village of Kedisan you should be at the top well before dawn. For information or guides, enquire at the local guesthouses.
Location: 4km east of Penelokan, near the village of Kedisan. Regular buses run from Denpasar and Kuta. Accommodation is available.

Gunung Bromo (Mount Bromo), see pages 72–3.

Gunung Merapi
One of Java's most formidable volcanoes, it last erupted in June 1998, so check locally for conditions before setting out. Mount Merapi is also one of Java's most rewarding, if difficult, climbs taking 4 or 5 hours to get to the summit and a further 3 hours to descend. For the easier approach, start from Selo just to the north of Merapi where guides are available. Take plenty of warm clothes and a torch. It is also possible to climb from Kaliurang, although this is a considerably tougher route taking a minimum of 6 hours to reach the summit.
Location: Selo lies 50km west of Surakarta (Solo), in Central Java. Buses leave for Kartusuro from the Umbunharjo bus station off Jalan Veteran. Change again for Boyolali and catch a bemo to Selo. Accommodation is available at Selo.

Gunung Rinjani
Dominating the whole of Lombok, this magnificent 3,726m mountain is the

To enjoy clear views of the mountains you must climb at dawn

second highest in Indonesia outside Irian Jaya. To climb it, you will need at least 2 days and considerable amounts of energy. Best to start in the town of Bayan, ascending via Senaru and returning the same way. Although there are now plenty of travellers doing the trip alone, you are strongly advised to take a local guide who can organise food and sleeping bags. For alternative and more testing routes, enquire locally.

Location: northern Lombok. Bemos leave from Cakranegara's Bertais terminal for Bayan, where you have to catch another bemo to Senaru. Basic accommodation is available at Senaru.

Distinguished sea-faring vessels in the port of Sulawesi

ISLAND HOPPING

To explore some of the dazzling islands that make up the Indonesian archipelago all you need is a handful of money, a grand sense of humour and lots of time. Boats leave from literally hundreds of ports, making their way by river and by sea to some of the least visited parts of the country.

Note, however, that schedules change from day to day and month to month, the only certainty being that boats leave when you least expect them to. The best season for island hopping is between May and October. During the rainy season it can be wet and rough, and extremely unpleasant.

For details about the national shipping line on Java, contact Pelni, Jalan Angkasa Kemayoran 18, Jakarta (tel: 424 1963).

For Bali, contact the Pelni office on Jalan Pelabuhan Benoa, Denpasar (tel: 228 962). For Lombok, contact the Pelni office at Jalan Industri 1, Ampenan (tel: 27212).

Sailing to Sumatra

Most passengers wishing to cross from Jakarta to Sumatra simply take a flight from Soekarno-Hatta Airport. Those looking for a more enjoyable alternative, however, can take the weekly Pelni ship from Jakarta's port of Tanjung Priok to Padang (and back). It's a relatively luxurious boat, with hot water and a restaurant, and you should make a reservation before departure. Tickets can be bought at Pelni's Jakarta office: Jalan Angkasa Kemayoran 18 (tel: 424 1963).

Visitors preferring a cheaper and

more authentic means of transport can take a boat from the island of Tanjung Pinang (off the coast of Singapore) to Pekanbaru in Central Sumatra. Generally it leaves three or four times a week, is typically crowded, hot, and when it rains, wet. Take food and reckon on a 36-hour journey, although as with everything in Sumatra, prepare for the exception.

Island chain
Beyond Bali, Java and Lombok lie countless other islands, many of them less than an hour away by air, others a few days by cargo boat. Some offer jungles, others uninhabited mountains, strange tribes and beautiful coloured lakes. Many are so small that they are not even named.

A Pelni passenger boat leaves every 2 weeks or so from Surabaya in East Java to the port of Lembar on Lombok and from there to Ujung Pandang (Sulawesi), Bima (Sumbawa), Wainngapu (Sumba) and Ende (Flores). Other passenger or cargo boats depart with far greater regularity between Lombok and the outer islands. For a real taste of adventure drop by the old port of Sunda Kelapa in Jakarta and try and get a passage on one of the old Bugis schooners that still occasionally make the voyage to the islands of Flores and Timor. You may have to sleep on the deck or work your passage, but you are likely to have a memorable experience.

Five-star cruising
Looking for a cruise without any hassle? These days there are plenty of opportunities, with good food, white wine and even hot showers. On Bali, for a short trip, take the Bali Hai Cruise

aboard a fully air-conditioned 34m luxury catamaran that accommodates 300 passengers and offers a range of full-day trips and sunset dinner cruises to the island of Nusa Lembongan leaving from Benoa Harbour, Bali Hai Pier (tel: 0361 720331).

If you have more time to spare and want comfort without the hassles, take the *Oceanic Odyssey*, a luxury cruise ship owned by Spice Island Cruises which goes east from Bali to Lombok, Sumbawa and Komodo. For further details contact Spice Island Cruises in Bali (tel: 0361 286283).

Slow boats off the Java coast, in Baluran National Park

FLORA AND FAUNA

At dusk, the sweet smell of frangipani mingles with the scented odours of Jepun trees and hibiscus. Great boughs of bougainvillaea cascade in sheer tropical splendour alongside scented capoka and dozens of varieties of orchids dazzle the senses.

On Java, Bali and Lombok alone you will find over 5,000 species of plants, plus more than 500 types of birds, from the white-bellied sea eagle and the olive-backed sunbird to the small blue kingfisher, as well as the famous Rothschild's mynah, Bali's

only endemic bird.

Despite massive deforestation and the rape of large areas of parkland, you can still spot a multitude of animals, from the long-tailed macaques to wild pigs and silvered leaf monkeys. Even leopards have been reported on the crowded island of Java, although these days sightings are exceptionally rare.

The best places to experience nature at its most beautiful are in the Javanese national parks of Ujung Kulon and Baluran, or at the Bali Barat

Left: rainforest, Java
Far left (main):
Baluran National
Park
Far left (inset): lotus
flowers
Below: wild flowers,
Lombok
Bottom: East Java

National Park. But wander away from
the towns, the cities and the endless
rice fields and you will catch a
glimpse not necessarily of tigers, but
of brightly coloured flowers and lush
countryside – remnants of one of the
earth's greatest tropical paradises.

NATIONAL PARKS

Nestling amid the hills and forests of Java and Bali lie a handful of fine national parks, although you may have to travel a considerable distance to get to them. Some are renowned as the homes of the few remaining Javanese rhinoceros, others are simply pleasant places to walk in. Before leaving Jakarta, contact the PHPA office on Jalan Merdeka Selatan 8–9 Blok G to enquire about permits and accommodation. Bring binoculars if you have them and a lot of patience. Note that in the wet season some of the parks may be inaccessible.

Baluran Taman Nasional

One of the greatest attractions of the Baluran National Park is its relative accessibility. The park lies just 37km from Ketapang, the main crossing point from Java to Bali, covering an area of 250 sq km and dominated by Mount Baluran. Although large areas of the park are arid and savannah-like, at dusk especially you can see herds of deer, wild pig and buffalo. Bring food if you intend to stay overnight and sign in at the main visitors' centre (see page 72).

Meru Betiri Taman Nasional

The Meru Betiri Reserve lies at the end of a potholed road that crosses half a dozen rivers, and forest and rubber plantations. Until the 1940s, this was a popular area for spotting the small Javanese tiger. These days, if you are lucky, you may come across black

Large tracts of forest and savannah are found at Baluran Taman Nasional

panthers, leopards and even turtles. There is basic accommodation in Sukamade village (Turtle Beach) or contact the PHPA Guesthouse at Rajegwesin village.

Location: 70km west of Genteng in East Java. Buses leave from the Banjarsari terminal in Banyuwangi for Genteng, where you have to take an irregular bus or hitch a lift to Sukamade.

Pulau Dua Bird Sanctuary

Ornithologists will have a field day in this sanctuary on Dua Island, which lies in Banten Bay off the coast of West Java. One of Indonesia's best-known bird parks, Pulau Dua boasts more than 50 species of bird including ibises and egrets. Get there between April and August to see it at its liveliest, and take food and water.

Location: 100km west of Jakarta. Buses depart from Jakarta's Kalideres station for Serang, from where you must catch a bemo to Banten. From the Karanghantu harbour in Banten, it is a half-hour boat ride. Currently there is a guesthouse, but no restaurant.

Taman Nasional Bali Barat (Bali Barat National Park)

Once upon a time visitors would have come across tigers in this sparsely populated region of Bali. These days the animals you are most likely to see in the 200 sq km of coastal forest are long-tailed macaques, barking and sambar deer, or, if you are really lucky, the Rothschild's mynah, which is Bali's only endemic bird. Several trails start out from Labuhan Lalang, 15km from the visitors' centre. Alternatively, take the delightful boat trip to Menjangan Island, a 30-minute trip from the mainland. To arrange a guide and accommodation go

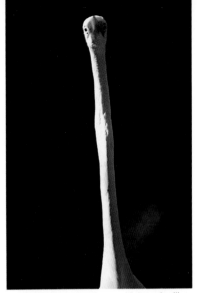

The opportunity of seeing rare bird species like the egret is the real attraction of Pulau Dua

to the visitors' centre, which is situated on the main road 3km from Gilimanuk.

Location: 134km northwest of Denpasar. Buses leave from Denpasar's Ubung terminal for Gilimanuk, taking 3 to 4 hours. Ask to be dropped off at the park headquarters.

Ujung Kulon Taman Nasional

Lying in the westernmost corner of Java, hemmed in by the Indian Ocean, this magnificent national park boasts several of the rare Javanese rhinoceros as well as leopards, gibbons, long-tailed macaques and herds of oxen. To get there, you can either catch a boat from Labuhan to Peucang island, which takes 5 or 6 hours, or arrange a tour. Make reservations and obtain a permit at the PHPA office on Jalan Perintis Kemerdekaan 43 in Labuhan.

Location: Labuhan is situated 120km west of Jakarta. Buses leave Jakarta's Kalideres station. Boats leave from Labuhan for Peucang Island twice weekly.

Collecting firewood in Java's central hills

HILL STATIONS

When the Dutch occupied Indonesia they not only constructed fine buildings and grand open squares, but also charming mountain retreats so they could escape the heat of the tropics. Many of these resorts offer unsurpassed views of distant volcanoes; others hot springs where you can rest your weary limbs. If you visit the hill resorts at weekends rooms may be hard to come by and the places inundated by crowds. At other times you may find yourself almost alone, but for the trees and bubbling streams.

Kaliurang

This pretty little resort, 900m up on Merapi's southern slope, is a fine weekday getaway with waterfalls, swimming pools and cool mountain air.

If you are here during the dry season, get up early to catch the spectacular sunrise and clear views of Mount Merapi. More active visitors can climb to Merapi's summit, although for your own safety you are advised to take a guide (see page 59).

Location: 24km north of Yogyakarta in Central Java. Regular buses leave from the main Umbunharjo terminal on Jalan Kemerdekan, taking 90 minutes.

Sarangan

This little town lies at the end of one of the most spectacular stretches of road on the whole of Java. Here, on the panoramic slopes of Mount Lawu, visitors can explore the crater and nearby waterfall, go speed-boating on the small lake as well as fishing and horse-back riding on fine-bred horses.

Not surprisingly, the Dutch took a liking to the place and built mountain villas commanding fine views of the area. If you come at weekends, be sure to have reserved a room. At other times of the year it's a perfect place to soothe nerves frayed by days of sightseeing in Solo and Yogyakarta.

Location: 55km east of Surakarta (Solo) in Central Java. Buses run from the Tirtonadi terminal on Jalan Jend Yani to Tawangmangu, from where you can catch a crowded bemo for the last 30-minute stretch.

Selekta

You will find all the pine trees and bubbling streams that you can dream of above this up-market hill resort, along with orchards, strawberries and fine mountain scenery. In the centre of town there is a recreational centre, built by the Dutch and containing a delightful rock garden and swimming pool.

Location: 23km from Malang in East Java. Buses leave from Malang's central bus station on Jalan Haryono. Alternatively, rent a taxi.

Tawangmangu

Dutch villas and simple *losmen* (bungalows) dot the hills around Tawangmangu, on the slopes of Gunug Lawu, which offers fine walks and mountain scenery. As a pleasant side trip, visit Sarangan (14km), or head west to the famous 15th-century Candi Sukuh, built during the Majapahit empire then mysteriously abandoned.

Location: 42km from Solo in Central Java. Buses leave from the Tirtonadi station on Jalan Jend Yani, taking 90 minutes.

The lush, tropical foliage around Jekut Waterfalls, near beautiful Tetebatu

Tetebatu

Surrounded by rice fields and offering magnificent views of Mount Rinjani, this is Lombok's most popular inland retreat. There are walks to a nearby waterfall, paddies where you can wander for days, as well as cooler mountain air (see page 129).

Tretes

This town in East Java is renowned for its popular hill resort and for its brothels. Nature lovers follow hiking trails around Mount Arjuna and Mount Welirang, visit waterfalls or go horse riding and swimming. Those in search of other activities can enjoy a no less varied menu.

Location: 55km south of Surabaya. Take the bus heading for Malang and ask to be dropped off at Pandakan. From here you can catch a bemo to Tretes.

OTHER ACTIVITIES

Birdwatching
Javanese kingfishers, blue-tailed bee-eaters, Sunda minnivets and white-breasted woodswallows are just some of the birds that can be seen on Java, Bali and Lombok, so long as you have the time and the patience. Good places to spot them include the Pula Dua Bird Sanctuary near Banten in West Java (see page 141), the Baluran National Park in East Java (see page 140) and the steep cliffs on the island of Nusa Penida (see page 88). For those wanting to observe birds the easy way, visit the Taman Burung (Bird Park) at Taman Mini Indonesia in east Jakarta (see page 39) or the Ragunan Zoo in south Jakarta (see pages 32–3) and the excellent two-hectare Bird Park in Bali (see page 161).

Cycling
Taking a bicycle around Java, Bali or Lombok may be hot, hard work, but it is a good way to see the countryside. Bicycles can now be hired in Kuta, Ubud and from many small *losmen* and guesthouses throughout the country.

Diving
There are plenty of opportunities for diving in Indonesia, ranging from Pulau Seribu (Thousand Islands, see page 48) a short distance from Jakarta, to Pulau Menjangan in the Bali Barat National Park (see page 141) and the increasingly popular Gili Islands on Lombok (see page 124). Keen divers also head for Balina Beach (see page 84) and Tulamben on Bali (see page 91), where you can rent gear. For enquiries, contact Oceana Dive Centre, Sanur Beach (tel: 288 652) which organises diving vacations.

Motorbiking
Although motorbiking is not popular on Java, on Bali almost everyone seems to use one. Bikes are generally 75cc and can be rented from anywhere in Kuta, Denpasar or Ubud. Most visitors tour the island from Kuta, and you can take a motorbike over to Lombok on the ferry. Wherever you go, however, remember to lock the bike securely, obtain insurance and, most importantly, drive carefully as accidents are common.

Diving off Benoa

DIRECTORY

> *The dominating fact about the islands is that, like Croesus and John D. Rockefeller, Jr., they are rich. They are the Big Loot of Asia.*
>
> **JOHN GUNTHER,**
>
> *Inside Asia*
> (1939)

Shopping

*F*rom beautiful wooden carvings to colourful batik and the eye-catching Wayang Kulit shadow puppets, Indonesia offers a bewildering choice of shopping opportunities. You can stock up on hand-woven textiles, musical instruments or even vast demonic stone carvings – although you may have trouble transporting these home.

On Bali, and especially around the village of Ubud, there is a wealth of artistic talent and this is reflected in the paintings, sculptures and silverwork on sale. On Lombok, beautiful terracotta jars made by the Sasaks can be found all over the island, as well as woven baskets. Indeed, the only thing that is both expensive and in short supply in Indonesia is electronic goods, so if that is what you are after, arrange a stop-over in neighbouring Singapore.

A way of life
Going shopping in Indonesia is not so much a necessity as a source of enjoyment. Prices can be as flexible as the attitude of the buyer and time an irrelevant commodity.

To see that attitude at its most prevalent you must visit the markets, but even in the shops and boutiques, where prices tend to be fixed, you will find a charm and helpfulness that is hard to come by in most European countries.

Don't buy the first thing that you set your eyes on though. A better approach is to spend a few days looking around to get an idea of what is on offer. That way you will avoid amassing too many second-rate tourist articles and should be better equipped to negotiate good prices.

Value for money
For cheap and cheerful items, but often of inferior quality, drop by the markets in the major towns. Next up the scale are the small studios and art galleries specialising in batik, woodcarvings or paintings. In Ubud and in Yogyakarta especially these studios provide greater choice and lower prices as they do not employ middlemen.

For comfort, take your pick of the modern shopping plazas that now abound in the big cities, especially in

Bird cages for sale in Pasar Ngasem, Yogyakarta

Sunday market in Kuta, on the island of Lombok

Jakarta. At Sarinah Department Store, on Jalan Thamrin, there is one of the widest choices of handicrafts in the whole country. Finally, at the top of the scale, are the larger hotels which sell arts and crafts from all over Indonesia.

As a rule, no matter where you are, always try to bargain by offering a considerably lower price than is advertised. At worst you will get a look of bemusement, at best a considerable discount. One last piece of advice: beware the ubiquitous touts, who will offer to take you shopping free of charge. They may not be getting money out of you directly, but they will certainly be paid a 10–20 per cent commission, which will be added on to the articles you buy.

MARKETS

Street markets can be found in towns and villages throughout Java, Bali and Lombok, selling everything from exotic fruits to water taps and from ancient magazines to fake Levi jeans. In some markets you can feast yourself on deep-fried dragonfly, stuffed duck or even pigs' balls. In others you will see beautiful woven baskets, sweet-smelling flowers or carved wooden monkeys. For antiques and imitation trinkets, Pasar Triwindu in Surakarta (see page 69), or Jalan Surabaya in Jakarta (see page 33) are worth a browse. For something more flighty, ask for the Pasar Ngasem, or bird market, in Yogyakarta (see page 54). Wherever you go you will find a rich tapestry of life second to none; take a camera and lots of film, you won't be disappointed. To find a market simply ask for *pasar*, and for the night market, *pasar malam*.

WHAT TO BUY

ANTIQUES

Renowned for its delightful antique masks, its *krises* (ceremonial daggers), and much prized betel nut sets, Indonesia is acquiring an even bigger reputation for its fakes. Unless you are a real expert or are content to buy an imitation, take the claims of any shop owner with a pinch of salt, especially in Jakarta's antique market on Jalan Surabaya, and concentrate on buying some more worthy article.

BRONZE AND BRASS CASTING

Bronze bells, musical instruments and cast statues are a speciality of the little town of Klungkung on Bali, but there are plenty of similar articles available in all the main cities on Java. Big tourist shops will have the widest choice of items and for a price they will be able to arrange shipment of the articles back to Europe.

CERAMICS AND PORCELAIN

Since the art was introduced from China more than 700 years ago, potters have been turning out fine ceramics and porcelain in Indonesia ever since. You'll find the most beautiful terracotta pots on Lombok and it is worth keeping an eye out for old Han dynasty pottery, T'ang ceramics and even choice Ming period porcelain.

PAINTINGS

Paintings on Bali are almost as abundant as rice fields, especially in the area around Ubud which has become the cultural capital of the island. You will

Local handmade baskets in Kuta village, Lombok

find plenty of the soporific village scenes, cock-fights and festivals that are churned out for undemanding tourists, but also some of the country's finest paintings that combine the traditional Balinese style with the influence of foreign artists like Walter Spies and Rudolf Bonnet. To get an idea of the quality, check out the Museum Neka in Ubud (see page 110) and when shopping for paintings, remember to be extremely selective.

SILVERWORK

If Ubud's *pièce de résistance* is its paintings, then Celuk's reputation is based on its silverwork (see page 101). Artisans in this little village run up bracelets, pendants and rings – all at relatively low prices. Elsewhere on Bali, and even Java, you'll find plenty of other ornate pieces, often decorated with filigree.

STONE CARVINGS

Most people take one look at the monstrous weight of these stone figures and move on to something more manageable. But these days, the more commercially minded masons will arrange to have them shipped anywhere in the world. To see what's on offer, check out the village of Batubulan (see page 100) on Bali. Here you can watch the artists at work and even order your own tailor-made stone demon.

TEXTILES

One of the finest of all Indonesia's arts, batik, which is cloth painted and dyed with bright colours, makes the perfect gift. The best places for batik include Yogyakarta and Surakarta in Central Java, as well as Ubud on Bali, but almost everywhere you will find beautiful silks and colourful sarongs – and occasionally even double Ikat, the finely woven and

To purchase the best stone carvings visit Batubulan on Bali

dyed cloth made in several Bali Aga villages.

WOODCARVINGS

Spectacular woodcarvings are a Balinese speciality, and nowhere more so than around Ubud and in the village of Mas (see page 114). Collectors' items range from teak fruit bowls to sandalwood statuettes and magnificent Garuda birds. There's no shortage of hideous wooden elephants and cheap, lurid carvings either, so be selective and shop around.

WOVEN GOODS

If a woven basket made from rattan is what you are after, then Lombok is the place to go, with a variety and price second to none. There are plenty of similar articles on Bali too, although at higher prices.

Jalan Surabaya, Jakarta

WHERE TO BUY

Wherever you go in Indonesia you will find beautiful hand-made items, carved wooden statues or pearl-studded bracelets. However, remember to be selective and bargain hard.

Below is a list of popular shops in the main centres. If these look expensive, simply check out others in the vicinity.

JAKARTA
Antiques
Archipelago Treasures, *Jalan Kemang Raya 90 (tel: 798 1359)*.
Grand Gallery, *Jalan Manggar Dua Raya, Grand Boutique Centre, Building 20 (tel: 612 2181)*.
NV Garuda Arts and Antiques, *Jalan Majapahit 12 (tel: 342 712)*.
Revin Art Shop Curio, *Jalan Ciputat Raya 88A (tel: 742 0066)*.
Shinta Art Antique Primitif, *Jalan Kebon Sirih Timur Dalam 5E (tel: 314 0258)*.

Handicrafts
Chic Mart, *Jalan Kamang Raya 55 (tel: 719 7813)*.
Dharma Mulia Gallery, *Jalan Ciputat Raya 50 (tel: 749 2850)*.
Irian Art & Gift Shop, *Jalan Pasa*

Baru 16A (tel: 348 3422).
Ita Nusa Traditional Arts, *Ground Floor, Atlantica Building, Jalan Kunungan Barat 7 (tel: 525 1655)*.
Pasar Seni, *Jaya Ancol Dreamland* Art market for bargains in shellcraft, Balinese woodcarvings, brassware, leather goods.

Jewellery and silverware
Dee Chan Jewellers, *Plaza Indonesia, Level 1 170–171 Jalan Thamrin 11 (tel: 310 7582)*.
Madonna Jewellery, *Pondok Indah Mall 30, Jalan Metro Pondok Indah (tel: 750 6843)*.
Perlini's Silver, *Plaza Senayan, Level 1, Shop K (tel: 572 5388)*.

Silk, cotton and batik
Batik Keris, *Jalan Kebon Sirih 111–115 (tel: 331 689)*.
GKBI, *Indonesia Government Batik Co-operative, Jalan Jend Sudirman 28 (tel: 571 3434)*.
Semar Batik, *Jalan Tomang Raya 54 (tel: 566 7568)*.

Shopping centres
For fixed-price shopping under one roof, these centres offer a huge selection of woodcarvings, batiks, puppets, silks, pottery, etc.
Pasaraya, *Jalan Iskandarsyah Raya 11/2 Blok M (tel: 726 0170)*.
Plaza Indonesia, *Jalan Thamrin Cav 28–30 (tel: 390 3728)*.
Sarinah Department Store, *Jalan Thamrin 11 (tel: 323 008)*.

YOGYAKARTA
Antiques
Ancient Arts, *Jalan Tirtodipuran 30*.

Ardijanto's, *Jalan Magelag, Km 5.8 (tel: 562 777)*.

Batik and cotton
Batik Keris, *Jalan Ahmad Yani 104 (tel: 512 492)*.
Batik Indah, *Jalan Tirtodipuran 6A (tel: 375 209)*.
Batik Juwita, *Jalan Ahmad Yani 64 (tel: 513 981)*.
Batik Plentong, *Jalan Tirtodipuran 28 (tel: 373 777)*.
Batik Winotosastro, *Jalan Tirtodipuran 54 (tel: 375 218)*.

Intricate textile design, Yogyakarta

Handicrafts
Art Shop Naga, *Jalan Malioboro 61*.
Tunas Asri, *Jalan Kasongan (tel: 370 523)*.
Yogyakarta Craft Centre,
Jalan Marsda Adisucipito.

Silver and jewellery
M D Silver Work, *Jalan Keboan, Kota Gede (tel: 515 323)*.
Moeljo's Silver, *Jalan Menteri Supeno UH XII/1 (tel: 588 042)*.
Silver Work & Art Shop, *Jalan Kemangan 69, Kota Gede (tel: 561 877)*.
Tom's Silver, *Jalan Ngeksi Gondo 60, Kota Gede (tel: 372 818)*.

Shopping centre
Malioboro Shopping Mall, next to the Ibis Hotel, has a range of handicraft shops.

DENPASAR
Art shops
Besakih Art Shop, *Jalan Surapati 20 (tel: 222 879)*.
Mega Gallery of Arts, *Jalan Raya Gianyar, Tohpati (tel: 225 120)*.
Pelangri Art Shop, *Jalan Gajah Mada 54 (tel: 224 570)*.
Timur Art Shop, *Jalan Legian Kuta 396B (tel: 751 537)*.

Handicrafts
Dastra Wood Carving, *Jalan Raya Sukawati 70X, Gianyar (tel: 298 224)*.
Kartika Jaya, *Jalan Raya Tuban (tel: 753 430)*.
Nogo Bali Ikat Centre, *Jalan Danau Tamblingan 98, Sanur (tel: 288 765)*.
Tapir Exclusive Souvenir and Gift Shop, *Matahari-Kuta Square, Jalan Pantai Kuta-Bali (tel: 757 593)*.

Popular batik, Yogyakarta

Entertainment

*Y*ou need never be bored on Java or Bali. Whether it's nightclubs in Jakarta or Sanur, shadow puppets in Yogyakarta, or Legong dances in Ubud, there is enough on offer to keep everybody happy. Many discothèques stay open until the early hours of the morning and even traditional entertainment like the Wayang Kulit shadow puppets can last until late at night. For something a little different, there are night markets, *gamelan* orchestras and sometimes illegal cock-fights. Most hotels will provide information on local events; or refer to the entertainment section of the local papers.

BARS

Visitors expecting to find an equivalent to neighbouring Bangkok's nightlife may not be entirely disappointed. While Indonesia does not have the go-go bars of Thailand, it does have the drinking establishments and massage parlours. Most of these are to be found in Jakarta's China Town, although Yogyakarta and even Surabaya can boast more than a handful, and on Bali's Kuta Beach you will find almost as many bars as there are on the rest of the archipelago put together. Only on Lombok is the bar scene almost non-existent, except for those in the big luxurious hotels at Senggigi Beach and among the plethora of little guesthouses on Kuta Beach and the Gili Islands.

For drama and violence Indonesian films are in a class of their own

Jakarta is the home to a mind-boggling range of nightclubs

CINEMAS

Cinemas abound in Jakarta and in all the major towns, although generally they show local films with no English subtitles. Any Western films that do make it tend to be heavily censored. For details of programmes, check the local newspaper or ask in your hotel. Also, while in Jakarta, check out the British Council, Jalan Jend Sudirman 57 (tel: 587 4411) and the Alliance Française, Jalan Salemba Rayes 25 (tel: 390 8580), both of which schedule weekly films.

COCKTAIL LOUNGES

All the luxury hotels have cocktail lounges where you can while away the time by a pool-side terrace or in a lush garden setting. Many hotels even host jazz bands or local musicians. For a glimpse of the real Java or Bali, however, you must leave these classy establishments, wander along the beaches or down the main streets and explore some of the places frequented by the local people. These will not only be cheaper, but they will give you a feel of what the real Indonesia is all about.

DISCOTHÈQUES AND LIVE MUSIC

People may dismiss Indonesia as a musical backwater, but Jakarta and the major resort areas not only have some of the biggest and most modern dance floors in the developing world, but some of the trendiest people on them. There is now a Hard Rock Café in Jakarta and Bali, countless discos, as well as several excellent venues for local bands. Elsewhere, new and exciting nightclubs are springing up every month. Entry to nightclubs is relatively cheap by Western standards, with a free drink often thrown in with the price. Expect to pay more at weekends.

KARAOKE LOUNGES

Although relatively new, karaoke lounges in Jakarta are already becoming big business. If singing along to a video is your idea of fun, there are plenty of places to choose from. Outside the major towns, however, karaoke is likely to mean little more than music in a massage parlour.

WHERE TO GO

JAKARTA
Cultural performances
Bharata Theatre
Traditional *wayang orang* dance drama performed nightly, except Saturday, between 8pm and 11pm.
Jalan Pasar Senen 15.

Sampan Bujana Sentra
Theatre restaurant and nightly cultural show.
Jalan Teuku Cikditiro II 1, Jakarta Pusat 10350 (tel: 392 3930).

Taman Ismail Marzuki
Regular cultural shows and performances. Check newspaper for details.
Jalan Cikini Raya 73, Menteng (tel: 315 4087).

Taman Mini-Indonesia
Sunday performances of drama, dance and music, taking place between 9am and 2pm.
10km southeast of Jakarta (see page 39).

Wayang Museum
Displays of shadow puppets every Sunday between 10am and noon. Telephone for details.
Jalan Pintu Besar Utara (tel: 692 9560).

Discos
Bengkel Nightpark, *Lot 14, Kawasan Terpadu Surdirman, Jalan Sendirman Kav 52 (tel: 515 5008).*
Ebony, *Kuningan Plaza, Jalan HR Rasuna Said (tel: 525 3775).*
Pitstop, *Sari Pan Pacific Hotel, Jalan Thamrin 6 (tel: 323 707).*
Stardust, *Jayakarta Tower Hotel, Jalan Hayam Wuruk (tel: 629 4408).*
Tanamur, *Jalan Abang Timur 14 (tel: 380 5233).*
Zanzibar, *Victoria 2nd floor, Jalan Sultan Hasanuddin, Kebayoran Baru (tel: 725 5527).*

Pubs
Fabrice's World Music Bar
Latin bands and salsa music.
Jalan Jend Sudirman Pintu V (tel: 570 3063).

Green Pub
Live music combined with Mexican food.
Djakarta Theatre Building, Jalan Thamrin (tel: 315 9332).

Hard Rock Café
Popular western bar/restaurant.
Jalan Thamrin (tel: 390 3365).

Jaya Pub
Live music and pub food.
Jaya Building, Jalan Thamrin No 12 (tel: 312 5633).

O'Reiley's Pub
Top-class hotel pub with beer on tap and band.
Grand Hyatt Jakarta, Jalan Thamrin 28–30 (tel: 390 1234).

The Tavern Pub
Live music and food.
Hotel Aryaduta, Jalan Prapratan (tel: 380 4777).

Shows
International Hailai Club
Las Vegas-style floor show, dance troupes, restaurant and disco.
Hailai Building, Jalan Lodan, Ancol (tel: 654 9868).

Taman Ismail Marzuki
Cultural and performing arts centre of Jakarta.
Jalan Cikini Raya 73, Menteng (tel: 315 4087).

YOGYAKARTA
Cultural Performances
Agastya Art Institute
Wayang Kulit performance every day from 3–5pm.
Jalan Gedongkiwo.

Ambar Budaya Craft Centre
Open: normally every night 8–10.30pm
but check with Tourist Office.
Jalan Adisucipto.
Arjuna Plaza Hotel (French Grill)
Wayang Golek performance on
Saturdays from 7–9pm.
Jalan Mangkubumi 48 (tel: 513 063).
Hanoman's Forest
Garden restaurant and traditional shows
of Wayang Golek, Wayang Kulit and
Javanese dance every night from 7–9pm.
Jalan Prawirotaman 9 (tel: 372 528).
Kraton Yogyakarta
Gamelan rehearsals at 10.30am–noon on
Monday and Wednesday; classical dance
rehearsals 10.30am–noon on Sunday.
Alun Alun. Enquire at your hotel.
Prambanan Ramayana Ballet
Open-air performances held at
Prambanan between May to October on
the nights of the full moon.
Tel: (0274) 496 408 for details.
Purawisata Open Air Theatre
Nightly performance from 8–9.30pm of
Ramayana Ballet and optional dinner at
the Gazebo Restaurant (tel: 374 089).
Jalan Brigjen Katamso.
Sono Budoyo Museum
Wayang Kulit performances held every
night, 8pm–10pm.
Northwest side Alun-Alun Lor (tel: 372 390).
Tirta Kencana Open Air Complex
Nightly performance of Ramayana Ballet
from 8pm and optional Indonesian buffet.
Jalan Ring Road Janti (tel: 385 550).

KUTA
Discos
BB Discotheque
Sophisticated disco and bar lounge.
*Hotel Ramada Bintang Bali, Tuban (tel:
753 292)*
Hard Rock Café
Latest hip disco with live music.

A temple celebration, Bali

Jalan Pantai, Kuta (tel: 755 661).
Peanuts
Popular pub/disco.
Jalan Legian, Kuta (tel: 754 149).

SANUR
Classical dance
Buffet dinner and classical dance, Monday,
Wednesday and Sunday at 7.30pm.
Sanur Beach Hotel (tel: 288 011).
Tanjung Sari Hotel
Jalan Tanjung Sari (tel: 288 441).

Discos
Grattan Bar
Nightly live jazz.
*Bali Hyatt Hotel, Jalan Danau Tamblingan
(tel: 288 271).*
Janger
Large disco with loud sound system.
Jalan Danau Tambigan, Sanur (tel: 288 888).
Melodi Music Bar
Cool, sophisticated and pricey.
*Radisson Bali Hotel, Jalan Hang Tuah 46
(tel: 281 781).*

UBUD
Cultural performances
Puri Saren Palace
Performances of the Ramayana, Legong,
Barong and Kecak held most nights of the
week. Enquire locally for details.
*Jalan Raya (next to the junction with
Monkey Forest Road).*

BALINESE FESTIVALS

The first light of dawn sees the locals already hard at work in the little bamboo huts that cluster around Lake Bratan, preparing their offerings of oil and betel nut, putting on their finest silks or simply placing gifts of rice and joss sticks on the ground for the local spirits.

Some of the men will have been up for hours, roasting the suckling pigs and ducks over a fire then placing them on banana leaves.

By 10am the first groups of women leave for the temple, carrying magnificent piles of fruit and other delicacies on trays above their heads. Inside the inner courtyard the offerings are blessed by the priests, sprinkled with holy water and offered up as food for the gods.

The *odalan* festival is not unique to this tiny village. Throughout Bali, similar festivals are held for a temple birthday, for a Hindu holiday, or simply to give thanks to the gods for creating this earthly paradise.

Around the Balinese new year especially, countless

ceremonies take place to celebrate the cleansing of the evil spirits or to honour the goddess of knowledge or the victory of virtue over evil. Some villages have temple ceremonies as thanks for the local rice crop, others to maintain equilibrium between the forces of good and evil.

Ceremonies are also held to celebrate each stage of a child's life from conception to birth through to death

and the joyous release of the spirit.

Whatever the ceremony, you will almost inevitably see great processions

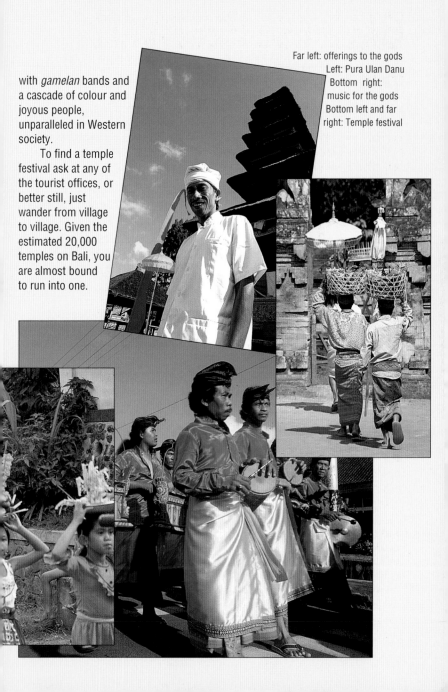

with *gamelan* bands and a cascade of colour and joyous people, unparalleled in Western society.

To find a temple festival ask at any of the tourist offices, or better still, just wander from village to village. Given the estimated 20,000 temples on Bali, you are almost bound to run into one.

Far left: offerings to the gods
Left: Pura Ulan Danu
Bottom right: music for the gods
Bottom left and far right: Temple festival

TRADITIONAL FORMS OF ENTERTAINMENT

Although disco dancing may be all the rage in the big cities, in the smaller towns and villages there are plenty of traditional forms of entertainment – just keep your eyes open and follow the crowds. Details of the larger, most popular events can be obtained from the local tourist authorities.

CLASSICAL DANCES

The most supremely elegant spectacle in Indonesia is not so much a form of entertainment as a work of art. Balinese girls as young as 3 learn the elaborate hand gestures and carefully prescribed movements of the Legong dance, and by the age of 11 or 12 they are said to be too old to perform. Nor are the dances purely traditional. These days there are bumblebee dances, masked dances and frog dances to add to the vintage Barong and Ramayana. You'll find plenty of special dances laid on for tourists, but if you are lucky you may find the real thing being performed at a temple or during a local festival. For information about classical dances ask at your hotel or in any tourist office.

Barong

This popular dance recounts the tale of the virtuous lion-like Barong and his duel with Rangda, the wicked witch. It's filled with colour, with magical battles and even a touch of comedy. Although mainly shown on Bali, you may occasionally find displays put on in Jakarta.

Kecak

The sound of monkeys chattering replaces the *gamelan* orchestra in this modern dance which tells a story from the *Ramayana*. Extremely popular, it is performed by candlelight on Bali and ends with the rescue of Sita by an army of monkeys.

Legong

One of the most beautiful and stylised of all dances, the Legong is performed by girls as young as 8 or 9 wearing elaborate jewelled costumes. The story tells of the kidnapping of Princess Rangkesari by Prince Lasem and her final rejection of his impassioned pleas.

Ramayana

Taken from the popular Hindu epic, this great tale recounts the kidnapping of Sita, the wife of Rama, and her eventual rescue by Hanuman, King of the monkeys. Anyone who is in the vicinity of Prambanan during the months of May and October at full moon will have the chance to witness the most spectacular performance of all.

GAMELAN MUSIC

You will hear the gentle combination of flutes, gongs and kettledrums at weddings, funerals and dances all over Indonesia. The grandest, most elaborate *gamelan* orchestras are made up of as many as 80 instruments. Others are composed of a

Hanuman, king of the monkeys

Scenes from Bali's famous Legong (above) and Ramayana (above right) dances

handful of local musicians playing for the fun of it. *Gamelan* performances take place every Sunday morning in the Kraton in Yogyakarta and in the National Museum in Jakarta. Elsewhere, in restaurants, markets or even hotels, you may find yourself being serenaded.

Tourist dances

WAYANG KULIT

The best place to see these boisterous, leather shadow puppets in action is either in Yogyakarta or in Surakarta, the traditional homes of the Wayang Kulit. But in Ubud, the cultural centre of Bali, in Jakarta and outside in the countryside too, keep your eyes open for one of Indonesia's favourite forms of entertainment.

LOCAL FESTIVITIES
While official Muslim holidays in Indonesia are fixed on the same date every year, many of the Hindu festivals on Bali depend on the position of the moon. To make sure you do not miss them, get hold of the list of local events issued by the tourist office. For details of national holidays, see the Practical Guide, page 185.

Children

*B*eautiful beaches, charming people and long sunny days means Indonesia can be the perfect holiday destination for children. Bali especially caters for the whole family, with a mind-boggling array of activities as well as paddling pools in many of the big hotels, and these days even child-minders can be found.

On Java and Lombok there are also plenty of attractions, although facilities are more basic and the standards of sanitation considerably lower.

Make sure that you pick the dry season to travel (June to August are the best months) and that you allow plenty of time for recuperation and acclimatisation after the long flight. Prior to departure, consult your physician for details of injections and any other necessary precautions that should be taken.

WHAT TO SEE

JAVA: JAKARTA AND SURROUNDINGS
Pasar Burung (Bird Market)
Parrots, doves and other exotic species of birds hang out in bamboo cages in this colourful little market (see page 37).
Pulau Seribu
Sun, sea and sand on dazzling tropical islands all within easy reach of Indonesia's capital city. Bring sun hats and high protection suntan oil (see page 48).
Ragunan Zoo
More than 1,000 animals, including the famous Komodo dragon, make this the perfect place for children and weary parents to escape to. Avoid at weekends (see page 132).

Taman Impian Ancol
Countless attractions for children of all ages, ranging from oceanarium to planetarium and jumping dolphins (see pages 38–9).
Taman Mini-Indonesia
Indonesia in miniature with giant snails, pleasure boats, birds and even a model train to take you around the various cultural sights (see page 39).

CENTRAL AND EAST JAVA
Handicraft Villages (Yogya)
Potters, silver-craftsmen and woodcarvers churn out every kind of work of art in these little villages (see page 55).
Pasar Ngasem Bird Market (Yogya)
Turtle doves, chickens and strange-coloured parrots are enough to tickle the fancy of the toughest toddler (see page 54).
Parangtritis
Escape to the seaside with sand dunes and donkey rides, but beware of big waves and dangerous currents (see page 59).
Sarangan
Cool hills, a crater lake filled with paddle boats and waterfalls nearby make this a pleasant retreat from the heat of the plains (see page 142).
Surabaya Zoo
About 500 species of animals and exotic birds, from flying squirrels to dwarf buffalo, can be observed here (see page 71).

BALI
Bali Bird Park
Over 250 bird species sure to delight children of all ages (see page 144).
Bali Festival Park
Huge theme park with plenty of activities for all the family (see page 82).
Goa Lawah
Bats by the million live in this legendary cave situated opposite the seafront (see page 85).
Monkey Forest (Ubud)
Hundreds of monkeys scramble up trees and demand to be fed with peanuts and bananas. Be very careful, however, as they can be vicious (see page 117).

A young Sasak weaver

Nusa Dua
Bali's most exclusive beach area with sea, sand, swimming pools and security (see page 93).
Sanur Beach
Fine beaches and a touch of luxury away from the crowds (see pages 82–3).
Waterbom Park and Spa
Water slides, pools, water volleyball in beautiful surroundings. Free entry for under-5s (see page 78).

LOMBOK
Sade Village
Thatched houses and rice farmers, with weavers merrily churning out tourist items (see page 128).
Senggigi Beach
Sun, sea and sand with good hotels and boat trips in the vicinity (see page 127).
Tetebatu
Cool mountain air, rice fields and horses and carts make this Lombok's perfect inland base for short walks and tours (see pages 128–9).

A smile for everyone

Sport

*I*n the heat of Indonesia's midday sun you would be foolish to exert yourself too much. Still, there are plenty of opportunities for golfing, swimming and sailing that will provide both relaxation and exercise. And for the less energetic, there is no shortage of spectator sports, from bull racing to scorpion fighting. For details of current sporting events enquire at the relevant tourist offices.

BULL RACING

You may have to visit the island of Madura to witness this exciting spectator sport (see page 75), but *aficionados* claim that it is definitely worth the trouble. The race involves two beautifully decorated bulls hurtling down a football pitch faster than Carl Lewis, tagging along 13-year-old boys on planks. There's plenty of excitement, too, from the bulls who are fed rice wine to lift their spirits and psyched up by the sounds of a *gamelan* orchestra. Competitions are held between August and September but enquire locally as locations vary from day to day.

COCK-FIGHTING

Bali is the place where you are most likely to encounter this activity. Although the government has banned cock-fights, the Balinese flout the laws with contempt. Have no doubts about the barbarous nature of this 'sport'; specially trained and manicured cocks attack one another with pecker and claws carrying razor blades in a raucous flutter of feathers that may only last a matter of seconds. Numerous observers place bets on the outcome.

DIVING, see Getting Away From it All, page 144.

GOLF

One of Indonesia's newly discovered sports, golf is fast becoming one of the country's biggest attractions. The scenery is second to none, courses are of a good standard, green rates are relatively low and caddies easy to come by. If you intend to play at weekends, however, book in advance. Courses within easy reach of the capital are the Jakarta Golf Club (tel: 489 1208), Pondok Indah Golf & Country Club (tel: 769 4906) and Kedaton Golf Club (tel: 590 9236). Bali's newest golf course, the Nirwana Bali Golf Club (tel: 244 374) outside Denpasar now competes with the Handara Country Club (tel: 288 944). In Lombok the best of the three is Rinjani Golf Club (tel: 33939).

RAM FIGHTING

This is one of the unlikeliest 'sports' that anyone could ever dream up but, cruelty aside, ram fighting is big business, especially in Bandung and other towns in West Java. Typically, two hyped-up rams charge blindly at one another to the sound of drums and gongs and the raucous cries of the locals, who place bets. Only when one of the animals is knocked out is the winner declared and two new specimens lined up for the next bout.

SAILING

Several companies now organise sailing holidays around Bali and Java ranging from just a day's outing to several weeks.

Above: watersports in Benoa
Right: paragliding on Bali

Modern cruisers or public ferry boats cover some of the most spectacular marine scenery in the East. In Bali contact Spice Island Cruises, Jalan Padang Galak 25, Sanur (tel: 0361 286 283) or Pelni, the national shipping line in Jakarta, Bali or Lombok. See also pages 136–7.

SURFING
Indonesia is ideal for surfing, although you should watch out for strong undercurrents which take their toll every year. Beginners and intermediate surfers flock to Kuta Beach on Bali. Experienced surfers opt for Uluwatu (Pantai Suluban), a short distance to the south (see page 90).

SWIMMING AND TENNIS
Almost all the big hotels have swimming pools. Some have tennis courts, Jacuzzis and fitness centres. If you are not a hotel guest, you can generally pay to use the facilities.

OTHER SPORTS
Boating, mountaineering, trekking and

riding are all popular sporting activities in Indonesia, along with less adventurous pursuits such as table tennis, badminton and bowling. For something a little different, you can even take an 8-day cycle tour around Lombok with Bidy Tours (tel: 0364 32127), or paraglide over the sparkling bay of Bali's Benoa Beach, north of Nusa Dua.

Food and Drink

*I*f you go to Indonesia expecting a gastronomic treat, you may find yourself disappointed. For while the country does offer a variety of delicious foods, the cuisine cannot for the most part compare with that of neighbouring countries.

Almost every meal revolves around *nasi* (rice), with the addition of vegetables, peanuts or dried fish. Indeed, if there is a national meal, then it is probably *nasi goreng*, a mixture of fried rice, meat and onions with occasionally a fried egg perched on top.

Most dishes use spices like garlic and ginger, but not liberally. Sometimes you may come across that most beloved of all Asian culinary additives, the deadly *cabe* (chilli), nestling surreptitiously under a mound of rice or turned into *sambal*, a sauce made with lime and brown paste. If you do take a mouthful of fire, the best way to cool it is neither water nor beer, but plain rice or a squirt of lime juice. To avoid this possibility, simply say *jangan terlalu pedas* ('not too spicy please').

As a rule Indonesians eat informally. If you are invited to somebody's house, however, remember never to finish your rice as this suggests that you have not been fed sufficiently. Use the right hand to pass food (the left is considered unclean) and wait for your host to start eating or drinking before you tuck in.

A TYPICAL MENU

Outside the big tourist centres of Kuta, Sanur, Nusa Dua and Jakarta, don't expect to find garnished steak and chips on the menu. A more likely alternative is *nasi rames*, which consists of white rice, meat or fish and vegetables, or *cap cay*, a delicious mixture of stir-fried vegetables with garlic.

If that does not suit, you can normally order *soto*, a thick soup with coconut milk, served with *krupuk*, which are large prawn crackers.

Gado gado is another popular local dish and is made up of half-cooked salad served with a spicy peanut sauce. Elsewhere there's plenty of *mi goreng*,

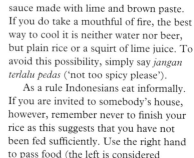

Street market, Bedulu

Red chillies have the heat of a furnace and the kick of a water buffalo

which is fried wheat flour noodles, or *nasi lemak*, which is rice with coconut milk, anchovies, egg and cucumber.

For dessert, Indonesians eat a variety of glutinous rice cakes often known as *jaja*. These are made from dough mixed with grated coconut, sweet potato or banana. If that is not to your taste, try *rumak*, made up of crisp, unripe fruit in a sweet and sour sauce, or simply ask for those delicious *pisang goreng* (fried bananas).

JAVANESE CUISINE

Although you will find rice served almost everywhere in Indonesia, each town and each region in the country also boasts its own speciality, with the *pièce de résistance* being fried worms and dragonflies.

In West Java, especially, Sundanese food is likely to feature on the menu. Popular dishes include *pepes usus* (chicken steamed in bamboo leaf), as well as spiced buffalo meat. For something a little different, order a plate of *petei* (spicy broad-bean salad) or *soto Bandung* (soup made from tripe).

In Central Java, and especially in Yogyakarta, the biggest speciality is a dish called *gudeg*, made from rice with boiled jack fruit, mixed with chicken, egg, coconut, cream and spicy sauce. *Ayam goreng* (chicken fried with spices and coconut) is another favourite, which is served with sweet chilli and rice. More adventurous eaters can opt for *opor* (barbecued sheep's brain)

In East Java, and especially Madura, soups are common, especially *soto madura* (spicy chicken broth). Almost everywhere you will come across *warungs* (food stalls) selling Padang food from West Sumatra. The food is cold, on occasions fiercesomely hot, but absolutely delicious. Added to that you are charged only for the dishes you eat.

BALINESE CUISINE

On Bali you can feast on roasted pig as well as steaks, fruits and almost every form of Western cuisine. Added to that is wonderful seafood freshly caught off the island's sparkling beaches.

If you fancy a *babi guling* (roasted pig), order it the night before to allow the restaurateur to prepare the pig for you by stuffing it with a spice-leaf mixture and then roasting it over a fire.

Another speciality is *betutu bebek*, a dish that consists of a whole duck stuffed with spices, wrapped in leaves then either steamed or roasted.

Other popular snacks on Bali range from unripe fruit to rice cakes.

OTHER CUISINES

Whilst nobody should miss an opportunity to try these exotic local titbits, there's no shortage of other Western restaurants in the main towns for those who do not take to such gastronomic novelties. Thai, Vietnamese, French, Italian and Indian food can be found in Jakarta, although at prices that are four or five times higher than local fare. In addition, almost all the major hotels will have Western-style restaurants. Certainly nobody should miss out on the traditional Dutch *rijstaffel*. This literally means 'rice table' and describes a whole banquet of side dishes such as kebabs and fried prawns.

STREET STALLS

Some of the most delicious food is to be found not in the five-star restaurants but in the humble little *warungs* (food stalls) or *rumah makan* (eating houses) which are frequented by appreciative locals.

Above, left: street vendor, Yogyakarta
Left: candies for sale, Bali

From noodles to Kebabs, Indonesia has plenty of fast food to offer

These *warungs* serve a variety of rice dishes or noodles as well as *satay* (kebabs), usually made from goat's meat and barbecued on a charcoal fire. To choose, just point at any dish that takes your fancy, sit down and feast on some of the cheapest and tastiest food that Indonesia has to offer. If you are nervous about your constitution, wait a few days before you venture out to the local stalls and always make sure that the food is freshly cooked.

DRINKS

You can drink Coca Cola or Fanta, or occasionally even expensive wine in the main towns of Bali, Java and Lombok, but the one thing that you should never miss out on is fruit shakes. These, made with papaya, pineapple, banana, lime and all the other luscious fruits that grow around the archipelago, can be bought from many restaurants catering for tourists and are the perfect antidote to a hot steamy day. To avoid stomach problems, ask for no ice (*tanpa es*).

For something a little stronger, Indonesia serves several good beers such as Heineken or the locally brewed Bintang, which was introduced by the Dutch. Finally, to avoid dehydration, drink as much water as possible. You can buy bottles of water in the shops or restaurants, although more up-market hotels will provide jugs of boiled water. Never, under any circumstances, drink tap water, which even the locals view with suspicion.

WHERE TO EAT

Eating in Indonesia is almost universally cheap. A good local meal will generally cost less than Rp40,000 a head (excluding alcohol) and only in the European restaurants in the big hotels will the cost be higher.

In the restaurant listings below, the following symbols have been used to indicate the average cost per person, not including alcohol.

R = Rp25,000–Rp50,000
RR = Rp50,000–Rpl00,000
RRR = Rpl00,000–Rp200,000

Service is generally charged at the rate of 10 per cent but expect extra taxes in hotel restaurants. Otherwise it is generally sufficient to leave Rp2,000 or Rp3,000 on the table as a tip.

JAKARTA
Indonesian food
Bengawan Solo Restaurant RRR
Very refined central Javanese cuisine in grand surroundings.
Sahid Jaya Hotel, Jalan Jend Sudirman 86 (tel: 570 4444).

Café Batavia RR
Extensive menu, lavish cocktails and open 24 hours.
Taman Fatahillah, Kota (tel: 691 5531).

Columbus Restaurant RRR
Fine Indonesian and continental dining.
Melia Jakarta Hotel, Jalan HR Rasuna Said Kav X (tel: 526 8080).

Jun Njan RR
One of the best-known seafood restaurants.
Jalan Batuceper 69, near Jalan Hayam Wuruk (tel: 381 4063).

Sari Bundo RR
One of the best padang restaurants in town.
Jalan Haji Juanda 27 (tel: 345 8343).

Sari Ratu R
Popular padang restaurant.

Plaza Indonesia (tel: 310 7534).
Satay House Senayan R
Renowned for its *gado gado* and *satay* (barbecued kebabs).
Jalan Kebon Sirih 31A (tel: 326 238).

European food
Ambiente Italian Restaurant RRR
Finest Italian cuisine in Jakarta.
Aryaduta Hotel, Jalan Prapatan 44–46 (tel: 386 1234).

Le Bistro RR
Bouillabaisse, *entrecôte* and some of the best French food in town.
Jalan Wahid Hasyim 75 (tel: 390 9249).

Memories RRR
Dutch cuisine with colonial trappings.
Wisma Indocement, Jalan Sudirman 70–71 (tel: 251 0402).

New George & Dragon RR
English/Indian food in popular expat establishment.
Jalan Talangbetutu 7 (tel: 310 2101).

The Ponderoso RR
Large steaks, salads and Mexican food are on the menu.
Jalan Sudirman 71 (tel: 522 3110).

Indian food
Hazara RR
North Indian food in authentic décor.
Jalan Wahid Hasyim 112 (tel: 315 0424).

YOGYAKARTA
Indonesian food
Hanoman's Forest Garden Restaurant RR
Indonesian and Western food with classical Javanese dance.
Jalan Prawirotaman 9B (tel: 372 528)

Rumah Makan R
Nasi goreng, seafood and Javanese specialities.
Jalan Gedong Kuning Selatan 5 (tel: 370 886).

Suharti's Ayam Goreng R
Specialises in fried chicken, the regional delicacy.
Jalan Laksda Adisucipto 208 (tel: 515 522).
Turangga Restaurant and Coffee Shop RR
Bright and airy décor with excellent service. A la carte, buffet and snacks.
Hotel Ibis Malioboro, Jalan Malioboro (tel: 516 974)

European food
Gita Buana RR
Delicious steaks, European dishes and Chinese fare.
Jalan Adisucipto 89 (tel: 561 164).
Legian Garden Restaurant RR
Delightfully situated with good Western and local food.
Jalan Perwakilan 9 (tel: 564 644).
Pesta Perak R
Wide selection of local and European food.
Jalan Tentara Rakyat Mataram 8 (tel: 563 255).
Superman's R
Pancakes, yoghurts and Indonesian dishes for backpackers.
Gang Sosrowijayan I (runs parallel with Marlboro).

SURABAYA
Indonesian food
Antika R
Reputedly the best Padang food in town.
Jalan Raya Darmo 1.
Oriental RR
Excellent Indonesian and Chinese food.
Jalan Taman AIS Nasutron 37 (tel: 534 4651).
Soto Ambengan R
Famous for its Madurese chicken soup with lemon grass.
Jalan Ambengan 3A.

European food
Café Venezia RR
International and Asian food in old villa.
Jalan Ambengan 16.
News Café RR
Bar and restaurant serving western and Indonesian food.
Jalan Panglima Suridrman 47–49.
Satellite Garden RR
Jalan Raya Kupang Baru 17.
Wendy's Fast Food Restaurant RR
Hamburgers, chips and soft drinks.
Jalan Pemuda.

BALI
Kuta Beach
Made's Warung R
Popular Indonesian and Western food.
Jalan Pantai Kuta (tel: 751 923).
Poppies R
Delightful setting, consistently good food.
Jalan Legian (tel: 751 059).

Sanur Beach
Bali Moon RR
Italian food in open-air setting.
Br Sindu Kaya, Sanur (tel: 288 486).
Kul Kul RR
Excellent Indonesian and Western food in garden setting.
Jalan Danau Tamblingan 166 (tel: 288 098).
Tanjung Sari Hotel Restaurant RRR
One of the most exquisite restaurants on the island.
Jalan Tanjung Sari (tel: 288 441).

Ubud
Ibah Restaurant RRR
For a regal Balinese dining experience. Reservations recommended.
Jalan Campuhan (tel: 974 466).
Murni's Warung R
Fine fruit salads, yoghurts and a huge variety of Western and local fare.
Jalan Raya (tel: 975 233).

Hotels and Accommodation

*I*ndonesia has some of the top hotels in the world, with swimming pools, restaurants and tropical gardens to match. At the lower end of the scale it has some of the friendliest homestays where you can stay with a family for less than US$5 a night.

Prices vary as much as the establishments. In Jakarta, a top suite at the Grand Hyatt Hotel will cost as much as US$600, whilst in the less exclusive hotels around the corner, standard rooms go for US$50–US$100 and less. Outside Jakarta prices are considerably lower, while on Bali you will find a bewildering choice of accommodation to suit every pocket.

Remember that in the high season (June to September), when the vast majority of Europeans take their holidays, it can be extremely hard finding accommodation if you turn up without a reservation. At other times of year it is quite possible to negotiate big discounts.

Tariffs are generally quoted in Indonesian *rupiah*, except in the big hotels where US dollars are the norm. A 21 per cent service charge and government tax is added to all bills, but enquire on arrival.

DO'S AND DON'TS

Although finding a satisfactory hotel in Indonesia is little different from finding one in any other country, there are a few points that are worth remembering.

The key to an enjoyable stay is a

Thomas Cook
Traveller's Tip

Travellers who purchase their travel tickets from a Thomas Cook network location are entitled to use the services of any other Thomas Cook network location, free of charge, to make hotel reservations.

central location, especially in Jakarta where a hotel on the outskirts may entail hours in a traffic jam. If you are making an advance reservation through a travel agent, always double-check the address, as often what you are told is central proves to be quite a distance from where you want to be. Generally, it is worth paying a little more to be close to the tourist sites.

Cheaper establishments in big towns tend to be dirty and noisy; sometimes, the small Chinese hotels may even double up as brothels. If you end up staying in a less than desirable establishment, make sure that you take security precautions and carry valuables in a money belt.

To be on the safe side, always arrive at your destination early to allow time to find a place to stay. Remember that the word hotel generally indicates a more expensive establishment, while the word *losmen* refers to a lower-price hotel or guesthouse.

Don't be afraid to check out the bedrooms and bathrooms and to ask for something larger or cleaner if what is on offer does not suit your taste. Many hotels will have several different standards of room with corresponding prices to match. Sometimes, you may even get breakfast included.

Never, under any circumstances, drink water from the tap. Most big hotels will provide jugs of boiled water. Finally, remember that phone calls and hotel meals are expensive, and that hotels add a hefty service charge to the bill.

SHOPPING AROUND

Although most hotels of a similar price bracket will offer comparable standards, it is always worth shopping around. Taxi or *becak* (tricycle) drivers are generally happy to take you to a selection of hotels because if you take a room they may get commission. At major airports like Jakarta and Denpasar special hotel reservation desks offer the full range of accommodation.

Right: five-star accommodation, Bali
Below: tropical comfort, Sanur Beach, Bali

PRICES AND FACILITIES

BALI

All the big international hotel chains like Hyatt and Sheraton are to be found on Bali, along with plenty of clean and pleasant hotels and homestays (*losmen*). Although prices at the top tend to be on a par with other international destinations, at the lower end simple, clean accommodation goes for a song.

Deluxe

Most of the deluxe accommodation is situated in the coastal areas and especially in the resorts of Nusa Dua and Sanur. Top-class hotels have every amenity from luxuriant gardens to swimming pools, fitness centres and restaurants. Almost all of them organise tours and will be able to arrange chauffeur-driven cars.

Rates can be as high as US$500 for a suite at the Amanusa, although most luxury establishments in Nusa Dua charge in the region of US$100-US$150 a night. Off season, however, you may be able to negotiate considerably lower prices. For peace of mind, book early, especially if you intend to stay during peak season.

Standard

Even mid-priced hotels and bungalows on Bali generally offer swimming pools and charming little gardens, as well as restaurants and travel services. Standard hotels vary in price from Rp40,000 to Rp100,000, although prices may be considerably lower during the low season.

Budget

Budget hotels and *losmen* (homestays) are found literally everywhere on Bali, offering clean and simple accommodation at bargain prices. In Ubud, prices for a small family owned *losmen* with a private *mandi* (a water tank from which to ladle water over yourself) can start as low as Rp6,000, breakfast included. These *losmen* are generally extremely friendly and a fine source of local information. Although security is generally high, always keep an eye on your belongings.

JAVA

Although hotels on Java as a rule cannot match those on Bali, Jakarta does have all the luxury amenities of any capital city – at a price. Outside the major tourist centres, standards tend to be considerably lower, with many small towns sporting little more than dingy Chinese hotels with an abundance of cockroaches.

Deluxe

From the Grand Hyatt to the Borobudur and the Mandarin Oriental, Jakarta has the full range of five-star accommodation with prices beginning at around US$100 per night before taxes. Outside Jakarta prices and standards are considerably lower. Make reservations well in advance as growing numbers of businessmen have led to high rates of occupancy.

Standard

There is not a huge amount to choose from in the standard range, except in the bigger cities which have plenty of mid-priced accommodation. Expect to pay between Rp60,000 and Rp100,000 in Jakarta and considerably less outside.

Budget

If you think you have stayed in some rough places in Asia, some of Java's basement accommodation can give you a run for your money. Rooms can be dingy in the extreme and security extremely poor. Prices range from as low as

Living in the lap of luxury at Jakarta's Grand Hyatt Hotel

Rp6,000, although you will pay higher rates in Jakarta. To find a satisfactory establishment, inspect the various rooms, and if you don't like any of them simply move on somewhere else.

LOMBOK
Lombok now offers quite a range of tourist accommodation, especially at Senggigi Beach where the Sheraton and Holiday Inn have been added to a growing number of small hotels and bungalows. At Kuta the luxurious Novotel Hotel contrasts with basic accommodation, while at Tetebatu and the Gili Islands there are several bungalows. Elsewhere, however, accommodation is hard to come by and less impressive.

On Business

Fifteen years ago Jakarta was one of the most chaotic business centres in the whole of Asia. These days, despite the financial crisis affecting the region, there is still good access to a significant economy and to the attractions of a relatively progressive city.

Here you will find foreign banks and plenty of multi-national corporations. On top of that, there is a stock market known as the Jakarta Stock Exchange, a bond market and an extremely active and optimistic business community.

Outside Jakarta, the only other real business centre is Surabaya which now serves the eastern part of the Indonesian archipelago and has become the focal point of the government's efforts to decentralise the economy. Surabaya has a big Chinese community, a selection of leading manufacturing concerns, and a private stock exchange.

ACCOMMODATION

Business accommodation in Jakarta is plentiful with at least ten major hotels offering every conceivable amenity. Prices for the top suites are in line with other business centres around the world and service of a high standard. To ensure room availability, book in advance.

BUREAUCRACY

If you are expecting to obtain a major business decision on your first trip to Indonesia, prepare to be disappointed. Doing business takes time and effort; much of it is a question of face, and at almost every level vast amounts of paper work and endless discussions with the country's notorious bureaucracy may be involved. The only real way to avoid hassles is to establish a joint venture with a reputable local partner. For details about investment requirements and government incentives, contact the

Indonesian Investment Co-ordinating Board (BKPM) in Jakarta (tel: 520 2047).

BUSINESS ETIQUETTE

Indonesian businessmen pride themselves on their appearance. They generally wear a suit and tie and expect visiting foreigners to do the same. Always shake hands and offer a business card, and when addressing a businessman use his full title. Initially you should expect to spend several hours in discussion, as long, drawn-out negotiations are usual. Any initial contact may skirt around the key issues which will often require further discussions.

If you are offered the opportunity of lunch or dinner, it is considered impolite to turn down the invitation. These days, breakfast meetings are on the increase. If you are the host in Jakarta, choose between the Grand Hyatt, the Mandarin, the Borobudur or the Hilton. Smaller hotels will be viewed as a reflection of inferior status.

BUSINESS TRANSPORT

All the big hotels offer a limousine service, charged either by the day or by the hour. Chauffeurs will take you to an appointment and pick you up later in the day. Bluebird taxis are also available and can be rented by the hour at considerably cheaper rates.

COMMUNICATIONS
Computers, printers, fax machines and photocopiers can be found in all the major hotels. Costs of hiring computers (generally by the hour) are, however, high. Local telephone services have improved dramatically over the last five years, but remain poor by Western standards. International calls on the other hand can be made very quickly and easily.

CONFERENCE AND EXHIBITION FACILITIES
Most of the big hotels offer conference and exhibition facilities catering for from 30 to several hundred guests. Contact the following for details:
Grand Hyatt Hotel, *Plaza Indonesia, Jalan Thamrin (tel: 390 1234).*
Hilton Hotel, *Jalan Jend Subroto (tel: 570 3600).*
Borobudur Hotel, *Jalan Lapangan Banteng Selatan (tel: 380 5555).*
Mandarin Oriental Hotel, *Jalan Thamrin (tel: 314 1307).*

MEDIA
Several publications offer local business news. These include the *Indonesian Business Monthly* and *Business Week Review.* The daily English-language newspapers are the *Jakarta Post* and the *Indonesian Observer.* All the big hotels sell the *International Herald Tribune*, the *Asian Wall Street Journal* and the

Financial Times, although you may find them a few days out of date.

OFFICE HOURS
Offices generally open between 9am and 5pm from Mondays to Fridays, although financial service companies may begin as early as 8am and close as late as 6pm. On Saturdays, many non-government offices in Jakarta are open for a half day. All offices are closed on Sundays.

SECRETARIAL AND TRANSLATION SERVICES
Secretarial and translation services are widely available in leading hotels. Costs are generally in line with other international business centres.

A selection of indonesian tabloids

Practical Guide

CONTENTS

ARRIVING

Entry formalities

Visitors to Indonesia must be in possession of passports valid for at least six months from the date of arrival and have proof of onward or return passage. Visas for a stay of up to 60 days are automatically granted on arrival to nationals of the UK, Australia, New Zealand and Canada. Nationals from South Africa will need a visa.

Travellers who require visas should obtain them in their country of residence, as it may prove difficult to obtain them elsewhere. In the UK, Thomas Cook Passport and Visa Service can advise on and obtain the necessary documentation. Consult your nearest Thomas Cook travel consultant.

By air

Indonesia's major international gateway is Soekarno-Hatta International Airport in Jakarta, which is served by airlines from Europe, North America, Australia and the Middle East, as well as by Garuda, the national flag carrier. Facilities are of a high standard, with banks, car rental, telephones, tourist information, left luggage, and even a hotel reservation service.

These days, an increasing number of tourists fly directly to Denpasar's Ngurah Rai International Airport on Bali. Flights arrive and depart from Amsterdam, Singapore, Hong Kong, Kuala Lumpur and Perth in Western Australia.

If you intend to fly during the high season, make sure that you reserve a seat early, and on the return trip remember to reconfirm your flight at least 72 hours prior to departure.

Tax: an airport tax of Rp50,000 is charged on departure for international flights and Rp11,000 on domestic flights.

To and from Jakarta Airport: a fleet of taxis connects Soekarno-Hatta International Airport with the centre of Jakarta, which lies 30km to the west. Fares are in the region of Rp75,000, including toll charges, and only if you take an expensive air-conditioned limousine will it cost you much more. During the week the journey should take 40 minutes to the centre of town, although to be safe allow more than an hour.

Airport buses depart every 30 minutes for the Gambir Train Station and Blok M in Kebayoran, as well as for various other points in the city where there are taxi connections.

To and from Denpasar Airport (Bali): taxis will take you from Ngurah Rai International Airport, which lies a short distance from Denpasar, to Sanur in less than 20 minutes and to Kuta in 15 minutes. Public buses run to the centre of town at frequent intervals.

By ship
Although not a popular method of entry, several luxury passenger vessels do sail between Singapore, Hong Kong, Jakarta and Bali, including the *QE2*, the *Oriana* and the *Sky Princess*. You can also catch boats from Singapore to the island of Sumatra. At Jakarta, boats berth at Tanjung Priok Harbour, 10km to the northeast of the city.

CAMPING
You will find opportunities for camping in several of the national parks but otherwise camping is not recommended. At best you may find yourself being woken up by a herd of inquisitive water buffalo, at worst by a group of locals who may be after more than your guy ropes.

CHILDREN
Up-market tourist hotels can generally arrange babysitters. Nappies are sold in shops and department stores in all the major cities. See also Children, pages 160–1.

Soekarno-Hatta International Airport

Sunny days in Padangbai, Bali

CLIMATE

May through to October are the best months to visit Java, Bali and Lombok as for the most part the weather is dry with only short bouts of rain in the early and latter parts. November to April is the monsoon season when tropical downpours alternate with sunshine. January and February are generally the wettest months of the year. Average temperatures are between 25°C and 28°C, but this may drop to 18°C or lower in the mountainous areas. Average humidity is 75 per cent. On Bali the rains tend to last longer, with the greatest concentration of sun between July and October.

CLOTHING, see page 25.

CONVERSION TABLES, see opposite

CRIME

Like any developing country, crime is on the rise in Indonesia, especially in

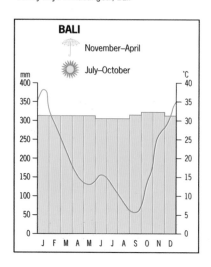

BALI

November–April

July–October

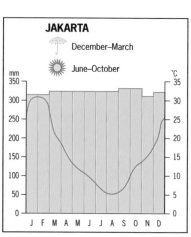

JAKARTA

December–March

June–October

Conversion Table

FROM	TO	MULTIPLY BY
Inches	Centimetres	2.54
Feet	Metres	0.3048
Yards	Metres	0.9144
Miles	Kilometres	1.6090
Acres	Hectares	0.4047
Gallons	Litres	4.5460
Ounces	Grams	28.35
Pounds	Grams	453.6
Pounds	Kilograms	0.4536
Tons	Tonnes	1.0160

To convert back, for example from centimetres to inches, divide by the number in the third column.

Men's Suits

UK		36	38	40	42	44	46	48
Rest of Europe		46	48	50	52	54	56	58
US		36	38	40	42	44	46	48

Dress Sizes

UK		8	10	12	14	16	18
France		36	38	40	42	44	46
Italy		38	40	42	44	46	48
Rest of Europe		34	36	38	40	42	44
US		6	8	10	12	14	16

Men's Shirts

UK	14	14.5	15	15.5	16	16.5	17
Rest of Europe	36	37	38	39/40	41	42	43
US	14	14.5	15	15.5	16	16.5	17

Men's Shoes

UK		7	7.5	8.5		9.5	10.5	11
Rest of Europe	41		42	43		44		45	46
US		8	8.5	9.5		10.5	11.5	12

Women's Shoes

UK		4.5	5	5.5	6		6.5	7
Rest of Europe	38	38		39	39		40	41
US		6	6.5	7	7.5		8	8.5

the big cities where pick-pockets and small-time thieves are commonplace. To protect yourself, make sure that you never carry around large amounts of cash or ostentatious jewellery, and use a money belt and the hotel safe.

Women should avoid travelling alone, especially on Java and Lombok. Locals regard single women as easy game and will pester them throughout their journey.

CUSTOMS REGULATIONS

The following items may be taken duty free into Indonesia: 2 litres of alcohol, 200 cigarettes or 50 cigars or 100 grams of tobacco. In principle, cassette recorders, typewriters and photographic equipment must be declared upon entry, although in practice customs officers will wave you through. All narcotics, arms and ammunition are prohibited. It is advisable to fully label all tablets and first-aid items, and to carry proof of purchase with you at all times.

Drugs

Possession or consumption of drugs is an extremely serious offence in Indonesia, punishable by life imprisonment. Never accept a package from any stranger, whoever they may claim to be, and never even consider smuggling drugs into or out of the country.

DISABLED TRAVELLERS

Besides lifts and ramps at the big hotels and wheelchairs at the international and domestic airports provided by Garuda, there is little in the way of facilities for disabled travellers in Indonesia.

ATTENTION

I. THOSE WHO ARE NOT ALLOWED TO ENTER THE TEMPLE ARE :
1. LADIES WHO ARE PREGNANT
2. LADIES WHOSE CHILDREN HAVE NOT GOT THE FIRST TEETH
3. CHILDREN WHOSE FIRST TEETH NOT FALLEN OUT YET
4. LADIES DURING THEIR PERIOD
5. DVOTEES GETTING IMPURE DUE TO DEATH
6. MAD LADIES / GENTLEMEN
7. THOSE NOT PROPERLY DRESSED
ALL DVOTEES ENTERING THE TEMPLE SHOULD MAINTAIN
CLEANLINESS AND ENVIRONMENTAL CONSERVATION

DRIVING

In theory, driving offers the perfect opportunity to escape the crowds. In practice, you may find Indonesian drivers to be among the worst in the world, especially in Jakarta which is a madhouse of traffic jams and one-way streets.

Few foreigners even bother to drive in the capital, preferring if necessary to hire a driver. On Bali and Lombok driving does make more sense, however, although even here nonchalant water buffalo and speeding buses can challenge even the most experienced drivers.

Those who do decide to take the plunge will need an international driving licence. You will also require insurance, although most reliable rental firms will be able to arrange this on the spot.

As a rule, main roads on Bali and Lombok are in a relatively good state of repair, although during the rainy season non-tarmac roads will be literally awash. Vehicles drive on the left (generally) with major towns signposted in English.

Petrol stations are few and far between, so always top up when you get the opportunity. Failing that, stop by one of the ubiquitous roadside stalls selling gasoline by the litre bottle.

Signs of the times

Car hire
Car-hire firms exist in many of the larger towns. To be safe, opt for a well-known international firm.

Jakarta
Avis Car Rental, *Jalan Diponegoro 25, Jakarta 10310 (tel: 314 2900).*
Golden Bird, *Jalan Mampang Prapatan Raya 9 (tel: 794 4444).*
Toyota Rentacar, *Jalan Hasyim Ashari 31, Jakarta (tel: 573 5757).*
Bali
Dwi Tunggal Tourist Information, *Jalan Padang Tegal, Ubud (tel: 976 301).*
Hertz Car Rental, *Grand Bali Beach Hotel, Sanur (tel: 288 511).*

Bicycle and moped hire
Bicycles and motorcycles can prove the perfect way to explore the countryside, so long as you can put up with the heat and the dust. On Bali, in Surakarta (Solo) and Yogyakarta especially, bicycles are relatively easy to come by, while in Kuta mountain bikes can be hired.

Daily rates are generally low but it is better to negotiate by the week. Before you depart, check that the bicycle or moped is in proper working order as you will be liable for any damage, and make sure that you lock the bicycle/motorbike at all times. Although insurance is not a legal requirement, everyone should make it a pre-requisite as accidents are by no means uncommon.

ELECTRICITY
Power supply is generally 220 volts in the big cities, but 110 volts is still used in some areas. Normal outlets take plugs with two rounded prongs. If in doubt, take an electrical adaptor.

EMBASSIES AND CONSULATES

The following is an abbreviated list of embassies and consulates in Jakarta. For a full list, see the telephone directory or any of the free hand-outs issued by the tourist authorities.

Australia, *Jalan HR Rasuna Said Kav 15–16, Kuningan, Jakarta (tel: 526 5661).*
Canada, *Wisma Metropolitan 1, 5th floor, Jalan Jend Sudirman 29, Jakarta (tel: 525 0709).*
Great Britain, *75 Jalan Thamrin, Jakarta (tel: 315 6264).*
New Zealand, *Gedung BRI II, Suite 2303, Jalan Jend Sudirman 44–46, Jakarta (tel: 572 7676).*
United States, *5 Jalan Merdeka Selatan, Jakarta (tel: 344 2211).*

EMERGENCY TELEPHONE NUMBERS

Jakarta
Ambulance: 118
Fire: 113
Police: 110
Bali
Ambulance: 118
Fire: 113
Police: 110

Jakarta hospitals

Gatot Subroto Hospital, *Jalan Abdul Rachman Saleh (tel: 344 1008).*
Pertamina Hospital, *Jalan Kyai Maja 43 (tel: 720 0290 or 725 0212).*
Rumah Sakit Pondok Indah, *Jalan Metro Duta 1 (tel: 765 7525)* – operates a 24-hour emergency service.

Bali hospitals

Sanglah Public Hospital, *Jalan Kesehatan 1, Sanglah, Denpasar (tel: (0361) 227 911).*
Wangaya Public Hospital, *Jalan Kartini, Denpasar (tel: 222 141).*

Dharma Usaha Clinic, *Jalan Jend Sudirman 50, Denpasar (tel: 227 560).*

The Thomas Cook Worldwide Customer Promise offers free emergency assistance at any Thomas Cook Network location to travellers who have purchased their travel tickets at a Thomas Cook location. In addition, any MasterCard cardholder may use any Thomas Cook Network location to report loss or theft of their card and obtain an emergency card replacement as a free service under Thomas Cook MasterCard International Alliance.

Thomas Cook Travellers Cheques (24-hour service – report loss or theft within 24 hours): tel: (44) 733 318 950.

Becak driver, Jakarta

HEALTH

There are no mandatory vaccination requirements for visiting Indonesia, but vaccination against tetanus, polio, typhoid and hepatitis A is recommended. Coastal areas are free of malaria, but anti-malarial tablets are advised for travellers intending to stay in inland rural areas either overnight or for longer periods of time.

Strict food and water hygiene is essential to avoid problems with diarrhoea. Make sure food has been properly washed and prepared and drink bottled water only (which means avoiding ice cubes).

Aids is present in Indonesia as elsewhere in the world, along with a host of other venereal diseases.

For the most part, the big hotels can arrange for a doctor to call or arrange hospital treatment. Jakarta and Denpasar have good medical facilities but in very remote places the only real alternative is to transport the person to the nearest big town.

HITCH-HIKING

Although occasionally visitors may find themselves being offered a free lift by locals, hitch-hiking is not a recommended way of getting around. What is more, since the cost of public transport is extremely low and most towns are served by buses or *bemos*, it is just not worth the risk.

INSURANCE

Anybody spending time in Indonesia should arrange insurance prior to departure. Ideally this should cover lost or stolen cash and credit cards as well as guaranteeing a return ticket in case of emergency. Make sure that you get additional cover if items like cameras or videos exceed the individual limit. If you lose anything or have anything stolen, report it immediately to the police and get an officially stamped statement.

BASIC PHRASES

Basics

Please	**Silakan**
Thank you	**Terima kasih**
Good morning	**Selamat pagi**
Good afternoon	**Selamat siang**
Good evening	**Selamat malam**
Good-bye	**Selamat tinggal**
Excuse me	**Permisi**
Welcome	**Selamat datang**
I don't understand	**Saya tidak mengerti**

Questions

What is your name?	**Siapa nama saudara?**
Where are you from?	**Dari mana?**
How much?	**Berapa?**
Do you speak English?	**Bisa berbicara bahasa Inggris?**
Do you understand?	**Mengerti?**
Where is?	**Dimana ada?**
When?	**Kapan?**

Places

Alley	**Gang**
Airport	**Lapangan terbang**
Beach	**Pantai**
Bus terminal	**Terminal bis**
Hospital	**Rumah Sakit**
Hotel	**Hotel**

Without this, most insurance companies will refuse to pay out claims money.

LANGUAGE

Bahasa Indonesia, which is the national language, is not only easy to pick up but will make your stay considerably easier and your experience of the country immeasurably richer. If you start with a few basic phrases before departure it

Market	**Pasar**
Mountain	**Gunung**
Restaurant	**Rumah makan**
River	**Sungai**
Street	**Jalan**
Temple	**Candi**
Village	**Desa**

Time

Yesterday	**Kemarin**
Today	**Hari ini**
Tomorrow	**Besok**
Hour	**Jam**
Week	**Minggu**
Month	**Bulan**
Year	**Tahun**

Useful Words

Bathroom	**Kamar Mandi**
Cheap	**Murah**
Drink	**Minum**
Eat	**Makan**
Expensive	**Mahal**
Good	**Bagus**
No	**Tidak**
Room	**Kamar**
Shop	**Toko**
Sleep	**Tidur**
Toilet	**Kamar kecil**
Yes	**Ya**

Food & Drink

| Beef | **Daging Sapi** |

Chicken	**Ayam**
Pork	**Babi**
Fish	**Ikan**
Egg	**Telur**
Vegetables	**Sayur**
Mixed vegetables	**Cap cai**
Noodles	**Mie**
Fried noodles	**Mie Goreng**
Rice	**Nasi**
Fried rice	**Nasi Goreng**
Soup	**Sop/soto**
Fruit	**Buah**
Beer	**Bir**
Boiled water	**Air putih**
Coffee	**Kopi**
Milk	**Susu**
Tea	**Teh**
Sugar	**Gula**

Numbers

One	**Satu**
Two	**Dua**
Three	**Tiga**
Four	**Empat**
Five	**Lima**
Six	**Enam**
Seven	**Tujuh**
Eight	**Delapan**
Nine	**Sembilan**
Ten	**Sepuluh**
Fifty	**Limapuluh**
Hundred	**Seratus**
Thousand	**Seribu**

won't take long to pick up new words and begin constructing simple sentences. Above is a list of useful words.

LAUNDRY/VALETING

Most hotels offer a fast and efficient laundry service with items returned the same day if they are given in before 9am. If you are in a real hurry, they can be laundered 'express service' and returned in as little as 4 hours.

LOST PROPERTY

If you lose something on a bus, train or in a public place, don't expect to get it back. Only in hotels and restaurants is ost property likely to be kept for a limited period of time.

MAPS

Several international cartographers produce good countrywide maps of Indonesia.

For Jakarta, try to get hold of the Falk Map which is available at most local book shops.

MEDIA

Although Indonesia's media remain tightly controlled by the government, there are several English-language newspapers such as the *Indonesian Observer*, the *Jakarta Post* and the *Surabaya Post* which are available in the major towns. The *Asian Wall Street Journal*, the *International Herald Tribune*, *Time Magazine* and *Newsweek* are also widely available in leading hotels and major book shops.

These days, most big hotels offer satellite television with live broadcasts from Hong Kong and London, as well as nightly films and videos. Radio Republik Indonesia broadcasts programmes in English.

MONEY MATTERS

The Indonesia currency is denominated in rupiahs. Indonesian notes consist of Rp50,000 notes, Rp10,000, Rp5,000, Rp1,000, Rp500 and Rp100. Indonesian coins are Rp1,000, Rp500, Rp100, Rp50 and Rp25 although these days small denominations are rarely used. As a rule take smaller notes, as in many places it can be difficult getting change for a Rp50,000 note. The Indonesian rupiah is freely convertible with other currencies, although in some of the more far-flung areas of Bali, Java and Lombok you may find foreign exchange banks hard to come by.

Bank services

Local and foreign banks provide standard services nationwide. Banking hours are 8am–3pm, Monday to Friday, and 8am–1pm, Saturday. Money can also be changed at authorised money-changers and at hotels, although they

Something for everyone

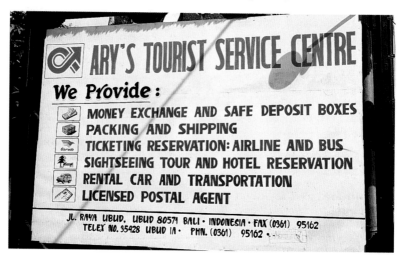

may offer a lower exchange rate. Official exchange rates are published in the daily newspapers.

Jakarta has several international banks. Visitors who are heading to more remote areas of Indonesia are advised to change money and travellers' cheques in advance.

Cheques and credit cards
Thomas Cook Travellers Cheques free you from the hazards of carrying large amounts of cash, and in the event of loss or theft can quickly be refunded (see Emergency Telephone Number, page 180). US dollar travellers' cheques are recommended, though cheques denominated in any of the major currencies are also accepted. Major tourist and business hotels accept travellers' cheques in lieu of cash.

The following branch of Thomas Cook can provide emergency assistance in the case of loss or theft of Thomas Cook Travellers Cheques.
P T Thomas Cook Indonesia, *Plaza Lippo, 9th Floor, Jalan Jend, Sudirman Kav 25, Jakarta 12920. Tel: 21–520 4540. Fax: 21–520 4539.*

Foreign banks in Jakarta
American Express, *Jalan HR Rasuna Said BI X–1, Kav 3 (tel: 521 6000).*
Chase Manhattan Bank, *Jalan Sudirman Kav 21 (tel: 571 2213).*
Citibank, *Jalan Jend Sudirman 1 (tel: 251 2007).*

NATIONAL HOLIDAYS
Indonesian national holidays vary from year to year, so you should always check with the tourist authorities or embassy. During public holidays, all forms of transport tend to get booked up.
1 January – New Year's Day
January/February – Mi'raj Nabbi

Mohammed (Ascension of the prophet Mohammed)
March – Nyepi (Balinese New Year)
March/April – Lebaran (religious festival marking the end of the Muslim fast)
March/April – Good Friday
April 21 – Kartini Day (celebrates women's emancipation)
May – Waisak Day (marks the birth and death of the Buddha)
June – Idhul Adha (Muslim day of sacrifice)
June/July – Muharram (Muslim New Year)
17 August – Independence Day
August/September – Maulid Nabi Mohammed (Birthday of the Prophet Mohammed)
5 October – Armed Forces Day
25 December – Christmas Day

OPENING HOURS
Shopping centres, supermarkets and department stores are usually open between 9am and 9pm Monday to Saturday and in larger cities even stay open on Sunday. Government office hours are 8am to 4pm, Monday to Friday, with prayer breaks on Fridays between 11.30am and 1.30pm.

ORGANISED TOURS
Tour operators around the world offer a bewildering choice of package tours to Indonesia with the majority of them starting or ending at Bali with optional stays in Jakarta, Yogyakarta, Borobudur and Mount Bromo. These days, growing numbers of international operators like Trailfinders and Jetset Tours combine trips to Indonesia with other popular regional destinations such as Thailand, Singapore, Malaysia and Australia.

For those wanting greater freedom to move about at will, locally organised tours can also be arranged in almost every major town and city. Make sure that you use a reputable organisation though, as unauthorised guides abound. Best to ask at your hotel or in the local tourist office.

For details about available international tours, contact your nearest Thomas Cook office or telephone Thomas Cook Holidays on (01733) 417000 (in the UK).

PHARMACIES

Pharmacies, known as *Apotiks*, can be found in almost all the main towns as well as many of the smaller ones. They generally sell a full range of all the items you would expect to find, from medicinal drugs and contraceptives to toothbrushes, shampoo and soaps. Although prescriptions are not generally needed for medicinal drugs, it is well worth knowing the generic name for any drug since they are often sold under different brand names. Also check the expiry date before purchasing a drug as they have a habit of staying on the shelves for a long time.

PHOTOGRAPHY

Indonesia is a veritable photographer's paradise. To ensure good results take your own film, since often what is available has been exposed to excessive heat. Keen photographers should take a polarising lens to reduce the glare and bags of silica gel to stop moisture getting into the camera. For really good results, concentrate on taking pictures in the early morning and late afternoon when the light is at its best. By midday, the heat and fierce shadows can spoil the most perfect shot. Generally you will be allowed free use of your camera. However, in some temples and museums

you will be charged for taking in a camera or a video and in certain museums the use of flash is prohibited. If in doubt, ask at the entrance.

Local shops will process film in less than an hour, and at prices considerably cheaper than neighbouring countries. Don't expect high quality though. Despite the savings, it pays to get your pictures developed back home.

PLACES OF WORSHIP

Although some 87 per cent of Indonesians are Muslim, there are plenty of other religious groups too, including Roman Catholics, Methodists and Anglicans. The following places of worship can be found in Jakarta and Bali.

Jakarta

All Saints Church (Anglican), *Jalan Prapatan, Jakarta (tel: 345 508).*
Gereja Immanuel (Protestant), *Jalan Merdeka Timur 10, Jakarta Pusat.*
Jemaat Anugerah (Methodist), *Jalan Daan Mogot 100, Jakarta.*
St Canisius College Chapel (Catholic), *Jalan Menteng Raya 64, Jakarta (tel: 325 546).*

Bali

Maranatha Church (Anglican), *Jalan Surapati, Denpasar.*
St Joseph Church (Catholic), *Jalan Kepundung, Denpasar.*

POLICE

You will be able to recognise the regular Indonesian police by their khaki caps, their neatly ironed shirts and their proverbial smiles. For the most part they are extremely friendly, and almost to the man unable to speak English. To report loss or theft, either go to Jakarta's police headquarters on Jalan Sudirman 45 (tel:

Post office and box, Yogyakarta

587 7777), or contact any other police office. Failing satisfactory progress, get in touch with your hotel or embassy.

POST OFFICES

Post offices can be found in almost all the main towns and villages, although they are generally extremely crowded and inefficient. A better option is to send mail through your hotel. When posting letters, make sure the stamps are properly stuck on, or better still, register them.

If you want to ship goods back home try to make arrangements through the shop where you purchased them. The alternative is to take your package to the central post office, fill in various forms, have the contents verified, then wait several months in the hope that one day the package will turn up.

The General Post Office has its head office in Jakarta at Jalan Pos Utara 2, Pasar Baru (open: Monday to Friday, 8am–4pm, Saturday 8am–1pm). On Bali,

the head office is on Jalan Raya Puputan, Denpasar (open: Monday to Thursday, 8am–2pm; Friday, 8am–noon; Saturday, 8am–1pm).

PUBLIC TRANSPORT
By air

The Asian monetary crisis has meant that smaller airlines are barely able to maintain a service and some have gone out of business. However, air transport is still the easiest and most comfortable means of travel in Indonesia and there are flights to almost any provincial and district capital. For details, contact the following:

Jakarta

Bouraq Indonesia Airlines, *Jalan Angkasa 1–3 (tel: 629 5270)*.

Garuda Indonesia, *Jalan Thamrin 5 (tel: 231 1101)*.

Merpati Nusantara Airlines, *Jalan Angkasa 2 (tel: 654 8888)*.

Bali

Garuda Indonesia, *Jalan Melati 61, Denpasar (tel: 0361 227 825)*.

Merpati Nusantara Airlines, *Jalan Merpati 51, Denpasar (tel: 0361 263918)*.

By *becak*

Pronounced 'baychahk', this is an antiquated tricycle generally able to seat two people (although locals occasionally squeeze in five), and is the perfect means of transport for short distances. Agree the price before you leave.

By *bemo*

These illustrious minibuses pile in more passengers than you could dream possible and then proceed to stop frequently to pick up more. *Bemos* operate on almost all the main routes, and although generally cheaper than buses they take considerably longer. Always check the destination and price, and if you are really in a hurry, rent the whole vehicle.

By boat, see Island Hopping, pages 136–7.

By bus

Buses are the most popular long-distance form of public transport serving most major towns and districts. Beware, however; while many of them travel like snails, others go like the wind and serious accidents are not uncommon.

For short trips there is little choice but to take the regular public buses which stop at every available opportunity, and will even do several circuits around town in order to pick up additional passengers. For longer trips, catch the express buses which rarely stop, are air-conditioned and on certain routes (Jakarta–Bogor) will use the toll roads.

Major towns often have several different bus stations, so always check prior to departure.

By train

Train services may be considerably slower than the buses, but they do offer the advantages of greater safety and, in executive or first-class carriages, considerably more comfort. Trains leave Jakarta for Bandung, Yogyakarta, Surakarta (Solo) and Surabaya. Always try to buy tickets well in advance and make sure that at all times you keep your eyes on your luggage.

The *Thomas Cook Overseas Timetable*, which is published bi-monthly, gives details of many rail, bus and shipping services worldwide, and will help you plan a rail journey around Java. It is available in the UK from some stations, any branch of Thomas Cook, or by phoning 01733 503571.

STUDENT AND YOUTH TRAVEL

Student discounts are regularly offered in museums and in some guesthouses and hostels. Make sure you have an official card and photograph with you.

TELEPHONES

Local and international telephone services are available in most hotels and post offices. Note, however, that it is expensive to dial internationally and that hotels generally add a hefty surcharge.

International codes for direct dialling:

Australia 61; Canada 1; Ireland 353; New Zealand 64; United Kingdom 44; United States 1

The Thomas Cook Traveltalk Card is a pre-paid telephone card supported by 24-hour multi-lingual customer service. Available from Thomas Cook branches in the UK in denominations of £10 and £20, the card can be re-charged by calling the customer service unit and quoting your credit card number.

Local transport

THOMAS COOK

See page 185 for details of Thomas Cook locations in Bali, Java and Lombok. Thomas Cook's World Wide Web site, at *www.thomascook.com*, provides up-to-the-minute details of Thomas Cook's travel and foreign money services.

TIME

Java is 7 hours ahead of Greenwich Mean Time (GMT) while Bali and Lombok are 8 hours head of GMT. That means when it is noon on Java, it is 1pm on Bali and Lombok, 5am in London, midnight in New York and 3pm in Sydney.

TIPPING

In most tourist restaurants an 11 per cent service charge will automatically be added to your bill. Where it is not, tip in the region of Rp1,000–Rp2,000 if the service has been satisfactory.

TOILETS

Where there are tourists, there are normally sit-down loos. Otherwise, you will have to make do with the aptly

named squat lavatory. If there is no flush, use the plastic dipper and bucket of water strategically placed alongside. To be on the safe side, take your own toilet paper, and if caught short, ask for the *kamar kecil*, or the WC (pronounced way say).

TOURIST OFFICES

Jakarta

Jakarta Theatre Building, Jalan Thamrin 9 (tel: 314 2067).

West Java

Jalan Cipaganti 151, Bandung (tel: (022) 81490).

Central Java

Jalan Malioboro 14, Yogyakarta (tel: 0274 566 000).

East Java

Jalan Gayung Kebonsari 173 (tel: 811 879).

Bali

Jalan Surapati Parman, Denpasar (tel: (0361) 222 387).

Lombok

Jalan Langko No. 70, Ampenan (tel: (0364) 21866).

Indonesia Tourist Offices Overseas

US: 3457 Wilshire Boulevard, Los Angeles, California (tel: 213 380 4876). **UK**: 38 Grosvenor Square, London W1X 9AD (tel: 0171 499 7661).

ACKNOWLEDGEMENTS

The Automobile Association wishes to thank the following photographers and libraries for their assistance in the preparation of this book: POWERSTOCK front cover; SPECTRUM COLOUR LIBRARY 6, 136, 156, 157
The remaining photographs are held in the Automobile Association's own photo library (AA PHOTO LIBRARY) and were taken by Ben Davies for this book with the exception of the spine taken by Dirk Buwalda and the back cover taken by Jim Holmes.
The author would like to thank: Guntur Purnomo, production manager of the Ramayana Ballet at Prambanan, the Borobudur Guesthouse and the tourist authorities in Jakarta, Denpasar and Ampenan. Also thanks to Thomas Renaut in Bangkok.

CONTRIBUTORS
Series adviser: Melissa Shales   **Copy editor:** Rebecca Snelling   **Indexer:** Marie Lorimer
Thanks to **Eric and Katerina Roberts** for their work on this revised edition.